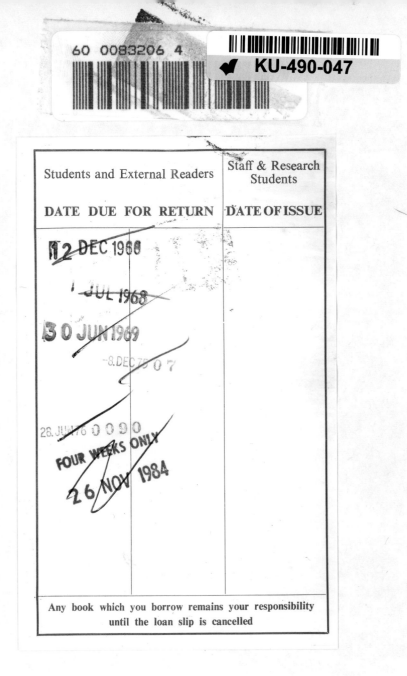

BAPTISMAL ANOINTING

ALCUIN CLUB COLLECTIONS
No. XLVIII

Baptismal Anointing

BY

Leonel L. Mitchell, Th.D.

LONDON

S·P·C·K

1966

First published in 1966
by S.P.C.K.
Holy Trinity Church
Marylebone Road
London N.W.1

Made and printed in Great Britain by
William Clowes and Sons, Limited
London and Beccles

We cannot properly evaluate or properly solve the problems of the present and the future unless and until we study the past. And the more involved and profound these problems, the more thorough must be our search into history. . . . History is a precious corrective of mere speculation, or subjective hypotheses. True knowledge of our present liturgy is knowledge based on the solid rock of historical facts; it is by studying the past that we can best learn how to shape the future.

Joseph Jungmann, *The Early Liturgy*

Contents

Acknowledgements

Thanks are due to the following for permission to quote from copyright sources:

Biblioteca Apostolica Vaticana: *Analecta Reginensia*, edited by André Wilmart (Studi e Testi 59).

Cambridge University Press: *The Liturgical Homilies of Narsai*, edited by R. H. Connolly and *The Apostolic Tradition of Hippolytus*, edited by B. S. Easton.

The Clarendon Press, Oxford: *Didascalia Apostolorum*, edited by R. H. Connolly; *Rituale Armenorum*, edited by F. C. Conybeare; and *The Apocryphal New Testament*, edited by M. R. James.

W. Heffer & Sons Ltd: *Woodbrooke Studies*, by A. Mignana.

The Henry Bradshaw Society: *Manuale ad Usum Percelebris Ecclesie Sarisburiensis*, by A. J. Collins.

Longmans, Green & Co. Ltd: *The Seal of the Spirit*, by G. W. H. Lampe.

Rivingtons Ltd: *The English Rite*, by F. E. Brightman.

Spicilegium Sacrum Lovaniense: *Les Ordines Romani du Haut Moyen Âge*, by M. Andrieu.

Abbreviations

P.K.	Papadopoulos-Kerameus, *Varia Graeca Sacra*
P.L.	*Patrologia Latina* (ed. Migne)
R.A.	Conybeare, *Rituale Armenorum*
R.E.D.	*Rerum Ecclesiasticarum Documenta*
R.O.	Denzinger, *Ritus Orientalium*
S.	Ambrose, *de Sacramentis*
Stowe	*The Stowe Missal* (ed. Warner)
Test.	*Testamentum Domini*
Wenger	*Jean Chrysostome: Huit Catéchèses Baptismales* (ed. Wenger)

Preface

This work was originally presented to the General Theological Seminary in New York City as a doctoral dissertation in the field of liturgics in February of 1964. It has since been revised and condensed, particularly by the elimination of many of the original footnotes. I am deeply indebted to the Reverend Professor H. Boone Porter, under whose supervision I prepared the original text, and to the Reverend Canon W. K. Lowther Clarke, for suggesting many revisions for this edition.

Introduction

In the slightly more than twenty years which separate us from the publication by the late Dom Gregory Dix of his paper *Confirmation, or Laying on of Hands?* a great deal has been written on the subject of Christian initiation. Very little of it, however, has been concerned with the liturgical texts of the initiatory rites, and certainly no comprehensive treatment of them has been attempted since Thompson's *The Offices of Baptism and Confirmation* appeared in 1914. In the present study we shall attempt to examine one aspect of these rites, the anointing with oil which accompanies baptism in all Christian liturgies from at least the third to the fifteenth centuries. Most of what has been written about the baptismal anointings has been from a theological point of view, attempting to prove that the anointing either is, or is not, the vehicle for the gift of the Holy Spirit. We shall be concerned rather with the examination of the *lex orandi* itself, in the firm belief that it is only by an accurate knowledge of what Christians of an earlier period did and said in the rites which they performed that we may be able to come to any conclusion regarding the meaning of these rites.

We shall examine the baptismal anointings, both those which precede and those which follow baptism, from their earliest appearance to the establishment of these rites in their modern "shape". This means that the final date of our inquiry will differ slightly for each rite, but that, in general, the tenth or eleventh century will be our *terminus ad quem*.

It will be impossible to refrain from all interpretative theological comment, nor would it be desirable to do so, for history is event plus interpretation. It is the duty, therefore, of the historian to present not only the record of events and the interpretation placed upon them at the time, but also to bring to bear upon them his knowledge of their subsequent effects, and to interpret them in the light of this knowledge. Our primary concern, nevertheless, will be with liturgical books, or with descriptions of the rites in literary or legal writings. The explanations with which we shall be chiefly concerned will be those of the men who used the rites, although we shall in no wise attempt to duplicate the monumental patristic study of A. J. Mason, whose *The Relation of Confirmation to Baptism* remains the classic study of the theology of Christian initiation.

Among the recent books on baptismal theology, Professor G. W. H. Lampe's *The Seal of the Spirit* occupies a pre-eminent place. He reviews the Scriptural and patristic doctrine with special reference to the concept expressed in his title.[1] We shall also refer to *Confirmation, its Place in the Baptismal Mystery*, by Fr Lionel Thornton, c.r. This work is admittedly an answer to Lampe's attack on the position maintained by Thornton and Dom Gregory Dix. It is particularly concerned with Scriptural background.

No student of the baptismal rite can fail to acknowledge his debt to the late Dom Richard Hugh Connolly, o.s.b., monk of Downside Abbey and head of Benet House, Cambridge. The breadth and depth of his patristic scholarship and interest is shown by the frequency with which his name appears as a leading authority in different aspects of the topic. It is he who established, at least for English-speaking students, the identity of the *Apostolic Tradition* of Hippolytus and the Ambrosian authorship of *de Sacramentis*. He is the editor of the Liturgical Homilies of Narsai and the *Didascalia Apostolorum*, and the author of important articles and introductions. In recent years his mantle has fallen upon another Benedictine, Dom Bernard Botte, who, following in Connolly's footsteps, has produced editions of Hippolytus and Ambrose, and important articles upon patristic and liturgical subjects.

One additional book requires notice. E. C. Whitaker has published for the S.P.C.K. *Documents of the Baptismal Liturgy*. The documents, it is true, appear frequently as unduly abbreviated excerpts, but the book is invaluable, both to the casual and to the serious student, for it collects many of the most important baptismal documents from sources not readily available, and presents them in readable English translations, together with a bibliographical note indicating the source of the original text. Although much important and interesting material is omitted, the convenience of having so many documents in a single volume outweighs its drawbacks as a working tool.

[1] A brief statement of the relation of our conclusions to Lampe's will be found in Appendix II.

Although it may seem paradoxical for one whose own liturgy does not include any baptismal anointings to undertake a study of their history, this effort will not, I hope, be without practical value. The Anglican Churches are at the present time undertaking a study of their initiatory rites almost unprecedented in their history, and many proposals are currently being put forward, both by official commissions and by interested individuals. The question of the place of anointing in the initiatory rites must be considered in this examination. The rejection of anointing out of hand by the Reformers as unscriptural and medieval can no longer be sustained, and it is only if the evidence of the tradition of Christian usage is available for those concerned to examine that an intelligent assessment of its proper place in any revised rite can be made.

I

The Apostolic Tradition

Although the earliest clear references to the anointing with oil as part of the baptismal rite are in the writings of Tertullian, it will be more convenient for us to begin our study with the *Apostolic Tradition* of Hippolytus, hereafter cited as *Ap. Trad.*, which gives us the text of a complete rite. This text is published in two English reconstructions, that of Burton Scott Easton, and that of Dom Gregory Dix, and in a French version by Dom Bernard Botte. These editions are necessarily reconstructions, as the text of *Ap. Trad.* does not survive except as it is embedded in other documents.

The recovery of the text and the establishment of its identity were largely the work of Dom R. Hugh Connolly, whose monumental patristic scholarship was an adornment both of Downside Abbey and of the University of Cambridge.[1] The principal documents used by Dom Connolly in his work of reconstruction were the Ethiopic, Arabic, and Coptic versions of the Egyptian Church Order, the Verona Latin fragments, the Canons of Hippolytus, the Testament of our Lord, the *Constitutiones per Hippolytum*, and the eighth book of the *Apostolic Constitutions*. Of these versions the Latin is the most important. The manuscript is described by Dr Easton in these terms:

> The Latin codex, now in Verona, is a palimpsest, probably of the sixth century, over which some two centuries later three books of Isidore of Seville's *Sentences* were written. The translation itself appears to have been made in the fourth century, and is a rendition of a Greek book of Church

[1] Reference should be made to his work *The So-Called Egyptian Church Order and Derived Documents* (*Texts and Studies*, Vol. VII, No. 4, Cambridge, 1916). An independent study reaching substantially the same conclusions, "Über die pseudoapostolischen Kirchenordnungen", was published by E. Schwartz in *Schriften der wissenschaftlichen Gesellschaft in Strassburg*, Strassburg, 1910.

laws, in which Hippolytus's book is preceded by portions of the Didascalia
and the complete Apostolic Church Order. The translator, who presumably
had no idea of the authorship of the closing portion, made his version
pedantically literal; a great advantage to the modern student. Unquestionably
neither the sixth-century copyist, the translator, nor the Greek text used was
infallible; the last certainly contained duplications. But the version is in-
comparably the best guide we have.[1]

Unfortunately the Latin text is not complete, and recourse must be
had to the Oriental versions, the earliest of which is from the eleventh
and the latest from the nineteenth century. To quote Easton again:

> The only other primary version, the Sahidic, is likewise incomplete, and the
> results of the moderate abilities of its translator have been further confused
> in later transmission. The Arabic is a secondary text, offering little that the
> Sahidic does not contain. The only practically complete version, the Ethiopic,
> is tertiary and is otherwise unreliable. All four of these versions presuppose
> a common Greek original, in which two different endings have been con-
> flated. The other sources, the Constitutions, the Testament, and the Canons
> are frank revisions, in which the original is often edited out of recognition
> or even flatly contradicted.[2]

In this study we shall quote from Easton's edition, unless the Latin
text or the readings of other editors seem important.

The description of baptism in *Ap. Trad.* begins with section 17 and
continues down to section 23, comprising Part II of Easton's edition.
The rite itself begins in section 21 with the blessing of the water at
cock-crow on Easter morning. The bishop, having hallowed the
baptismal water by his prayer, proceeds to "give thanks over the oil"
which is called the "oil of thanksgiving", and then to exorcize other
oil called the "oil of exorcism". Two deacons bring these oils to the
presbyter who will perform the anointing, the deacon with the oil of
exorcism standing on his left, and the deacon with the oil of thanksgiving on his right.

The candidates are presented naked before the presbyter, who bids
each in turn renounce the devil. When each has renounced, he immediately anoints him with the oil of exorcism, using the formula:

> Let all spirits depart far from thee.

The candidate is at once led down into the water and baptized by the
presbyter;[3] who lays his hand upon his head and asks him the threefold

---

[1] Easton, *op. cit.*, pp. 28f.   [2] ibid., p. 31.
[3] Or possibly by the bishop; cf. Easton, p. 46, n. 1; Dix, p. 35, n. 11.

interrogative form of the creed. He is baptized at each of his three replies.

> And afterward, when he has come up [out of the water], he is anointed by the presbyter with the oil of thanksgiving, the presbyter saying: "I anoint thee with holy oil in the name of Jesus Christ." And so each one, after drying himself, is immediately clothed, and then is brought into the church.[1]

The sequence of events to this point should be noted. The blessing of the water, the disrobing of the candidates, their renunciation, anointing with the oil of exorcism, baptism, and anointing with the oil of thanksgiving have taken place in the baptistery. The candidates are now clothed and brought back into the church. The conclusion seems inescapable that Hippolytus, while requiring most rigorously that the candidates go down into the water naked, wishes them to be properly attired when they are presented to the congregation.[2] We must also realize that by anointing *Ap. Trad.* means more than touching a person, or signing him with a cross made in oil. It expects the oil to be applied directly to the body of the person being anointed.[3]

When the newly-baptized have been clothed and brought from the baptistery into the church, they are brought before the bishop. Easton, following the text of the Verona Latin fragment, describes the liturgical action which follows in this way:

> Then the bishop, laying his hand upon them, shall pray saying:
> "O Lord God, who hast made them worthy to obtain remission of sins through the laver of regeneration of the Holy Spirit, send into them thy grace, that they may serve thee according to thy will; for thine is the glory, to the Father and the Son, with the Holy Spirit in the holy church, both now and world without end. Amen."
> Then pouring the oil of thanksgiving from his hand and putting it on his forehead, he shall say: "I anoint thee with holy oil in the Lord, the Father Almighty and Christ Jesus and the Holy Ghost."
> And signing them on the forehead he shall say: "The Lord be with thee"; and he who is signed shall say: "And with thy spirit." And so he shall do to each one.[4]

---

[1] *Ap. Trad.*, 21. 19–20, Easton, p. 47.

[2] This same sense of modesty seems to lie behind the direction, in 21. 4–5, that the children be baptized first, then the men, and finally the women. Each candidate would be clothed and led into the church after his own baptism and anointing.

[3] cf. Ps. 133. 2.

[4] *Ap. Trad.*, 22. 1–4, Easton, pp. 47f.

Dix, on the other hand, makes a substantial change in the meaning of the prayer, translating:

> O Lord God, who didst count these worthy of deserving the forgiveness of sins by the laver of regeneration, make them worthy to be filled with thy Holy Spirit and send upon them thy grace . . .[1]

His critical note reads (expanding the abbreviations), "So Testament of our Lord, Ethiopic, Boharic, Canons of Hippolytus; omit Latin, which is corrupt here." A full discussion of the critical question raised by Dix will be found in Lampe, *The Seal of the Spirit*.[2] Whether or not one agrees with Professor Lampe's conclusions as to the theological merits of the emendation, he has marshalled the evidence strongly in favour of accepting the reading of the Latin text (*per lavacrum regenerationis spiritus sancti*). In support of his conclusion, Lampe quotes from the preface to Dom Bernard Botte's edition of *Ap. Trad.*, "To add to, or subtract from the Latin on the authority of other witnesses is always a risky adventure. This kind of correction can only be assigned the value of conjecture."[3]

Even if we are unwilling to follow Dix in preferring them to the Latin text, we must recognize the significance of the Oriental readings as witnesses to the liturgical practice and theological interpretation of those who "corrected" the earlier material with which they worked. This prayer, according to the Oriental versions followed by Dix, accompanies the giving of the Holy Spirit to those who have received the washing of regeneration. Presumably the gift is associated with the liturgical action which follows the prayer, that is, the anointing and laying on of hands.

A variant of more importance to our immediate purpose is the omission of the second anointing, that by the bishop, from the Canons of Hippolytus. In the Canons, the close of the prayer is followed at once by the signing of the forehead:

> Then he signs their foreheads with the sign of charity and kisses them, saying: "The Lord be with you."[4]

J. M. Hanssens, in his extensive study of *Ap. Trad.*, raises the question of the genuineness of the second, or episcopal, anointing, on the basis

---

[1] Dix, p. 38.   [2] pp. 138–41.

[3] Botte, *La Tradition Apostolique* (Paris, 1946), p. 13. Quoted by Lampe, op. cit., p. 140.

[4] D. B. de Haneberg, *Canones S. Hippolyti*, XIX, 13, p. 77.

of its absence from the Canons.[1] He seems, nevertheless, to offer no evidence which would justify disregarding the combined testimony of the Latin and Oriental versions, particularly in the light of the low evidential value assigned to the Canons by Connolly.[2] It is more likely that the editor of the Canons has "corrected" his source in the light of his own liturgical tradition.

Let us consider again the nature of the ceremonies. The neophytes have returned from the baptistery to the church. After their baptism their bodies have been anointed with the oil of thanksgiving, and they have been dried and clothed. The bishop gives his final blessing by laying on of hands, and anoints the heads of the neophytes, pouring oil over them from his hand and marking their foreheads with the sign of the cross (*consignans in frontem*). The prayer *Domine Deus*, we must note, is in the plural, and the rubric before it speaks of laying hands on them (*manum illis imponens*). The rubric for the anointing and signing, on the other hand, is in the singular, and concludes, "Ita singulis faciat". This suggests that the prayer was said over the group of neophytes by the bishop with hands extended, while the anointing and signing were performed for each individually. Since the anointing as described in *Ap. Trad.* would necessitate the bishop's actually touching the head of each neophyte, there would be a tactual laying on of hands in close association with the consignation. This may account for the apparent confusion of the two practices in later rites.

The signing of the neophytes is followed by their participation for the first time in the prayer and offering of the faithful, the exchanging of the kiss of peace, and the reception of the Holy Eucharist. The distinctive feature of the baptismal Eucharist is the administration of three cups to the newly-baptized: of water, of milk and honey, and of wine.[3] The third cup is, of course, the Eucharistic chalice.

This section of *Ap. Trad.* ends with a reminder of the *disciplina arcani* and a direction to the bishop to impart "any other thing that ought to be told" to the converts privately after their baptism.[4]

In addition to the baptismal section, two other passages in *Ap. Trad.* are relevant to our discussion. The first is the blessing of oil which follows the Eucharistic prayer in the consecration of a bishop. Although

---

[1] J. M. Hanssens, *La Liturgie d'Hippolyte*, p. 471
[2] Connolly, op. cit., pp. 132f.   [3] *Ap. Trad.*, 23. 7, Easton, p. 49.
[4] *Ap. Trad.*, 23. 13–14 (the passage is not in the Latin).

this oil is probably not the "oil of thanksgiving" mentioned in the baptismal rite, the form of blessing reveals certain associations which oil held for early Christians.

> If anyone offers oil, he shall give thanks as at the offering of the bread and wine, though not with the same words but in the same general manner (*non ad sermonem . . . sed simili virtute*), saying: "That sanctifying this oil, O God, wherewith thou didst anoint kings, priests and prophets, thou wouldest grant health to them who use it and partake of it, so that it may bestow comfort on all who taste it and health on all who use it."[1]

The association of the anointing of Christians with the anointing of priests and kings in the Old Testament recurs continually in liturgical and theological writings.

The second passage deals with the sign of the cross.[2]

> But imitate him always, by signing thy forehead sincerely; for this is the sign of his Passion, manifest and approved against the devil if so thou makest it from faith; not that thou mayest appear to men, but knowingly offering it as a shield. For the adversary, seeing its power coming from the heart, that a man displays the publicly formed image of baptism, is put to flight; not because thou spittest, but because the Spirit in thee breathes him away. When Moses formed it by putting the blood of the Paschal lamb that was slain on the lintel and anointing the side-posts, he signified the faith which we now have in the perfect Lamb.[3]

With this passage should be taken the related:

> By signing thyself with thy moist breath, and so spreading spittle[4] on thy body with thy hand, thou art sanctified to thy feet; for the gift of the Spirit and the sprinkling with water, when it is brought with a believing heart as it were from a fountain, sanctified him who believes.[5]

The *Apostolic Tradition* has presented us with a complete baptismal rite with sufficient directions for its actual performance. This rite includes anointing with oil before and after the baptismal immersion.

---

[1] *Ap. Trad.*, 5, Easton, pp. 36f.

[2] This passage is found twice in the Latin text in slightly different versions. They may be seen arranged in parallel columns, together with the Coptic and the Canons of Hippolytus, in Connolly's study, op. cit., pp. 100f.

[3] *Ap. Trad.*, 37, Easton, pp. 56f.

[4] The Latin has *spm*. Hauler fills it out "sp(iritu)m", but comparison with the Sahidic reveals that Easton is correct in interpreting it as "sputum"; cf. Hauler, *Fragmenta Veronensia Latina*, LXXIX, 19–24; Horner, *The Statutes of the Apostles*, p. 330.

[5] *Ap. Trad.*, 36. 11, Easton, pp. 55f.

Two other passages in the treatise give us hints as to the meanings which its compiler saw in the use of oil and in the signing with the cross. As we shall see later, these hints will be followed up in other authors, while the general outline of the rite, with significant variations, will continually reappear.

The distinctive ceremonies connected with the anointings in *Ap. Trad.* which we shall observe particularly as we examine other rites are principally these:

1. The blessing of the "oil of thanksgiving" before the exorcism of the "oil of exorcism", that is, in the inverse order of their use.

2. The exclusive use of exorcized oil before baptism, reserving the "eucharistized" oil for post-bapismal anointings.

3. The double anointing after baptism, that of the body by the presbyter, and that of the head by the bishop.

4. The association of the episcopal laying on of hands with the episcopal anointing and signing with the cross.

The meaning of the rites is less easy to codify. Certainly the anointings were associated with the anointings of priests and kings in the Old Covenant, but to say this is not to exhaust their meaning. The use of oil was in some way related to its healing use, both in medicine and unction of the sick, and we shall see other meanings, not suggested in *Ap. Trad.*, attached to anointing in other early writers.

The passages on the sign of the cross quoted above make clear the importance of the baptismal signing. For a Christian to sign himself with the cross was to display his baptism, although the precise relationship between the sign of the cross, the *lavacrum* of baptism, and the Spirit is not immediately evident. We must therefore suspend judgement on the interpretation of these ceremonies until we have looked more fully into their background and their treatment in other writers.

There is, nevertheless, one further question which must be asked about *Ap. Trad.*, namely: what is this liturgy? The traditional answer is that of Connolly, Dix, and Easton. To quote Dr Easton:

They represent the normal practices at Rome in Hippolytus's younger days, and he is quite sincere in believing that they are truly apostolic and therefore unalterable. And that they actually are rules of real antiquity is shown by the corroboration they receive from other early Christian writers, among whom Tertullian in particular describes usages extraordinarily like those expounded by his Roman contemporary. The *Apostolic Tradition*, consequently, is more than a source for Roman customs at the beginning of the third century; it may with equal safety be invoked for the practices of even fifty years earlier. In the words of Harnack: "Here is the richest source that we in any form possess for our knowledge of the polity of the Roman church in the oldest time, and this Roman polity may, in many regards, be accepted as the polity held everywhere."[1]

I call this the traditional view, because it has been generally accepted since the publication of Connolly's study in 1916. There is, however, a minority view, and Fr Hanssens argues with great learning, if not with great clarity, that the liturgy of *Ap. Trad.* is, in fact, Alexandrian in origin and "ideal" in character.[2] By "ideal" Hanssens means that the liturgy of Hippolytus was not the actual liturgy of any Church, but that it was composed in accordance with what the author believed to be the "correct" liturgical practice. There is undoubtedly some truth in this position, and more caution than Dr Easton's words seem to imply must be used in identifying the present text of *Ap. Trad.* with the actual rite of the Roman Church. On the other hand, it was surely not composed in a liturgical vacuum and must reflect the actual practice of a particular Church, even if it has been "corrected" according to its editor's theological and liturgical presuppositions. Furthermore, since we do not possess the Greek original, nor any version which is not a part of some larger work, there is the additional problem of distinguishing the "corrections" of Hippolytus from those of the later editors and translators through whose hands it has passed.

The supposed Alexandrian origin of *Ap. Trad.* seems to this writer to have less to commend it, although Hanssens' argument certainly deserves a more thorough study than it has yet received. His theory, briefly, is that Hippolytus was an Alexandrian by birth and upbringing, who later became a presbyter of the Roman Church. The relationship between *Ap. Trad.* and the later Roman rite, which we shall examine in Chapter V, he sees as deriving from northern Italy and southern Gaul, "propagated by means of the Gelasian Sacramentary and the Germano-Roman Pontifical". To determine whether or not this hypothesis is tenable is really beyond the scope of the present investigation. We may note, however, that it is an hypothesis which involves explaining away a large body of evidence connecting *Ap. Trad.* with Rome. Whether it be considered tenable or not, Fr Hanssens' view is certainly

---

[1] Easton, op. cit., pp. 25f.
[2] Hanssens, *La Liturgie d'Hippolyte*, pp. 506–11 and *passim*.

not proven, and for the purposes of this study its effect is simply to raise tentative questions in a few places. There is no doubt that *Ap. Trad.*, either directly or indirectly, exercised a profound influence over the later rites, and that its discovery clarifies many points which are obscure in other sources.

Even if Hanssens' case should prove stronger than it seems at present, the practical situation remains much the same. Even if not Roman, *Ap. Trad.* remains our oldest complete rite of Christian initiation. Even if considerably "idealized", the rite of *Ap. Trad.*, or something very like it, to which the present text provides our clearest clue, has influenced almost all subsequent Church orders, at least indirectly.

II

Origins of Baptismal Anointing

EARLY PATRISTIC EVIDENCE

If we seek to go behind *Ap. Trad.* to find the origin of the rites of anointing in Christian baptism, we shall be hard pressed to find unambiguous references. Some attempt must, nevertheless, be made to account for the existence of the anointings, even if it involves an element of uncertainty. The first step, at least, is on solid ground.

Tertullian composed his treatise *de Baptismo* about the year 200. The following passage in this work refers directly to the post-baptismal rites:

> Then having come up from the font we are thoroughly anointed with a blessed unction, in accordance with the ancient discipline whereby, since the time when Aaron was anointed by Moses, men were anointed unto the priesthood with oil from a horn: from which ye are called "christs" (*christi dicti a chrismate*) from the chrism, that is the anointing, which also lent its name to the Lord. This was done spiritually (*spiritalis*) since he was anointed with the Spirit by God the Father, as in Acts: "They have gathered together in that city against thy holy Son whom thou hast anointed." Likewise in us the anointing flows over our body but aids our spirit (*carnaliter currit unctio sed spiritualiter proficit*), just as the bodily action (*carnalis actus*) of baptism itself, that we are immersed in the water, has a spiritual effect (*spiritalis effectus*), that we are freed from sin. In the next place the hand is laid on in blessing, invoking and inviting the Holy Spirit (*Dehinc manus imponitur per benedictionem advocans et invitans spiritum sanctum*).[1]

Pre-baptismal ceremonies are mentioned in *de Corona*.[2] They include a renunciation of "the devil, and his pomp, and his angels" and an imposition of hands by the bishop (*sub antistitis manu*). The threefold immersion and the post-baptismal rites described above followed. The

---

[1] *de Baptismo*, 7–8 (C.C., Vol. 1, p. 282).   [2] *de Corona*, 3.

rite is basically similar to that of *Ap. Trad.*, although no pre-baptismal
unction with the "oil of exorcism" is mentioned. Water baptism is
followed by anointing and the imposition of hands. The anointing is
connected with the anointing of Aaron, that is with the anointing of
priests under the Old Covenant, and also with the Messianic anointing
of Christ by the Holy Spirit, with which the baptismal *chrisma* identifies
the Christian.

Tertullian nowhere mentions anointing in connection with the laying on of hands. He seems to know only one anointing, that immediately following baptism, i.e. the presbyteral chrismation of *Ap. Trad.*
He does, however, know a signing distinct from the anointing. This is
brought out in *de Resurrectione Carnis*, in which he interprets the initiatory rites in this way:

> Flesh is washed, that the soul may be cleansed: flesh is anointed, that the
> soul may be consecrated: flesh is signed, that the soul may be fortified:
> flesh is shadowed by the imposition of the hand, that the soul may be
> enlightened by the Spirit: flesh feeds on the Body and Blood of Christ,
> that the soul also may fatten upon God.[1]

The sequence of rites is baptism, anointing, signing, the imposition
of hands, and communion: a sequence similar to that in *Ap. Trad.*
Tertullian identifies the sign of the cross on the forehead with the *taw*
of Ezek. 9.4, which will be "upon our foreheads in the true and catholic
Jerusalem".[2] But he never states that the sign is made in oil.

Undoubtedly the most startling statement in *de Baptismo* is, "Not
that we obtain the Spirit in the water, but that cleansed in the water
under the angel (*sub angelo*) we are prepared for the Holy Spirit."[3] It is
clearly the imposition of hands and not the consignation to which
Tertullian is referring, since he does not even mention the signing in *de
Baptismo*. We shall therefore be justified in accepting the conclusions of
Fr Paul Galtier, "It is with the person of Christ and not with the Holy
Spirit that chrism and unction are placed in relation [by Tertullian]."[4]

By this division of the baptismal rite into two parts and the association of the gift of the Spirit with the second part, Tertullian provided
the theological basis for much later discussion. The single anointing
which he mentions belongs to the baptism, not to the laying on of

[1] *de Resurrectione Carnis*, 8 (*C.S.E.L.*, Vol. 47, pp. 36f).

[2] *adversus Marcionem* III, 22.

[3] *de Baptismo*, 6.

[4] P. Galtier, "La Consignation à Carthage et à Rome" in *Recherches de Science
Religieuse*, Vol. II (1911), p. 352.

hands. Its primary reference is to the baptism of Christ and to the share
which Christians have through their baptism in his anointing. Although
he calls the unction *spiritualiter*, as opposed to *carnaliter*, he does not
identify the baptismal anointing with the gift of the Holy Ghost.

Moving backward from Tertullian, we move out of the realm of
concrete evidence and into that of reconstruction and conjecture. A
great deal has been written about the initiatory rites of the second
century, but evidence for the use of anointing in orthodox Christian
practice is difficult to find. Irenaeus, for example, is definitely familiar
with Gnostic anointings, and baptisms in a mixture of oil and water,[1]
but he never mentions anointing unequivocally as an orthodox baptismal rite. Two passages from Irenaeus may be cited as evidence for such
an anointing. In *The Demonstration of the Apostolic Preaching* he says:

> The Son, as being God, receives from the Father, that is from God, the throne
> of the everlasting kingdom, and the oil of anointing above his fellows. The
> oil of anointing is the Spirit, wherewith he has been anointed; and his fellows
> are the prophets and righteous men and apostles, and all who receive the
> fellowship of the Kingdom.[2]

Similarly, in the *adversus Haereses* he declares:

> The Spirit of God descended upon Jesus, for he had promised through the
> prophets that he would anoint him, that we, laying hold of the abundance
> of his anointing, might be saved.[3]

Certainly these passages are perfectly consistent with an external rite
of anointing, but they do not require it. Even Dix, who considers
Irenaeus a witness for the primitive antiquity of anointing, admits,
"None of these passages *need* be more than metaphorical."[4] Whether
or not Irenaeus understood them of an actual anointing conferred at
baptism, his statements would, at least, have lent authority to the
ceremony when it was practised. By his identification of the Spirit with
the oil of anointing, even if his use was completely metaphorical, he
would have encouraged the identification of the external rite of anointing with the gift of the Spirit at baptism.

One earlier writer who seems to refer to an actual anointing is
Theophilus of Antioch. In his *Apologia ad Autolycum* he chides a
heathen friend for laughing at his calling himself a Christian, reminding

---

[1] *adversus Haereses* I, 21.3–5.
[2] *Demonstration.* 47 (ed. J. A. Robinson, London, 1920, p. 112).
[3] *adversus Haereses* III, 9.3 (*P.G.*, 7, 872).
[4] *Confirmation, or Laying on of Hands?*, p. 19.

him that the anointed (τὸ χριστόν) is serviceable. Only an anointed ship, he goes on to say, is seaworthy, and all of us were anointed when we entered this life and when contending in the games. He concludes:

> Do you not wish to be anointed with the oil of God? For we are called Christians, because we have been anointed (χριόμεθα) with the oil of God.[1]

It is possible, of course, that this too is metaphorical, but the parallel to Tertullian's "*christi dicti a chrismate*" seems to indicate that the Christians have actually been anointed.

When we go back to Justin Martyr, we find the situation has become even more obscure. Justin's famous account of Christian baptism in his First Apology describes no rite other than the baptismal washing and the Eucharist.[2] Whether this is due to the apologetic nature of the work, or to the lack of any additional rites to describe, has been argued extensively in the pages of the journal *Theology* by Professor J. E. L. Oulton, Dom Gregory Dix, Professor E. C. Ratcliff, and Canon A. H. Couratin.[3] The last three of these articles argue that Justin did know rites connected with Christian initiation other than water baptism, and Canon Couratin specifically argues that anointing with oil was one of these rites. In the opinion of the present writer there is not sufficient evidence to justify adopting his thesis as established, and counting Justin as a witness to the baptismal anointing. On the other hand, we have certainly been delivered from having to count him as a witness against the anointing.

The evidence of the *Apology* must be considered first. This work clearly does not make provision for any post-baptismal rites other than the Eucharist. Dix, however, has justly pointed out:

> Justin, in his Apology, is setting out to answer the popular charges against the Christians, including the dangerous charge of magic. His whole account of the Christian rite is adapted to demonstrate the harmlessness of these rites from the point of view of the charges brought against them, and is less naïve than appears on the surface.[4]

To this judgement, Ratcliff adds:

> We may take it, indeed, that Justin's sketches of Baptism and the Eucharist

[1] *Apologia ad Antolycum*, 1.12 (P.G., 6, 1041).   [2] *Apology* I, 61–5.
[3] Oulton, "Second-Century Teaching on Holy Baptism", Vol. 50 (1947), pp. 86–91; Dix, "'The Seal' in the Second Century", Vol. 51 (1948), pp. 7–12; Ratcliff, "Justin Martyr and Confirmation", Vol. 51 (1948), pp. 133–9; Couratin, "Justin Martyr and Confirmation—A Note", Vol. 55 (1952), pp. 458–60.
[4] art. cit., p. 9.

are so carefully drawn as to present the appearance of being adequate and self-explanatory, and not wholly unfamiliar, to his pagan readers.[1]

This should be sufficient to establish the neutrality of the First Apology on the question of the anointing. It does not mention an anointing, but a perfectly acceptable reason for the omission can be shown. We must therefore turn to Justin's other works for a hint.

In the Second Apology, Justin, in discussing the Name of God, mentions that the Son is called χριστός because he has been anointed (κεχρῖσθαι) by God,[2] but he does not apply the name to the Christians. It is in *The Dialogue with Trypho the Jew* that Couratin believes he finds reference to baptismal anointing. He quotes two passages from the *Dialogue*. In chapter 41 Justin states that the oblation of flour which Leviticus commands to be offered for those cleansed from leprosy is a type of the eucharistic bread. Because this discussion follows that concerning the paschal lamb in chapter 40, Couratin believes that Justin is thinking of the baptismal Eucharist at Easter. He sees the connection in Lev. 14, in which the rites of the seventh/eighth day in the cleansing of the leper correspond to the Christian initiatory rites held over the night between Saturday and Sunday.

The sequence beginning at Lev. 14.9 with the washing of the leper on the seventh day, and continuing with the offering of the lambs, wheat, and oil on the eighth day, corresponds to the order of the Christian rites. First the leper is baptized on Saturday night, then he is anointed with oil (verses 14–17), and the remainder of the oil poured over his head (verse 18). Finally, the offering of the flour and the animal sacrifice complete the rite (verses 19 and 20). It is this offering which Justin calls a type of the eucharistic bread. Couratin concludes:

> If the suggestion made in this note is correct, it follows that Justin was familiar with an initiatory rite which included Anointing with Oil as well as Baptism with Water and the Offering of the Eucharist.[3]

He also quotes chapter 86 of the *Dialogue*, which connects all anointings in the Old Testament with Christ, as evidence that

> when Justin's mind starts running on Christian baptism, he begins by thinking about water, and produces Old Testament references of a more or less apposite kind; he then goes on to think about oil and produce similar references to prefigurations of the anointing of Christ and to the anointing of

---

[1] art. cit., p. 134.   [2] Apology II, 6 (ed. Otto, Vol. I, p. 214).
[3] Couratin, art. cit., p. 459.

kings and priests; and he next proceeds to quote from Isa. 11 with an implied reference to the sevenfold Spirit, which the Christ imparts to those who believe in him.[1]

In spite of Couratin's suggestions, we cannot state definitely that Justin knew the sequence of water, oil, Spirit, found in Tertullian, but there is certainly nothing in his manner of writing incongruous with his having known it, and it may well be that Couratin is correct.

Moving back from Justin, we find no reference to the baptismal anointing until we come to the New Testament. A passage in St Ignatius of Antioch requiring the bishop's supervision of baptisms has been taken by some to refer to the necessity of his administering the unction, or at least consecrating the oil. It need mean nothing more, however, than that the bishop is the minister of the sacrament, either personally or by deputy, and that to baptize apart from him is an act of schism. This would be parallel to Ignatius' immediatly preceding statement concerning the Eucharist:

> Let that be considered a valid (βεβαία) Eucharist which is celebrated by the bishop, or by one whom he appoints.[2]

NEW TESTAMENT EVIDENCE

There is naturally no unambiguous reference to baptismal anointing in the New Testament. There are, however, certain passages which speak of an anointing, and which may refer to an actual unction at baptism.

In 2 Cor. 1.21, 22 St Paul says:

> But it is God who confirms (βεβαιῶν) us with you in Christ, and has anointed (χρίσας) us; he has sealed (σφραγισάμενος) us and given us the earnest (ἀρραβῶνα) of the Spirit in our hearts.

In this passage he applies to the Christian community what were to become the technical terms of the initiatory rites: confirmed, anointed, and sealed. They need not have been technical terms to St Paul, but his use of them in a single passage is striking.

In 1 John 2.20 we read, "You have an anointing (χρῖσμα) from the Holy One." In Johannine writings "the Holy One" is a title of Christ, as is seen in the Petrine confession in John 6.69, "You are the Holy One of God." The Christian, then, is one who has received an anointing from

---

[1] ibid., p. 460.
[2] *Smyrnaeans* 8.1 (ed. K. Lake, *The Apostolic Fathers*, Vol. 1, L.C.L., Cambridge and London, pp. 260–1).

Christ. The anointing is mentioned again in 1 John 2.27, which says that his χρῖσμα remains in you and will teach you all things. Clearly, this is parallel to the gospel passage John 14.26, "The Holy Spirit, whom the Father will send in my name, will teach you all things."

The background of these passages is our Lord's baptism in Jordan, in which "God anointed Jesus of Nazareth with Holy Spirit and power",[1] as St Peter explained to Cornelius. The identification of the descent of the Spirit at the baptism of Christ with an anointing is attributed by St Luke to our Lord himself, when he places on his lips the passage from Isa. 61 read by Jesus in the synagogue as the first public act of his ministry, "The Spirit of the Lord is upon me, because he has anointed me . . .".[2] The same note is sounded in Acts when St Stephen speaks of Jesus as the Holy Child, or Servant (παῖς), whom God has anointed,[3] in a passage quoted by Tertullian in explanation of an actual external anointing.[4] Indeed, the picture of the baptism of Christ in Jordan underlies much Christian baptismal practice. G. R. Beasley-Murray, in his recent *Baptism in the New Testament*, can comment:

> It is all but universally agreed that the occasion for the impartation of the chrism was baptism and that the chrism was the Holy Spirit.[5]

Most writers, nevertheless, do not accept the view that the Johannine and Pauline passages quoted above refer to an actual external rite of anointing. Beasley-Murray, for example, in spite of his words quoted above, believes that the chrism represents the Gospel into which the Christian is initiated at baptism,[6] while Lampe considers it a metaphorical reference to our participation in the Messianic unction of Christ through membership in him in baptism.[7]

On the other hand, Dix believes that these passages "cannot without strain be interpreted metaphorically",[8] and Thornton contends that "the 'chrism' here referred to is definitely a concrete object (as in the Greek version of Ex. 30.25). Moreover, in typical Hebrew fashion, this holy oil is personified and actually identified in function with the Holy Spirit."[9] For him, 1 John is "good reason for thinking" that baptismal anointing was practised in Ephesus fifty years before Justin Martyr.

---

[1] Acts 10.38.   [2] Luke 4.16f.   [3] Acts 4.27.
[4] *de Baptismo* 7.   [5] p. 233.   [6] op. cit., p. 236.
[7] *Seal of the Spirit*, p. 81.
[8] *Confirmation, or Laying on of Hands?* p. 10.
[9] *Confirmation, its Place in the Baptismal Mystery*, p. 21.

On this side also must be counted T. W. Manson, who, in an article in the *Journal of Theological Studies*, sees in this passage from 1 John the *raison d'être* of the Syrian use in which anointing precedes the baptism. He assigns the composition of 1 John to Syria and considers it evidence for the existence of a liturgical anointing before baptism.[1]

The evidence does not appear to the present writer sufficiently conclusive to make possible a firm stand on either side of this controversy. A liturgical anointing at baptism may have been known in New Testament times. The evidence is consistent with such an anointing, but does not require it. Whether the New Testament passages quoted refer to an actual anointing or not, there can be no reasonable doubt that Christians who did have a liturgical anointing used these passages as Scriptural justification for the practice.

The "Messianic anointing" of Jesus by the Holy Ghost at his baptism is the type of Christian baptismal anointings. Because Jesus Christ was anointed with Holy Spirit at his baptism, the Christian is anointed with chrism at his. Indeed, to a Greek-speaking person "christening" would inevitably suggest anointing rather than washing.

In addition to these passages referring specifically to an anointing, there are other relevant New Testament passages. T. W. Manson, in the article previously mentioned, speaks of two different traditions in the New Testament regarding the gift of the Holy Spirit. Although his line of inquiry is different from ours, his findings shed certain light on the background of the anointings.

In the first of these traditions, which Manson believes to be the oldest, the gift of the Holy Spirit precedes baptism. It is best illustrated by the account of the baptism of Cornelius and his household in Acts 10.44-8, in which St Peter baptizes the Gentiles after they have received the Spirit. This tradition is reflected in such passages as Gal. 3.3, in which we are said to have begun with the Spirit; Rom. 8.15 and Gal. 4.6, in which it is the Spirit sent into our hearts which enables us to cry "Abba"; and 1 Cor. 12.3, "No one can say, 'Jesus is Lord,' except in the Holy Spirit." This also appears to be the order of Paul's own conversion in Acts 9.17f.

The passage from 1 Corinthians seems to the present writer to be most relevant. From *Ap. Trad.* we learn that baptism in the name of the Trinity was not by the recitation of a declarative formula, but that the candidate was baptized confessing the name of the Trinity by replying

[1] "Entry into Membership of the Early Church", in *J.T.S.*, Vol. 48 (1947), pp. 25-33.

credo to the interrogative creed. It is reasonable to conjecture, on the basis of this example, therefore, that baptism "in the name of the Lord Jesus" (as in Acts 8.37) meant that the baptismal confession was "Jesus is Lord." If then "Jesus is Lord" in 1 Cor. 12.3 is indeed the baptismal confession, the passage means that it is the previous gift of the Spirit which enables us to make this confession and be baptized.

The second tradition is that of Acts 8.14–24 and 19.1–7, in which the Holy Spirit is given after baptism by the laying on of Apostolic hands. To this tradition also belongs the sermon of St Peter on Pentecost in Acts 2.38, calling upon those who hear him to be baptized and receive the Holy Spirit. This tradition also claims the support of the Markan and Matthean accounts of the baptism of Christ, in which the gift of the Holy Spirit follows the water baptism.

Manson sees in these traditions the two liturgical usages represented on the one hand by *Ap. Trad.*, Tertullian, and the overwhelming practice of both Eastern and Western Church, and on the other by the Syrian custom of pre-baptismal chrismation.

Most writers who treat the theology of baptism and confirmation discuss these passages, reaching a variety of conclusions as to their significance. For the purposes of the present investigation, we must admit that the passages cited do not refer directly to baptismal anointing. They may have played an important rôle in determining the order of the initiatory rites, however, and were quoted by later writers as Scriptural authority for their liturgical practice.

The New Testament accounts of the healing miracles of Christ also contributed to the development of the baptismal liturgy. Washing, anointing, and the laying on of hands are all associated with healing in the New Testament, and the healing miracles were often considered to be types of baptism.

The most direct influence of a healing miracle upon the liturgy can be seen in the account of the healing of the blind man in John 9.1–7. The cure involved two healing ceremonies: first, Christ anointed the eyes of the blind man with an ointment compounded of clay and spittle; then, he sent him to wash in the pool of Siloam. The actions are obviously symbolic. John emphasizes the fact by his Messianic interpretation of the name of the pool. A similar anointing is described at the healing of the deaf mute in Mark 7.32–6. It is this account which contains the word *ephphatha*, ἐφφαθά, which was adopted into later baptismal rites to accompany an anointing. It is not hard to see how later Christians could identify the spittle of the χριστός with the oil of the χρῖσμα. Mark 6.13 mentions actual anointing with oil as used by the Apostles in casting out devils and healing the sick, and it is possible that this use may be the origin of the anointing with the "oil of exorcism" before baptism.

Jesus anointed with his own spittle as a means of healing, and the Apostles anointed with oil for the same purpose. Luke 10.34 reminds us that oil was also used medically. The use in *Ap. Trad.* of the typology of priestly and royal anointing in the blessing of the oil for the sick has already shown us the association between baptismal anointing and healing, and this relationship will become a liturgical and homiletical commonplace.

Tertullian and a multitude of later writers connect the baptismal anointing with the anointing of priests in the Old Testament. In this context the attribution of a royal priesthood to the Christian people in 1 Pet. 2.5 and 2.9, and in Rev. 1.6 and 5.10 provides a link between the liturgy and the Old Covenant.

Another strand woven into the rite of baptismal anointing is suggested by Rev. 7.3. The angel is here described as sealing the servants of God on their foreheads with the "seal (σφραγίς) of the living God". This seal was the mark by which the elect of God could be identified, and it was frequently interpreted as the sign of the cross made in baptism on the foreheads of the believers. There is no indication in Revelation that the seal was made with oil, nor that it was in the form of a cross, although the parallel with Ezek. 9.4 where the mark of the *taw* was in the shape of an X would lead to the assumption that a cross (or *chi* for χριστός) was made. The identification of this sign with the mark borne by the Christian is already found in Tertullian,[1] and, considering the liturgical character of Revelation, it is not impossible that this sealing reflected an existing practice.

Massey Shepherd, in his analysis of this chapter in *The Paschal Liturgy and the Apocalypse*, sees in it a reflection of the rites of Christian initiation, although he is unwilling to ascribe definitely to the Seer of the Apocalypse a knowledge of the liturgy described by Hippolytus and Tertullian.

We may well be dealing here ... with influences which the Apocalypse itself has had upon the development of the baptismal rites. But at least these aspects of the ceremonial and ritual seem to be implied:

---

[1] *adversus Marcionem* III, 22; *de Corona* 3.

1 The renunciation of Satan
2. The profession of faith
3. The washing
4. The sealing with the Name
5. The investment with white garments

It is possible too, that the sealing carries further recollections of the chrismation and laying on of hands in "Confirmation". But this cannot be so definitely read out of the text.[1]

Certainly the eschatological seal which marked the faithful for the day of redemption came to be an element in the interpretation of the baptismal signing, and in this development Rev. 7 played a part.[2]

From the New Testament the Church drew two elements which it expressed in its baptismal anointings. The first was the Messianic anointing of Jesus with the Holy Spirit. With this the first post-baptismal anointing of *Ap. Trad.*, and the corresponding anointings in other rites are identified. The second is the sealing, or signing, which has its roots in the eschatological seal. In this element it is the mark of the cross, not the oil with which it was customarily applied, which is of primary significance. Although separate in origin, these two elements merged in the practice of signing the cross with chrism, and were frequently confused both in practice and in theory.

Unfortunately the evidence does not permit us to come to a definite conclusion as to the liturgical reference of the New Testament passages we have cited. It is certainly possible that the author of 1 John was familiar with a liturgical anointing, but the opposite view can also be maintained. It is also possible that the Seer of Revelation knew the baptismal signing with the cross, but on the other hand the typology of Ezekiel would be sufficient to account for the reference without his having known any such external practice. In the latter case the Apocalypse itself may have influenced the development of the rite. It is certain that these baptismal ceremonies developed as a continuation of the tradition represented in the New Testament passages discussed above and as consistent with them.

OLD TESTAMENT BACKGROUND

As the previous section has amply demonstrated, it is impossible to discuss the New Testament evidence without considering the Jewish

---

[1] op. cit., pp. 90f.
[2] cf. Lampe, *The Seal of the Spirit*, p. 15; Thornton, *Confirmation*, pp. 45–55.

and Old Testament background. Many Old Covenant types were applied to the Christian baptismal anointings. The most important of these is, of course, the actual anointing with oil.

The Old Testament uses three words for anointing. *Dāshēn* means literally "to make fat" and is found only in Ps. 23. It is rendered λιπαίνειν in the Septuagint, and need not detain us longer. *Sûk* means "to pour" and is rendered ἀλείφειν in the Septuagint. It occurs in Deut. 28.40 and Ruth 3.3. Religious anointing is always *māshah*, which means "to smear or spread with oil". It is, of course, the root of Messiah. It is rendered in the Septuagint by both χρίειν and ἀλείφειν, both of which are translated "to anoint".

In the Old Testament oil has its normal, secular, Near Eastern uses. The most important of these was as a cosmetic.[1] It was not so used in times of mourning, of which its absence was a sign.[2] It was also used in the preparation of food,[3] in lamps,[4] and as a medicine.[5] It was a principal item of commerce,[6] and became a symbol of wealth.[7] Oil usually connoted a joyous celebration, and in Ps. 45.7. it is called "the oil of gladness". This phrase was to become a technical term for a Christian baptismal oil,[8] probably because of the Messianic associations of Psalm 45.

Considerable religious use was made of oil in the Old Testament, not only for the lighting of the tabernacle and the temple,[9] but also in the anointing of persons and things. The oil used was customarily olive oil. The compounding of a "holy anointing oil" is prescribed in the Priestly Code in Ex. 30.22–5:

> Moreover the Lord said to Moses, "Take the finest spices: of liquid myrrh five hundred shekels, and of sweet-smelling cinnamon half as much, that is two hundred and fifty, and of aromatic cane two hundred and fifty, and of cassia five hundred, according to the shekel of the sanctuary, and of olive oil a hin; and you shall make of these a sacred anointing oil blended as the perfumer: a holy anointing oil it shall be.

With this oil Moses was directed to anoint the tabernacle and the ark and all of the vessels of the sanctuary, including the altar.

---

[1] Deut. 28.40; Ruth 3.3; Ps. 104.15; Judith 16.8
[2] 2 Sam. 14.2.   [3] 1 Kings 17.12; Ex. 29.2; Lev. 2.4.
[4] Ex. 27.20; 1 Chron. 9.29; cf. Mishna, *Shabbath* 2.1f.
[5] Isa. 1.6; Ezek. 16.9.   [6] Ezek. 27.17; Hos. 12.1.
[7] Deut. 33.24.   [8] In the Coptic and Byzantine rites.
[9] Ex. 27.20; Lev. 24.2; 1 Chron. 9.29.

You shall consecrate them, that they may be most holy; whatever touches them will become holy.[1]

With this oil he was directed to anoint Aaron and his sons as priests. Its use was restricted to this purpose, and its confection and use for other purposes was forbidden under pain of excommunication. According to Talmudic tradition, the oil compounded by Moses was used to anoint the priests and kings of Judah until the time of Josiah, who hid the anointing oil with the holy ark, the rod of Aaron, and the pot of manna. It is believed that the anointing oil will reappear in the days of the Messiah.[2]

As we have already seen, the anointing of Christians was identified with the anointing of Aaron by Moses, and Christian rites of anointing commonly referred to the anointing of prophets, priests, and kings.

The anointing of priests is found in Ex. 28.41 and 29.36, in Lev. 8.12, and Num. 3.3 in the P tradition. The Holiness Code restricts the anointing to the high priest in Lev. 21.10, and the Rabbinic tradition accepts this distinction.[3] The consecration of objects by anointing is found also in the earlier JE tradition of the anointing of the pillar at Beth-el by Jacob.[4] Its purpose appears always to have been to make objects holy, or to indicate their holiness.

Of unusual interest is the description of the method of anointing priests found in the Talmud. In the tractate *Kerithoth* we read:

Our Rabbis have taught: In anointing kings one draws the figure of a crown, and with priests in the shape of the letter *chi*. Said R. Menashia: The Greek [letter] *chi* is meant. One [Tannā] teaches: The oil was first poured over the head and then smeared between the eyelids; whereas another [Tanna] teaches: the oil was first smeared between the eyelids and then poured over the head.[5]

And in *Horayoth*, another tractate, we read:

Our Rabbis taught: How were the kings anointed? In the shape of a wreath. And the priest?—In the shape of a *chi*.[6]

It has not usually been observed by Christian scholars that the priestly anointing with which the Fathers identified the baptismal unction was also an anointing in the form of a cross, nor that it involved the pouring

[1] Ex. 30.29.   [2] *Horayoth* 12a.   [3] ibid., *Kerithoth* 5b.
[4] Gen. 28.18; 31.13; 35.14.
[5] Epstein, *The Babylonian Talmud, Kerithoth*, p. 36.
[6] ibid., *Horayoth*, p. 85.

of oil upon the crown of the head and the anointing of the forehead. The similarity of Jewish and Christian practice is astounding.

The anointing of prophets is mentioned only in the cases of Elisha and the author of Isa. 61, the passage which our Lord applies to himself in Luke 4.16f. In the latter case the reference may be metaphorical, and it is uncertain to whom the reference was intended. For Christians, of course, its use by Jesus is sufficient guarantee of its importance as background for the baptismal anointings.

The anointing of kings appears to be the chief unction of what might be termed a sacramental nature in the Old Testament. It is considered to be of Egyptian origin, and to have been in use in Canaan before the conquest.

> By the pouring of the consecrated oil upon the head, there was effected a transference to the person anointed of a part of the essential holiness and virtue of the deity in whose name and by whose representative the rite was performed.[1]

The anointing of kings was, therefore, similar to the anointing of priests in meaning. It was an essentially theocratic act, by which the king became the "Anointed of Yahweh". It was more than a ceremony and actually conveyed the power for the exercise of regal authority.

The anointing of Saul, the first anointed Hebrew king, is described in 1 Sam. 10.1, that of David in 1 Sam. 16.13, and that of Solomon in 1 Kings 1.39. Other royal anointings mentioned in the Old Testament are of Jehu (2 Kings 9.6), Joash (2 Kings 11.12), Jehoahaz (2 Kings 23.30), and Absalom (2 Sam. 19.10). Of particular interest is the description of the anointing of David:

> Then Samuel took the horn of oil, and anointed him in the midst of his brothers; and the Spirit of the Lord came mightily upon David from that day forward.

In this case, at least, the oil served as the vehicle for the bestowal of the Holy Spirit, and Christians saw in this act the type of their *unctio Spiritus sancti*.

The prophet Samuel anointed Saul and David, and Elisha anointed Jehu, but the regular minister of the anointing was the priest. In the anointing of Solomon both Zadok the priest and Nathan the prophet had a part, and this may have been the point of transition to a regular priestly anointing.

[1] A. R. S. Kennedy, "Anointing", in Hastings' *Dictionary of the Bible*, New York, 1909, p. 35.

In Hebrew usage "The Anointed" means primarily the king, and it appears that the anointing of the high priest was a later extension of the rite. An important element in Christian thought concerning this anointing is the designation of the anointed person as "holy to the Lord".

It is beyond the scope of this study to trace the development of the Messianic concept in Judaism, but it was obviously the Messiahship of Jesus which brought to Christian notice the concept of the Anointed King.

Reference has been made to various other Old Testament typologies, such as the use of oil in the healing of a leper in Lev. 14, as they occurred in Christian sources, and they need not be repeated here. The concept of the seal in Ezek. 9.4, nevertheless, is sufficiently important to require treatment.

> And the Lord said to him, "Go through the city, through Jerusalem, and put a mark (*taw*) upon the foreheads of the men who sigh and groan over all the abominations that are committed in it."

The mark, or *taw*, was a cross. It is the regular Hebrew word for the X branded upon the thigh or neck of horses to designate ownership, and for the mark made by the illiterate. In the old form of the Hebrew alphabet, seen, for example, on the coins of the Maccabees, the letter *taw* is represented by × or +.

Christians, quite naturally, saw in this marking of the faithful with a cross a prophetic sign that the power of the cross of Christ would save them from destruction. Whether they identified Ezekiel's *taw*, and its parallel in Rev. 7.3 with their own practice of signing the newly baptized with the cross, or began the custom in imitation of it is impossible to say. There is, in either case, a close relationship between the *taw* and Christian practice.

This *taw* was identified by Justin Martyr with the Septuagint reading of Num. 21.8, "Make for yourself a serpent, and place upon it a sign", and with the sign in the blood of the Paschal lamb in Ex. 12.13,[1] both passages with definite christological associations. The combined effect of these references would have been to strengthen the influence of the *taw* typology on Christian thinking. The sign of the cross became the sign which, by the shedding of the blood of Christ, saves the faithful from the Evil One and from eternal death. Thornton believes that this identification had already been made by the time

[1] *Dialogue* 94, III, 112.

of the writing of Revelation, and lies behind the sealing recorded there.[1]

We have found two aspects of the baptismal anointing prefigured in the Old Testament: consecration to the service of God by anointing with holy oil, and the signing with the mark of the *taw*. Both signified consecration and protection, and these qualities Christians ascribed to their baptismal unction. Jesus is the Messiah, the Anointed One, and for Christians anointing had a specifically christological significance, but this significance was rooted in the Hebrew idea of anointing.

PAGAN AND SECULAR USE OF OIL

A thorough study of the importance of oil in the classical world will be found in the article "*oleum*" by A. S. Pease, late professor of classics and president of Amherst College, in Pauly-Wissowa, *Real-Encyclo-pedie der Classischen Altertumswissenschaft*. Among the many secular uses of oil cited by Pease with copious references to the works of classical authors, the use of oil at the bath and in the gymnasium are of particular concern to us.

"In connection with the bath," says Dr Pease, "there was an anointing with oil from the time of Homer and Hesiod." Its use is mentioned in both the *Iliad* and the *Odyssey* and in *Works and Days*.[2] From the *de Medicina* of Celsus we learn the custom of the Roman bather in the reign of Tiberius:

> When he went to the bath, first he would sweat a little under a garment in the warm room, be anointed there, and then go into the hot baths . . . again to wash and be anointed.[3]

The use of oil corresponded to the modern use of soap. This is made clear by various references to such diverse sources as the *History of Susannah* in the Apocrypha and *The Golden Ass* of Apuleius. *Susannah* 17 speaks of oil as needed for washing, while Apuleius says of his friend Aristomines, whom he found in great misery and calamity:

> And on the spot I dragged him to a private bath, and I myself anointed and scrubbed him.[4]

[1] *Confirmation*, p. 52. If his theory identifying the anointing with the "seal of circumcision" is true, it provides us with still another line of Old Testament types.
[2] *Iliad* 10.577; 14.171; 18.350; *Odyssey* 3.466; 4.252; *Works and Days* 522f.
[3] *de Medicina*, 1.4.
[4] Apuleius, *Metamorphoses*, 1.7.

Apuleius refers to the use of oil in bathing in at least two other passages. In both he tells of being received as a guest in the home of an acquaintance,

> Take his luggage into the bedroom ... and then fetch from the cupboard oil for anointing and a towel for rubbing, and the other things I am accustomed to use, and take my guest to the nearest public bath.[1]

In the second passage, he and his friends have been offered food and a hot bath.

> They at once took off their clothes, and naked and refreshed by the steam of a tremendous fire, they splashed themselves with hot water and anointed themselves with oil (*oleo peruncti*) and then sat down to tables heaped bountifully with a feast (*mensas dapibus largiter instructas*).[2]

Similarly, the satiric poet Martial tells of a man who did not give the *unctor* sufficient oil to anoint his whole body.[3]

Many other references to classical literature may be found in Dr Pease's definitive article, but these will suffice to show the almost essential connection in the ancient world between washing and anointing. We cannot go so far as to state that in this secular use of oil in bathing we find the source of the Christian baptismal anointings, but we may observe that to a Roman or Hellenistic Greek anointing would be associated with washing as naturally as we associate soap with water. When a Roman went to the bath he took a towel and oil.

The Greeks and Romans anointed themselves not only for bathing, but also for exercise. The anointing of all types of athletes is mentioned repeatedly in classical authors. Ovid speaks of the discus-throwers as "gleaming with rich olive oil",[4] and Virgil tells of rowers whose "naked shoulders glisten, moist with oil",[5] Not only professional athletes, but the ordinary citizen as well anointed himself to participate in the exercises of the gymnasium. From Galen we learn that the anointing customarily both preceded and followed the exercise, and that in the larger baths and gymnasia there was a separate room for the anointing.[6] From this we can see the appropriateness with which St John Chrysostom, for example, could speak of those about to be baptized as being anointed as "athletes of Christ".

---

[1] Apuleius, *Metamorphoses*, 1.23.   [2] ibid., 4.7.
[3] Martial, *Epigrammata*, 12.70.   [4] *Metamorphoses*, 10.176.
[5] *Aeneid*, 5.135.   [6] Galen, 11.476; cf. Pease, art. cit., col. 2463.

Oil was also used in pagan religious rites. Pagans, holding an anthropomorphic conception of their deities, tended to reproduce the secular uses of oil in religious rites. The gods were not expected to drink the oil, but their shrines were lighted with oil lamps and their images anointed with oil. The anointing of the cult-image was believed to be a meritorious act.

A further religious use of oil was in conjunction with sacrifice, particularly burnt sacrifice, in which the pouring of oil over the victim served the practical purpose of causing it to burn more readily.

Those who approached the cult-image or the sacred precincts were also frequently anointed. Pease describes this as a sacramental act giving special purity to those engaged in the sacred work. He mentions specifically the anointing of Egyptian, Hebrew, and Christian priests, and the anointing of the kings of Israel as examples of this use of oil.

In the mystery religions the anointing of people was not common. Ovid describes the apotheosis of Aeneas in *Metamorphoses* 14. Venus, Aeneas' mother, has been speaking to the river god Numicius:

> The horned god obeyed the commands of Venus, and in his waters cleansed and washed away whatever was mortal in Aeneas. His best part remained to him. His mother washed his body and anointed it with divine perfume, and touched his mouth with ambrosia mixed with sweet nectar and made him a god . . .[1]

The mystic bath, the mystic anointing, and the mystic food which make the Roman hero a god are a striking parallel to the baptism, anointing, and communion of the Christian initiate, which make him a partaker of the divine life of Christ. We would in no way wish to imply that the rites described by Ovid were a source of Christian baptismal practice, but the existence of this passage in a well-known classical work does provide a framework within which a Roman convert to Christianity could interpret the rites of his own initiation.

Pausanias describes the mystic rite at the oracle of Trophonius, in which children were washed and anointed in the name of Hermes, and the geographer Strabo describes the anointing of naked youths in the rites of the grotto of Charon at Nysa.[2] By far the most interesting description is that furnished by Firmicus Maternus of the rites of Attis:

On a certain night an image (*simulacrum*) is laid supine on a litter and is

---

[1] *Metamorphoses*, 14, 602–7.
[2] Pausanias, *Graeciae descriptio*, 8, 39, 7; Strabo, *Geographia*, 14, 1, 44.

mourned with measured laments set to music. Finally when they have sated themselves with their false lament, a light is brought in. Then the necks of all who mourned are anointed by a priest. When he has anointed them, he whispers in a soft voice: "Be of good cheer, initiates, the god has been saved; and for us too there shall be salvation from sufferings."[1]

The great majority of the Gnostic sects evidently practised unction in their initiations in the second century, but it is by no means clear whether their use is dependent upon Christian practice, or derived from pagan sources. A detailed examination of the Gnostic evidence is made by Professor Lampe in *The Seal of the Spirit*.[2]

The use of oil in magic appears to have been well established by the second century, and, although there does not appear to have been any direct influence upon Christian practice, authorities in the field believe that the influence of the magical papyri upon Gnostic usage is definitely established.[3]

Pease believes the practice of anointing with oil to be derived from the anointing with the fat of a sacrificial animal in primitive religion. By means of this anointing the virtue and power of the animal sacrificed passed into the person anointed. He does not believe this interpretation to have been known to the classical practitioners of anointing, and contends that the rite remained in use although its meaning had been long forgotten.

From these references we can see the importance which oil had in the life of the average Roman. Not only did he cook with it, burn it in his lamps, and wash with it, but he used it as a medicine, as a cosmetic, and in religious rites. The association of washing and anointing was extremely close both in religious ceremonial and in daily life. Certainly the idea of a sacred anointing would not have been alien to the mind of a neophyte coming to the Church from the pagan Roman world.

When we add to the pagan and secular background the use of oil to anoint kings and priests in the Old Testament, and view all in the light of the New Testament proclamation of Jesus as the Christ, the Anointed One, and the Christian people as a royal priesthood, the expression of these ideas in the visible anointing of Christians at their baptism becomes almost inevitable. Whether or not 1 John describes an actual

---

[1] *de errore profanarum religionum*, 22.1.

[2] pp. 120–8.

[3] cf. G. Anrich, *Das Antike Mysterionwesen*, pp. 103f, 209; J. Coppens, *L'Imposition des Mains*, pp. 321f.

baptismal anointing, it provides a *raison d'être* for the introduction of the ceremony in imitation of the anointing of Christ by the Spirit at his baptism. We are Christians because we are χριστοί, anointed as kings and priests, as athletes of Christ, baptized into his death and resurrection.

III

The Ancient Syrian Rites

THE "DIDASCALIA APOSTOLORUM"

There is one family of rites of Christian initiation which does not follow the general pattern of *Ap. Trad*. This is the Syrian family, in which the anointing with consecrated oil precedes, rather than follows, baptism. The exemplar for this type of rite is the *Didascalia Apostolorum*.

Although written in Greek, the *Didascalia* is known to us only through a complete Syriac text, extensive Latin fragments, and its use by the compiler of the first six books of the *Apostolic Constitutions*. Of the document itself, Dom Connolly says it is third in point of time to the *Didache* and *Ap. Trad.*, but of a different nature. It is "much more an elementary treatise on pastoral theology" than a rudimentary sacramentary.[1] Our interest in it is focused on a single passage at the beginning of chapter XVI "On the Appointment of Deacons and Deaconesses":

> In the first place, when women go down into the water, those who go down into the water ought to be anointed by a deaconess with the oil of anointing; and where there is no woman at hand, and especially no deaconess, he who baptizes must of necessity anoint her who is being baptized. But where there is a woman, and especially a deaconess, it is not fitting that women should be seen by men: but with the imposition of hand do thou anoint the head only. As of old the priests and kings were anointed in Israel, do thou in like manner, with the imposition of hand, anoint the head of those who receive baptism, whether of men or of women: and afterwards—whether thou thyself baptize, or thou command the deacons or presbyters to baptize— let a woman deacon, as we have already said, anoint the women. But let a man pronounce over them the invocation of the divine Names in the water.

[1] R. H. Connolly, *Didascalia Apostolorum*, p. xxvi.

And when she who is being baptized has come up from the water, let the deaconess receive her, and teach and instruct her how the seal of baptism ought to be [kept] unbroken in purity and holiness.[1]

On one hand, certain affinities with the rite of *Ap. Trad.* will immediately be observed. Anointing is clearly that of the whole body; otherwise the concern for modesty would be meaningless. The anointing of the head is reserved to the bishop and is connected with the "imposition of hand". The anointing of women by a deaconess, although not in *Ap. Trad.*, is a reasonable development. On the other hand, the elimination of all mention of a post-baptismal unction, and the clear similarity of the pre-baptismal unction here described to the twofold post-baptismal anointing in *Ap. Trad.* are striking differences, and are the distinctive mark of this family of rites. There is no anointing after baptism, and what are usually considered distinctively post-baptismal acts—the anointing of the forehead by the bishop and the laying on of hands—precede the baptism.

This lack of a post-baptismal anointing becomes particularly clear when this passage is read with *Ap. Con.*, 3.16, which is based on it. In *Ap. Con.* the conclusion of the passage reads:

And let a deacon receive the man and a deaconess (ἡ διάκονος) the woman, that so the conferring of this inviolable seal (σφραγίς) may take place with a becoming decency. And after that, let the bishop anoint with chrism (μύρον) those that have been baptized.[2]

Here the final sentence has been altered to permit the addition of a post-baptismal unction. The probable reason for this change will be discussed later, when we turn our attention to *Ap. Con.*, but the alteration accentuates the lack of a post-baptismal anointing in the *Didascalia*.

Ap. Con., 3.16, nevertheless, places its stress upon the pre-baptismal unction, for which additional directions and theological explanations are given. When the women come to be baptized,

the deacon shall anoint only their foreheads with the holy oil (ἅγιον ἔλαιον), and after this the deaconess shall anoint (ἀλείφειν) them ... but in the laying on of hands (χειροθεσία) the bishop shall anoint her head only.

As in the *Didascalia* this anointing is likened to that of priests and kings, but the reference is expanded by adding,

[1] ibid., p. 146.
[2] F. X. Funk, *Didascalia et Constitutiones Apostolorum*, Vol. I, p. 211; Whitaker, p. 27.

4

not because those who are now being baptized are being ordained priests, but as being Christians (anointed) from Christ (the Anointed),[1]

and by quoting 1 Pet. 2.9. The anointing of the heads of those about to be baptized is explained as being done for a type (εἰς τύπον) of the spiritual baptism. It is therefore the pre-baptismal anointing with which *Ap. Con.*, 3.16 associates a theological meaning, while the post-baptismal unction is presented as a bare fact without explanations. This is consistent with the view that the post-baptismal anointing was an addition made by the Constitutor, as the editor of *Ap. Con.* is customarily called, to the complete rite found in his source.

If we examine these two passages together, it will not be difficult to reconstruct the basic outline of that rite. The first baptismal ceremony is the anointing performed by the deacon. In the case of male candidates, the deacon anoints the entire body, while in the case of women, he simply begins the anointing by pouring oil on their foreheads and allows the actual anointing of the body to be performed by the deaconess, while the male ministers withdraw. The candidates of both sexes are then led to the bishop, who pours oil upon their heads "for a type of the baptism of the Spirit". This anointing is followed by the leading of the candidates to the water. The deaconesses seem to have gone into the water with the women and the deacons with the men, while the presbyter or deacon standing beside the font pronounced the invocation of the Name. The women were then received by the deaconesses, and presumably the men by the deacons, and instructed, before being led into the church for the Eucharist.

The *Didascalia* implies that in the absence of a deaconess another woman might anoint the women, but recognizes the possibility that the baptizing minister might have to anoint them himself. There is also a certain confusion as to the rôle of the various ministers in the baptism. This can be explained on the basis of practical necessity. If the requisite number of deacons, deaconesses, and presbyters is not available, as might well be the case in the rural parts of Syria, provision is made for others to perform their liturgies. The bishop alone, however, is to anoint the heads at the laying on of hands. This is in accordance with the ceremonies of *Ap. Trad.*, but it is the exact opposite of the later Roman custom, which permitted the presbyter to anoint the head, but restricted the anointing of the forehead to the bishop.

[1] F. X. Funk, *Didascalia et Constitutiones Apostolorum*, Vol. I, pp. 209ff.

THE "ACTS OF JUDAS THOMAS"

We find the order of the *Didascalia* maintained in other Syrian sources, of which the earliest appears to be the Gnostic *Acts of Judas Thomas*. This work exists in both Syriac and Greek, and although the precise relationship between the two versions is not clear, the weight of scholarly opinion tends towards accepting the Syriac as original.[1]

Two of the five accounts of baptism in the *Acts* are quite brief, but four of the five mention anointing with oil before baptism, and the fifth mentions the giving of the *rushmâ*, or seal, but without specifying that oil was used.[2]

The first of the longer descriptions is of the baptism of King Gundaphar. In this account the Apostle enters the bath-house by night with the king and his brother. He first pours oil upon their heads while reciting a florid invocation, then baptizes them in the Triune Name, and at dawn administers the Eucharist.

The description of the baptism of Mygdonia in the Syriac provides a complete parallel to the *Didascalia*. The Apostle first anoints her head, then tells her nurse to anoint her and put a linen cloth about her loins, after which he baptizes her and celebrates the Eucharist.

In the description of the baptism of Vizan (Iuzanēs in the Greek) and certain women, Mygdonia performs the office of the deaconess. The Apostle anoints with oil the heads of those to be baptized:

> And he commanded Mygdonia to anoint them, and he himself anointed Vizan. And after he had anointed them, he made them go down into the water in the Name of the Father and the Son and the Spirit of holiness. And after they had been baptized and were come up, he brought bread and the mingled cup.

Admittedly these are Gnostic writings, and cannot be accepted at face value as testimony to the usage of orthodox Christians, but their supporting value is nevertheless high, when they are taken with the description of baptism in the *Didascalia*. Unquestionably the anointing was most important in the Gnostic sect which these *Acts* represent. The

[1] cf. F. C. Burkitt, "The Original Language of the Acts of Judas Thomas", in *J.T.S.*, Vol. I (1900) pp. 280–90.

[2] These are most conveniently examined in Whitaker, *Documents*, pp. 10–16. The Syriac text, with English translation, is published as *The Acts of Thomas*, ed. A. F. J. Klijn, Leiden, 1962. The Greek is in Lipsius and Bonnet, *Acta Apostolorum Apocrypha*, Vol. II, Part 2, Leipzig, 1891.

Greek versions actually omit all reference to the use of water in two cases.[1]

Leaving aside the complex question of the relationship of the Greek and Syriac texts, we are, nevertheless, presented with testimony to a rite which laid great stress upon a pre-baptismal unction, and which identified it in some sense with the gift of the Spirit.

MAR EPHRAEM SYRUS AND MINOR SYRIAN WRITERS

St Ephraem, the fourth-century Biblical exegete and ecclesiastical writer, is the great doctor of the Syrian Church. His third and fourth hymns for the Epiphany provide further evidence for the distinctive Syrian order of the baptismal rites. The third hymn speaks of the anointing and the fourth of baptism. The latter hymn begins, "Descend my sealed brothers, put ye on the Lord", indicating that they have already received the *rushmâ*.[2] The third hymn dwells at length on the typology of the anointing:

> Christ and chrism are conjoined, the secret with the visible is mingled: the chrism anoints visibly—Christ seals secretly, the lambs newborn and spiritual, the prize of his twofold victory; for he engendered it of the chrism, and he gave it birth of the water.

The hymn goes on to refer specifically to the anointing of Christ by the sinful woman, to the oil multiplied by Elijah, to the olive branch brought into the ark, to the oil poured out by Jacob at Bethel, to the anointing of Aaron by Moses, to the anointing of Saul and David, and to the anointing of the Levites. The purpose of the seal is declared to be the separation of Christ's people from the peoples of the world, and the making of the body holy as a Temple of the Spirit, "for the Father and Son and Holy Ghost have moved and come down and dwelt in you".

Mar Ephraem refers again to the baptismal anointing in the seventh of his hymns on virginity.[3] It is clear from this hymn also that the anointing precedes the baptism. In 7.2 he says, "April recreates those who are fasting, anoints, baptizes, and whitens them", clearly referring to the Easter baptisms, and in 7.8 he says simply, "The anointing precedes."

[1] That of Gundaphar (Lipsius and Bonnet, p. 142) and of a demoniac woman (ibid., p. 165).

[2] Post-Nicene Fathers, Vol. 13, pp. 269–72.

[3] Latin and French versions are given by Dom Edmund Beck in an article "Le Baptême chez Saint Ephrem", in *L'Orient Syrien*, Vol. I (1956), pp. 111–36.

The Syriac doctor describes the meaning of the unction in several ways. In strophe five, he compares it to the paint with which the image of a king is painted, declaring that with the visible oil the hidden image of the hidden King is painted. In strophe seven he attributes to the anointing the cleansing of the stained body, comparing baptism to another womb in which the sinner is new born as was Naaman in the river. There is a certain confusion between oil and water as the agent of washing, and in strophe nine he compares the destruction of sin by holy oil to the destruction of sinners by the flood. For our purpose, the most important passage is strophe six:

> The oil is the agent of the Holy Spirit and his minister, and followed him as his disciple. Through oil the Spirit signed priests and kings. The Holy Spirit through oil imprinted the seal upon his sheep, as a ring which impresses its seal in wax. Even so the Spirit impresses the hidden seal upon the bodies through oil when they are anointed in baptism and signed in baptism.

Most evidently the oil is the vehicle of the Holy Spirit, which marks the faithful as the sheep of Christ. It is intimately bound to baptism in Ephraem's thought and cannot be separated from it.[1] It appears that he was familiar with baptism both at Epiphany and at Easter, since his hymns speak of it both at Epiphany and in April after the fast. It is also clear that he expected the anointing to precede baptism.

Two other Syriac accounts of baptism are contained in Overbeck's *S. Ephraemi Aliorumque Opera Selecta*. The first describes the baptism of Rabbûla, the famous fifth-century bishop of Edessa. The order described is confession of faith, anointing, baptism, and Eucharist.[2]

The second account is a Syriac description of the baptism of Constantine attributed to Mar Ephraem Syrus, but possibly dating from the sixth century. In this account Constantine is described as a leper who is cleansed from his leprosy by the pre-baptismal anointing. This is particularly interesting in the light of Justin Martyr's discussion of the relation between the rites for the cleansing of a leper in Lev. 14 and the Christian initiatory rites.[3]

The order of events described at Constantine's baptism was blessing of the water, anointing, baptism, and reception of the Eucharist. The formula for the anointing was:

---

[1] Brief references to anointing also occur in *contra Haereses* 7.23 and *de Fide* 49.4.
[2] *Vita Rabbulae*, op. cit., p. 165.
[3] Dialogue 41, see above, pp. 14–15.

By this with which I anoint thee be thou made clean.[1]

In this context we may note a passage from St Ephraem's fourth hymn for Epiphany:

> When the leper of old was cleansed, the priest used to seal him with oil, and to lead him to the waterspring. The type has passed, and the truth has come: lo! with chrism have ye been sealed, in baptism are ye perfected, in the flock ye are intermixed, from the Body ye are nourished.[2]

It would appear that this passage from the real Ephraem lay behind the "leprosy" of Constantine in the pseudo-Ephraem.

The Acts of John the Son of Zebedee claims to be a Syriac translation of a history "composed by Eusebius of Caesarea concerning St John", although Dom Connolly believes it to be a native Syriac composition.[3] It contains two accounts of baptism. In both cases the oil is blessed first, then the water. After this follow the profession of faith, anointing, and threefold baptism.

In the first case the formal profession of faith follows the anointing, and after baptism the neophytes are clothed in white and given the kiss of peace. There is no mention of the Eucharist. The anointing is described thus:

> When he had stripped, the holy [man] drew nigh, and took oil in his hand, and made him a cross on his forehead, and anointed his whole body.

In the second case the Eucharist is mentioned after the baptism. The work is believed to date from the late fourth century.[4]

ST JOHN CHRYSOSTOM

Turning from Syriac to Greek-speaking writers, we come to the baptismal homilies of St John Chrysostom.[5] Chrysostom describes in detail the baptismal rites of the Church of Antioch, in which the homilies were delivered, in the second of a collection of eight homilies

---

[1] Overbeck, op. cit., p. 360. I am deeply indebted to the Reverend Professor Robert C. Dentan, Ph.D., for reading these selections for me in Syriac and translating the necessary parts.

[2] Post-Nicene Fathers, Vol. 13, p. 270.

[3] *J.T.S.*, Vol. VIII, pp. 249–61.

[4] Wright, *Apocryphal Acts of the Apostles*, Vol. II, pp. 38–42 and 53–5. cf. Whitaker, pp. 18–20. For the sake of completeness two other references should be noted: *Clementine Recognitions* 3.37 and Aphraates, *Homily* 12.13.

[5] cf. my article, "The Baptismal Rite in Chrysostom", in *Anglican Theological Review*, Vol. 43 (1961), pp. 397–403.

published by Fr Antoine Wenger from a manuscript found by him in the Stavronikita monastery on Mount Athos. A parallel description occurs in the third of another series of homilies published in 1902 by the noted Byzantine scholar A. Papadopoulos-Kerameus in a rare volume entitled *Varia Graeca Sacra*. An English translation of both series of homilies has recently been published under the title *St John Chrysostom: Baptismal Instructions*.[1]

The baptismal ceremonies described in the Stavronikita manuscript (Wenger) begin with the renunciation of Satan and adherence to Christ. This is followed by the anointing, which is described in this way:

> He anoints you upon the forehead with the spiritual chrism (μύρον) as a soldier enrolled for the spiritual arena, and places the seal (σφραγίς) upon you, saying, "So and so is anointed in the name of the Father, and of the Son and of the Holy Ghost."

Although no subject for the verbs is expressed in the Greek, the context makes it clear that the same priest who has accepted the renunciation and adherence is meant. In the parallel passage in P.K., Chrysostom states, "God himself anoints you by the hand of the priest", and quotes 2 Cor. 1.21. It is also clear that the seal in Wenger means the sign of the cross. The corresponding passage in P.K. removes any possible doubt by saying, "They gave you the cross upon your forehead".

In the following chapter Chrysostom describes the effects on the devil of seeing the soul he thought under his tyranny joined to Christ:

> For this reason [the priest] anoints your forehead and gives you the seal, so that when That One sees it, he will turn away his eyes.

The oil with which the anointing is performed is called μύρον. This is the same name used in *Ap. Con.*, 3.16 for the post-baptismal oil and is the regular Greek term for the oil which in the West is called chrism. The oil is described in P.K. in this way:

> This ointment (χρῖσμα) is at once both oil (ἔλαιον) and chrism (μύρον): chrism to anoint the bride, and oil to anoint the athlete.

The rest of the ceremonies take place when it is dark, and as there is no mention of the interval of a day, we may assume that the renunciation and sealing took place on the afternoon of Holy Saturday and the

[1] Wenger, *Jean Chrysostome: Huit Catéchèses Baptismales*, pp. 145ff; Papadopoulos-Kerameus (P.K.), *Varia Graeca Sacra*, pp. 173ff; P. W. Harkins, *St John Chrysostom; Baptismal Instructions* (Ancient Christian Writers, Vol. 31), pp. 213-55, 161-72.

baptism itself at Easter Even. It is not clear whether the renunciations were held late in the day and formed a continuous service with the evening ceremonies, or whether there was an interval between the two parts of the rite.

At the beginning of the evening ceremonies the initiate is divested of all his clothing and his whole body anointed with the holy oil. Whether this oil is the μύρον used for the seal or another oil is not clear, but the use of the word χρῖσμα to describe both chrism (μύρον) and simple oil leads one to believe that the same oil is meant. The purpose of this unction is to fortify and defend all the bodily members against the darts of the enemy. After the anointing the initiate goes down into the sacred waters. Chrysostom describes this in these words:

> Through the words of the priest and his hand the visitation of the Holy Spirit comes upon you and another man arises.[1]

This is the only reference to the Holy Spirit, other than in the Trinitarian formulas, in Chrysostom's account of baptism. Undoubtedly the picture he has in mind is the baptism of Christ in Jordan, with the hand of John the Baptist upon the head of Jesus. At the moment of baptism the ἱερεύς (who is unquestionably the bishop) lays his hand upon the candidate's head and the Holy Spirit descends upon the new man in Christ.

The baptism is by triple immersion with the customary Trinitarian formula, with the verb in the passive.[2] Chrysostom explains that the passive is used because the priest is simply acting for Christ, by virtue of his ordination to that function by the Holy Spirit, and that the true minister of the sacrament is the indivisible Trinity.

After they come up out of the water, the initiates are welcomed into the congregation, given the kiss of peace, and led to the Holy Table where they receive the Eucharist. There is mention of neither anointing nor laying on of hands after baptism.

The account from St John Chrysostom is thoroughly consistent with the rest of the Syrian evidence. There is first the signing of the forehead, then the anointing of the whole body, and after that baptism and the Eucharist. Chrysostom connects the signing and anointing with protection against the devil, and therefore probably with the eschatological seal of Ezekiel and Revelation. His particular reference, however, is

---

[1] Wenger 25, p. 147.
[2] "So-and-so is baptized in the Name of the Father, and of the Son, and of the Holy Spirit."

more immediate: it is to protect the catechumen from the wrath of the devil at the moment when he is passing out of his sovereignty into the Kingdom of Christ. He is anointed as an athlete in the spiritual arena and perfumed as a bridegroom for the spiritual marriage.

It would be possible to say, in modern terms, that for Chrysostom baptism and confirmation are administered simultaneously, for he associates the gift of the Spirit with the words and hands of the priest at the moment of baptism. Although he does not connect the anointing of Christians with the anointing of Christ, the position of the anointing in the rite, immediately after the adherence to Christ, must have made the relationship obvious between χριστός and the verb χρίειν.

It would be possible to contend that Chrysostom did know a post-baptismal anointing, but omitted all mention of it in his pre-baptismal lectures because of the *disciplina arcani*. This would, nevertheless, be pure conjecture. All the evidence we possess places Chrysostom's baptismal instructions in the Syrian tradition of no post-baptismal unction, as we should expect, if they were indeed delivered in Antioch. The rite he describes is of the *Didascalia* pattern, although he differs from Ephraem Syrus in not ascribing the gift of the Holy Spirit to the anointing.

THEODORE OF MOPSUESTIA

An account parallel to that found in Chrysostom is given in the Mystagogical Lectures ascribed to Theodore of Mopsuestia, a contemporary and friend of Chrysostom. Unfortunately, the writings of Theodore are not preserved in the original Greek, but come down to us in a Syriac translation, dating (probably) from the fifth or sixth century.[1]

The rites described by Theodore are very similar to those described by Chrysostom. The renunciation of Satan is phrased in almost the same words in both authors, although Theodore's description of it is much more extended. After the adherence to Christ, the priest approaches "clad in a robe of clean and radiant linen", and signs the initiates on the forehead with the holy chrism, saying, "So-and-so is signed in the name of the Father, and of the Son, and of the Holy Spirit." This corresponds exactly to the signing in Chrysostom.

---

[1] Syriac text and English translation published by A. Mignana in *Woodbrooke Studies*, Vol. 6. The selections are from sermons 3 and 4, pp. 46–68. They are also reprinted in Whitaker, pp. 36–42.

Theodore calls this ceremony the first-fruits of the sacrament and gives the following explanation:

> The sign with which you are signed means that you have been stamped as a lamb of Christ and as a soldier of the heavenly King. Indeed, immediately we possess a lamb we stamp it with a stamp which shows to which master it belongs, so that it may graze the same grass as that which the rest of the lambs of the owner graze, and be in the same fold as that in which they are. A soldier who has enlisted for military service, and been found worthy of this service of the State because of his stature and the structure of his body, is first stamped on his hand with a stamp which shows to which king he will henceforth offer his service; in the same way you also, who have been chosen for the Kingdom of Heaven, and after examination have been appointed a soldier to the heavenly King, are first stamped on your forehead, that part of your head which is higher than the rest of your body ... The sign (with which you have been signed) demonstrates that you have communion with, and participation in, all these things.

It is the sign of the cross, and not the chrism with which Theodore is here concerned. It is the mark of chrism, not the anointing which he expounds.

After the signing, the candidate's head is covered with a linen *orarium* by his godfather. The baptism proper follows, presumably immediately. Theodore's description of baptism follows a lengthy discourse on its meaning, which quotes Eph. 1.13, 14 and 2 Cor. 1.21, 22 with their references to anointing and sealing. For the baptism the candidate removes all his garments and his whole body is anointed with chrism, "a mark and sign that you are receiving the covering of immortality, which through baptism you are about to put on".

The anointing is begun by the priest, who says, "So-and-so is anointed in the name of the Father, and of the Son, and of the Holy Spirit", and then "the persons appointed for this service" anoint the whole body. The ceremony is clearly the same as that which Chrysostom describes, although he gives no formula for this anointing. Perhaps "the persons appointed for this service" are the deacons and deaconesses mentioned in the *Didascalia* and *Ap. Con.*, 3.16. The latter passage in particular appears to envisage a rite similar to that described by Theodore and Chrysostom, for, like them, it disassociates the anointing of the whole body from the anointing of the head, restricting the latter to the bishop, but allowing the former to be performed by assistants.[1]

---

[1] In all probability the *priest* in Theodore and Chrysostom is the bishop, not the presbyter. St Ambrose regularly uses *sacerdos* to mean bishop.

At the baptism the priest lays his hand on the candidate's head and recites the Trinitarian formula, as in Chrysostom. The neophyte is then clothed in white.

The great difference between Theodore's account and that of Chrysostom is that following the clothing, Theodore has a second sealing, corresponding to the post-baptismal chrismation in other rites. He says:

> After you have received the grace of baptism and worn a white garment that shines, the priest draws nigh unto you and signs you on the forehead and says: "So-and-so is signed in the name of the Father, and of the Son, and of the Holy Spirit." When Jesus came out of the water he received the grace of the Holy Spirit who descended like a dove and lighted on him, and this is the reason why he is said to have been anointed.

There follow as proof texts the passage from Isa. 61 quoted by our Lord in Luke 4.18, and Acts 10.38. The meaning of this anointing is:

> The Holy Spirit descended on you also, and you were anointed and received grace: and he will remain with you, as it is through him that you now possess the firstfruits.

Theodore then moves on to a discussion of the meaning of baptismal rebirth and concludes with his account of the baptismal Eucharist.

His brief description of a post-baptismal signing sets Theodore's account apart from the others we have considered, except *Ap. Con.*, 3.16, to which it is parallel. It is the belief of the present writer that this account of the post-baptismal signing represents a later addition to the rite. It is a doublet of the pre-baptismal signing, using the same formula. The description of its meaning requires only a few lines, as opposed to the four pages of Mignana's edition devoted to the pre-baptismal signing. It is the opinion of the distinguished Syriac scholar Mgr Gabriel Khouri-Sarkis that this passage is not original, but should tentatively be assigned to the sixth-century translator of Theodore's work into Syriac.[1] If his view proves to be acceptable, it places Theodore firmly in line with the rest of the Syrian evidence. If, on the other hand, it must be regarded as unproven, we have, none the less, in Theodore an account parallel to that in *Ap. Con.*, 3, in which the signing before baptism received greater emphasis.

Whoever wrote it, the passage on the post-baptismal unction in Theodore's fourth sermon does give a good account of what this

---

[1] Mgr Khouri-Sarkis expressed this opinion in a personal letter to me in March 1962. As far as I am aware, he has not published his conclusions.

unction was believed to do. It was based upon the anointing of Christ at his baptism and completed the picture of the baptism in Jordan by adding to the voice of the Father represented by the invocation and hand of the priest, the descent of the Spirit who anointed Christ and anoints us. Whenever the post-baptismal anointing was added to these rites, this explanation conforms to the general Eastern view of its meaning.

THE LITURGICAL HOMILIES OF NARSAI

Narsai was a professor in the school of Edessa from 437 to 457. He then founded the Nestorian school at Nisbis. He was a disciple of Theodore of Mopsuestia. The seemingly omnicompetent Dom Hugh Connolly has edited and translated his liturgical homilies.[1]

The anointing and other pre-baptismal rite are described in the homily "On Baptism", while the baptism proper is described in the homily "On the Mysteries of the Church and on Baptism".[2]

The rite begins with the renunciation of the devil and confession of faith. The candidate is then presented before the priests, who enter his name in the book. The priest then blesses the oil:

> The three names he casts upon the oil, and consecrates it, that it may be sanctifying the uncleanness of men by its holiness. With the name hidden in it he signs the visible body; and the sharp power of the name enters even unto the soul.

He administers the seal (*rushmâ*), signing the face with the oil in the name of the Trinity:

> The three names he traces upon the face as a shield; that the tyrant may see the image of the Divinity on the head of a man.

In performing the anointing, the priest says,

> Such a one is the servant of the King of kings that are on high and below; and with his name he is branded that he may serve [as a soldier] according to his will.

This signing was apparently followed by the anointing of the whole body, for Narsai goes on immediately to say:

> The name of the Divinity he mixes in his hands with the oil; and he signs and

---

[1] *Texts and Studies*, Vol. 8.

[2] These are called B and C respectively by Connolly. Mignana numbered them 22 and 21, but there is no doubt that Connolly's order is correct.

says "Father" and "Son" and "Holy Spirit". "Such a one", he says, "is signed with the three names that are equal, and there is no distinction of elder or younger between One and Another." ...

The three names he recites, together with [the rubbing of] the oil upon the whole man; that hostile demons and vexing passions may not harm him.

Narsai likens the newly anointed Christian to an athlete going down into the arena, and says:

The Spirit gives power to the unction of the feeble oil, and it waxes firm by the operation that is administered in it. By its firmness it makes firm the body and the faculties of the soul, and they go forth confidently to wage war against the Evil One ... The name of the Divinity looks out from the sign on the forehead; and the eyes of the crafty ones are ashamed to look upon it.

The homily concludes with a call to prayer, and the following homily describes the water baptism and the baptismal Eucharist.

Narsai presents us with the same picture which we obtained from the other Syrian sources. Post-baptismal unction is unknown. The pre-baptismal anointing and the water baptism seal and confirm the candidate as a soldier and athlete of Christ.

A post-baptismal anointing did, nevertheless, find its way into the Syrian rites. We have already seen such an anointing in the third book of *Ap. Con.* and in the homilies of Theodore of Mopsuestia. Even if we deny that these references are parts of the original texts, their presence in the extant manuscripts shows that they were added by someone accustomed to a post-baptismal anointing. We must therefore look at those Syrian sources which do have a post-baptismal unction.

ST CYRIL OF JERUSALEM

If the mystagogical catecheses of St Cyril of Jerusalem are genuine, they were probably delivered in 347 or 348. They are frequently attributed, however, not to Cyril, but to John, his successor in the see of Jerusalem.[1] Fortunately, the solution of this problem does not affect directly the testimony they bear to the practice of the Church of Jerusalem in the fourth century.

Cyril's rite, like the others we have examined, begins with the

[1] A discussion of their authenticity is found in the introduction to F. L. Cross's edition, *St. Cyril of Jerusalem's Lectures on the Christian Sacraments*. Quotations are from his translation.

renunciation and adherence. The latter takes the form of a short formal creed. The ceremony then moves into the inner chamber of the baptistery, where the candidates take off their clothes and are anointed from head to foot with exorcized oil. The use of exorcized oil rather than chrism for this pre-baptismal anointing is reminiscent of *Ap. Trad.* and the Roman tradition, which always used exorcized oil before baptism. Cyril explains this anointing as making the candidates partakers of Jesus Christ, the good olive tree.[1] The reference is to St Paul's figure in Rom. 11 of the wild olive branches grafted into the good tree. The exorcized oil also removes sin and chases away the invisible powers of the devil. Although the olive tree figure appears here for the first time in our discussion, the second explanation, as we have seen, is almost standard.

The similarity of Cyril's rite to *Ap. Trad.* is again shown in the baptismal formula, which is interrogative in form, instead of the declarative formula found in Chrysostom, Theodore, and Narsai.

The anointing which follows baptism is described in detail by Cyril:

> Now ye were made Christs by receiving the emblem (ἀντίτυπον) of the Holy Ghost; and all things were in a figure wrought in you, because ye are figures (εἰκόνες) of Christ.

He then explains that as the Holy Ghost came upon Christ when he came up out of Jordan, so the Christian receives the χρῖσμα, the antitype of the Holy Spirit with whom Christ was anointed. He quotes Isa. 61.1, Acts 10.38, and Ps. 45.7, concluding:

> As he was anointed with the spiritual oil of gladness, the Holy Ghost, who is so called because he is the author of spiritual gladness, so ye were anointed with ointment (μύρον), having been made partakers and fellows of Christ.[2]

Cyril likens the change wrought in the chrism by its blessing to the change in the eucharistic bread wrought by the invocation of the Holy Spirit, and says that after the invocation over the chrism it is "the gift of Christ; and by the presence of his Godhead, it causes in us the Holy Ghost".[3] For Cyril the bodily anointing is the accompaniment of the santification of the soul by the Holy Spirit.

The anointing itself was quite complex. First the forehead, then the ears, then the nostrils, then the breast were anointed as symbolizing the whole of the divine armour with which the neophyte is to fight against the devil. The Eucharist follows the anointing.

---

[1] op. cit., 2.3.   [2] 3.1, 2.   [3] 3.3.

Cyril also connects the name Christian with the χρῖσμα, and affirms that it is the anointing which really entitled the Christian to that name.[1] The anointing, Cyril affirms, is prefigured in the anointing of Aaron and Solomon, but the anointing of the Christian was not in a figure (τυπικῶς) but in truth (ἀληθῶς), "because ye were truly anointed by the Holy Ghost".

Cyril's rite is quite different from that found in other Syrian sources. It follows the pattern of *Ap. Trad.* rather than the *Didascalia*, and is comparable to the rites of other parts of the Christian world which will be discussed in the following chapters. Apparently Jerusalem did not share the native Syrian rite with its neighbours, and Etheria's simple comment, "The Paschal vigils are kept as with us", indicates the cosmopolitan nature of the Holy City, which kept it in touch with the rest of the Christian world. The existence of this rite in Jerusalem would, of course, bring it to the notice of other Syrian Churches, and it may be from here that the post-baptismal anointing spread to other parts of Syria. Nevertheless, the universality of post-baptismal anointing outside Syria makes any conjecture in the absence of concrete evidence hazardous.

THE "APOSTOLIC CONSTITUTIONS"

The *Apostolic Constitutions (Ap. Con.)* contain three accounts of the baptismal rite. That in 3.16, which we have already examined, is based upon *Didascalia*, 16; that in 7.22 is based upon *Didache*, 7.1; while the source of that in 7.39-45 is unknown. All three of these accounts include a post-baptismal anointing with chrism. Many questions concerning the *liturgica* of *Ap. Con.* remain to be answered, and upon their answers will depend ultimately the position and authority of this compilation. It is almost certainly of Syrian provenance, and from the latter half of the fourth century. Its editor (the Constitutor) has sometimes been identified with the author of the longer recension of the Ignatian epistles.

Just as the rite in 3.16 includes a post-baptismal anointing not found in *Didascalia*, 16, so too the rite in 7.22 includes anointing. *Didache*, 7.1 contains no mention of any ceremony other than water baptism, but *Ap. Con.*, 7.22 reads:

But thou shalt first anoint the person with holy oil, and afterward baptize him with water, and finally thou shalt seal him with the chrism; that the

[1] 3.5.

anointing with oil may be a participation of the Holy Spirit, and the water a symbol of the death, and the chrism a seal of the covenants.[1]

The Constitutor has brought the baptismal rite of the *Didache* into line with what he believes to be the correct usage, providing a pre-baptismal anointing with holy oil and a post-baptismal seal (σφραγίς) with chrism. It is interesting to note that the Constitutor is enough of a Syrian to connect the participation of the Holy Spirit with the pre-baptismal anointing. With this explanation of the rite in 7.22 may be read his explanation of the rite in 3.16:

> This baptism therefore is given into the death of Jesus: the water is instead of the burial, and the oil instead of the Holy Ghost; the seal instead of the cross; the chrism is the confirmation of the confession.[2]

A further insight into the thinking of the author of *Ap. Con.* is provided in the passage immediately following that quoted above from 7.22:

> If there be neither oil nor chrism, the water is sufficient both for the anointing, and for the seal, and for the confession of him that is dead, or indeed is dying together with [Christ].

Apparently the oil was not essential!

In both of these descriptions *Ap. Con.* has brought the baptismal rite of its source into line with the Constitutor's idea, providing the rite with two anointings, one with oil before the water baptism, and one, called the seal, with chrism afterward. He seems to have been influenced by the practice of the Jerusalem Church in this, although he does not accept Cyril's interpretation of the signing with chrism.

The third of the baptismal rites of *Ap. Con.* is the most detailed. Its source is unknown. Professor E. C. Ratcliff has suggested that it represents the Constitutor's correction of the Antiochene usage with which he was familiar,[3] and this seems the most reasonable hypothesis.

The instruction of catechumens is discussed in 7.39, and the baptismal rites begin at 7.41 with the renunciation and adherence, the latter taking the form of a baptismal creed. This is immediately followed by the

---

[1] Greek text is in F. X. Funk, *Didascalia et Constitutiones Apostolorum*, Vol. I, p. 406, Translation is from Whitaker, *Documents*, p. 28.

[2] 3.17; Funk, p. 211; Whitaker, p. 28.

[3] Ratcliff expressed this view in a letter to me in March 1963. The liturgical forms given in *Ap. Con.* he believes to be proposed departures from Antiochene usage.

anointing with oil, which is blessed by the priest[1] for the remission of sins and preparation for baptism. The oil is sanctified "in the name of the Lord Jesus". The blessing of the water and baptism follow.

After the baptism, the priest anoints the neophyte with chrism and prays that the ointment may be effectual for maintaining the sweet odour of Christ upon him firm and fixed. The priest is directed to say these things over everyone who is baptized, "For this is the efficacy of the laying on of hands on every one". The Constitutor goes on to explain that unless such an invocation (ἐπίκλησις) is pronounced by the priest over each, the baptism is no more effectual than Jewish washings.

The passage is not immediately clear, and I am indebted to Professor Ratcliff for suggesting to me what I believe to be its correct interpretation. The first problem is the meaning of "the laying on of hands". In *Ap. Con.* this is not a distinct rite, but is the act which accompanies the two anointings and the baptism. The priest necessarily lays on hands when he anoints and, according to the ceremonial envisioned by *Ap. Con.*, he would have laid on hands at each of the three baptismal immersions.[2] The Constitutor is anxious to insist that an ἐπίκλησις accompany the laying on of hands on each candidate, for unless this is done, the actions are deprived of their proper power.

This passage might also be interpreted to apply to the post-baptismal anointing alone. Dom Gregory Dix so interprets it, and suggests that the Constitutor is protesting against the frequent omission of post-baptismal anointing in Syria,[3] but as Fr Damien Van den Eynde has pointed out, there is no reason to believe that the Constitutor attached any greater importance to the post-baptismal unction and its accompanying laying on of hands than to any other rite.[4] The post-baptismal prayer, with its emphasis upon the fragrance of the chrism, certainly does not suggest any deep theological attachment to the post-baptismal unction. If *Ap. Con.* copied the post-baptismal anointing from the Jerusalem usage, the Constitutor did not take over the theological meaning which Cyril attached to it. Perhaps, as Ratcliff has hinted, he used a version of *Ap. Trad.* as the basis of his revision, but

---

[1] *priest* here as elsewhere is more probably bishop than presbyter.

[2] cf. D. Van den Eynde, "Baptême et Confirmation d'après les Constitutions Apostoliques VII, 44, 3", in *Recherches de Science Religieuse*, Vol. 27 (1937), pp. 196–212; and in the same volume, P. Galtier, "Impositions des Mains et Bénédictions au Baptême", pp. 464–6.

[3] Dix, *Confirmation, or Laying on of Hands?*, p. 4.

[4] Van den Eynde, art. cit., p. 211.

was unable to accept the post-baptismal prayer of *Ap. Trad.* because his Syrian background drove him to associate the gift of the Holy Spirit with the pre-baptismal anointing. Certainly *Ap. Con.*, 3.17 requires us to believe that the Constitutor did not consider the sealing with chrism to be an essential rite of baptism.

The rite concludes with the recitation of the Lord's Prayer by the initiate. The Eucharist is not mentioned, but this does not imply that the rite was not customarily a part of the Eucharistic liturgy, which is treated in *Ap. Con.*, 8.

If the baptismal rite of *Ap. Con.* is the actual liturgy of a particular Church, it is the earliest Syrian account of post-baptismal anointing outside Jerusalem. If, on the other hand, it is, as we have suggested, an "ideal" liturgy embodying the Constitutor's own views, it need reflect only his own acquaintance with other rites, and is important primarily because of its influence upon later developments.

The rite of *Ap. Con.*, 7.39-45 may well reflect acquaintance with a form of *Ap. Trad.* Certainly the eucharistic liturgy of *Ap. Con.*, 8 shows the influence of Hippolytus' work. But if the Constitutor adopted the format of *Ap. Trad.*, he did not adopt its content. The post-baptismal prayer in *Ap. Trad.*, for example, is associated primarily with the laying on of the bishop's hand; in *Ap. Con.* it is the prayer for the anointing with chrism. The Jerusalem usage may be responsible for the Constitutor's introduction of the post-baptismal chrism, but there is no hint in *Ap. Con.* that the chrism conveys the Spirit.

CONCLUSION

Certainly Cyril has a theology of the post-baptismal anointing. He connects it with the gift of the Spirit. Just as certainly, this is not the theology, or even the practice, of large parts of the Syrian Church. If the passage in Theodore describing post-baptismal unction is genuine, then the rite had spread to Mopsuestia by the early fifth century. Certainly the Greek-speaking Churches of the metropolises of Jerusalem and Antioch would be the first to adopt it, while the Syriac-speaking country Churches would have been slower moving. Chrysostom, writing at Antioch about 390, knew no post-baptismal anointing. Cyril (or perhaps John) in Jerusalem considered it important. *Ap. Con.* introduces this unction into rites which did not originally contain it. We may definitely affirm, in any case, that the pattern of the *Didascalia* was followed throughout the Syrian Churches other than Jerusalem at least until the end of the fourth century, and longer in some places.

Fr Lionel Thornton sees in the traditional Syrian order of initiatory ceremonies a parallel to the Jewish rites, in which the male proselyte was first circumcised and then baptized. In Fr Thornton's view the anointing replaces circumcision in Christian usage.[1] He sees the scriptural basis of this order in the healing miracle described in John 9.6-7. Dix makes the same point in " 'The Seal' in the Second Century", in which he contends that the Syrian is the original Christian order.[2]

More light is shed on this by T. W. Manson in two articles in the *Journal of Theological Studies* for 1947.[3] In the first article he carries the evidence for the Syrian order of rites back into the pages of the New Testament itself, and interprets 1 John as evidence for the existence of these rites at the time of its composition. The three witnesses of "Spirit, water, and blood" in 1 John 5.7,8 he interprets in the light of 1 John 2.20-7 as referring to the anointing, baptism, and the Eucharistic chalice.

It is Manson's contention that 1 John provides the *raison d'être* for these Syrian baptismal rites, namely: it is only the prior gift of the Holy Spirit in our hearts which enables us to make the baptismal confession of faith. Manson equates this gift of the Holy Spirit, "while we are yet sinners", with the good news of the Gospel.

He also notes the similarity between the order of the Syrian rites and the Jewish order of circumcision, baptism, and sacrifice, and feels that this similarity may have been responsible for the adoption of the "normal" order by the rest of the Christian world. He concludes:

> In favour of the antiquity of the Syrian practice is the consideration that it has all the rest of the practice of Christendom against it, and that it is very unlikely that a difference of such magnitude would have been an innovation. It is more likely to be a survival.[4]

The testimony of Manson does much to strengthen the Thornton-Dix position, which for them is secondary to the maintenance of a particular theological view of the relation of anointing to the gift of the Spirit. Certainly the Syrian liturgical practice is different from that of the rest of Christendom, East and West. Man is by nature traditional

---

[1] *Confirmation, Its Place in the Baptismal Mystery*, pp. 27f.

[2] *Theology*, Vol. 51 (1948), p. 8.

[3] "Entry into Membership of the Early Church", pp. 23-33, and "Miscellanea Apocalyptica III", pp. 59-61, both in *J.T.S.*, Vol. 48.

[4] art. cit. p. 26.

in his religious practice, and Greeks and Syrians appear to be particularly so. Once the pre-baptismal anointing was established in the Syrian rites, the custom would tend to maintain itself against, or even alongside, the post-baptismal unction. It would do this, even without any consistent theological explanation of why it was done, simply because it had always been done that way.

The theological explanation of the Syrian order given by Manson seems to give a reasonable and coherent reason for the practice. In addition to the reasons given by Manson for the all but universal adoption of the reverse practice, I would add the desire to imitate the baptism of Christ, at which the anointing with the Spirit was the final act. Whether or not 1 John can be cited as actual evidence for the Syrian baptismal anointing, its spirit unquestionably lies behind these rites. The opposition to the false gnostics by the true Gnostic to whom the anointing of the Holy Spirit reveals the truth is the proper background against which to view the Syrian baptismal rites.

IV

The Eastern Rites

Although the principal concern of the remainder of this study will be the Western rites, we cannot neglect the rites of Eastern Christendom, in which the anointing with holy chrism plays such an important part. Unfortunately, we do not possess liturgical documents of the Eastern Church comparable in age and importance to the Latin sacramentaries and *ordines*, and such documents as we do possess have not been subjected to the same intensive study. Our consideration of the Eastern rites must necessarily, then, be less detailed than that of their Western counterparts, both because of the limited availability of materials, and because of the Western background, training, and interest of the present writer.

THE PATRISTIC PERIOD

A theological consideration of the testimony of the Fathers was undertaken in the last century by Arthur J. Mason, to whose book, *The Relation of Confirmation to Baptism*, we have already made reference in our introduction. An opposing view was presented by A. Theodore Wirgman in *The Doctrine of Confirmation*. These books remain classics, and we should accomplish little by going afresh over the ground they have covered so adequately; we shall therefore confine our citations to those which seem most directly to promote our study.

The evidence of Clement of Alexandria, head of the famous catechetical school at the end of the second century, is far from clear. He undoubtedly knew the practice of anointing with oil from Gnostic sources, but his own references to orthodox practice need not be more than metaphorical. He does, nevertheless, speak of myrrh (μύρον) as a symbol of the Holy Spirit.[1] He also refers to the offering to God of the

[1] *Paedagogus* 2.8.

first-fruits of food, drink, and χρῖσμα, and, while this may well be a reference to the Eucharistic elements and baptismal oil, there is no necessity so to interpret it.[1]

Clement frequently uses the term σφραγίς, but there is no definite proof that he connected it with any external rite, and Lampe is probably correct in asserting that for Clement "the shining character of righteousness" stamped upon the soul by Christ is the seal.[2] On the other hand, even Lampe admits, "It would be surprising if he knew no ceremony of chrismation after baptism."[3]

Clement's successor as head of the catechetical school, Origen, was unquestionably familiar with baptismal anointing as an orthodox rite. "We have been baptized", he says, "in visible water, and in visible chrism."[4] Unfortunately he tells us little else about the anointing, although we may assume from the order in which he customarily mentions the washing and anointing that chrismation followed baptism. The baptismal washing (λουτρόν) and anointing (χρῖσμα) were closely connected in Origen's thought, and the term βάπτισμα in his writings covers both.

Origen gives us an explanation, or rather two explanations, of the anointing. "The anointing", he says, "is the indwelling of the Holy Spirit."[5] His second explanation is that to have been anointed is to have believed in Christ.[6] The anointing derives its meaning from belief in the Anointed One.

Lampe argues that although the unction of the Spirit conferred in baptism may be represented figuratively by the anointing, it is not, according to Origen, bestowed by this means.[7] To this writer, the evidence does not warrant such a conclusion. Origen clearly knew and used an anointing with chrism, or μύρον, at baptism. He identifies this anointing closely with the baptismal washing and with the gift of the Spirit. The oil, he says, represents the indwelling of the Spirit, and the anointing the belief in Christ. He does not, it is true, actually say that the anointing is an efficacious ceremony, as opposed to a symbolic one, but his continued mention of oil and water together show the importance which he attached to it. Origen so evidently considered the anointing and the washing to be a single rite that he did not raise the question of what part of the baptism conveyed what grace. Lampe's statement, therefore, seems too strong. Origen's words need not mean

[1] *Stromateis* 7.7.   [2] Lampe, *Seal of the Spirit*, pp. 153ff.   [3] ibid., pp. 156f.
[4] *in Romanos* 5.8.   [5] *Selecta in Ezek.* 16.   [6] *Selecta in Exod.* 12.7.
[7] Lampe, op. cit., p. 167.

that he believed the Holy Spirit to be given by the anointing, but they are perfectly congruous with his having held such a view. The case, for the present, must remain "not proven".

A letter of Athanasius to Serapion contains an important reference to the anointing. It identifies the anointing with the seal, and both with the Spirit, quoting 1 John 2.27, Isa. 61.1, and Eph. 1.13 in support of the identification. "The Spirit", it concludes, "is anointing (χρῖσμα) and seal (σφραγίς), in which the Word anoints and seals all."[1]

St Basil, in *de Spiritu Sancto*, refers to the signing with the cross, the blessing of oil and water, and the renunciation of Satan, as ceremonies not specifically mentioned in Scripture which the Church practises at baptism.[2] St Gregory of Nyssa, his younger brother, speaks of the oil as consecrated like the eucharistic bread.[3]

Didymus the Blind, whom Athanasius placed over the catechetical school at Alexandria, and who numbered among his pupils St Gregory Nazianzen, St Jerome, and Rufinus, likens the anointing of the Saviour with the Holy Spirit to the anointing of the creature at his baptism with created, hallowed oil.[4] In this context he quotes the familiar Scripture passages, Isa. 61.1, Ps. 45.7, 1 John 2.20, 27. He identifies the Spirit who descended upon Jesus in the form of a dove with the dove sent from the ark, and he derives the use of oil from the olive branch held by the dove when he returned to Noah. Oil, he concludes, is therefore a symbol of peace.[5]

From Didymus we learn that the anointing was given to a convert received from heresy, and that only a bishop has the grace to consecrate the chrism.[6] This is our first indication that the anointing could be separated from actual baptism, and that it was the link binding the individual Christian to the bishop, by whom the oil had to be hallowed. Our earlier sources had envisaged the bishop as the minister of baptism, and although there must have been occasions upon which this was not the case, this is our first statement that he, and not an officiating presbyter, must perfect the chrism.

Two canonical enactments may be read in conjunction with the statement of Didymus. Canon 48 of the Council of Laodicea reads:

[1] *Ep. I to Serapion* 23 (P.G. 26, 584C).
[2] *de Spiritu Sancto* 27.66 (P.G. 32, 188).
[3] *in baptismum Christi* (P.G. 46, 581).
[4] *de Trinitate* 2.6.23 (P.G. 39, 556–60).
[5] ibid. 2.14 (P.G. 39, 692–6).
[6] ibid. 2.15 (P.G. 39, 720–1).

Those who have been enlightened must after the baptism (τὸ βάπτισμα) be anointed with the heavenly anointing (χρῖσμα) and be made partakers of the Kingdom of Christ.[1]

Little is known of the Council of Laodicea, but its canons can safely be attributed to the middle of the fourth century. Post-baptismal chrismation is here required, because it makes us sharers in the royal anointing of Christ.

The other is canon 7 of Constantinople (A.D. 381), which is, however, considered to be spurious by Duchesne and Bright,[2] and probably represents fifth-century practice. It describes in detail the anointing of certain heretics who return to the Catholic and Apostolic Church. They are to be anointed with the holy chrism on the forehead, the eyes, the nostrils, the mouth, and the ears. This is described as "sealing", and the accompanying formula is given as: "The seal of the gift of the Holy Spirit". Other heretics are required to receive the entire initiatory rite, beginning with the catechumenate. The canon appears again as Canon 95 of the Trullan Synod of 692,[3] and, whatever its actual date, the formula and complex anointing which it describes are similar to later Eastern rites.

THE PRAYER BOOK OF BISHOP SERAPION

The oldest of the liturgical documents which we shall examine in this chapter is the "euchologion" ascribed to Serapion, Bishop of Thmuis, a contemporary and friend of Athanasius. The Greek text of this document was published by F. E. Brightman in the first volume of the *Journal of Theological Studies*, and an English edition under the title *Bishop Sarapion's Prayer Book* was brought out by Bishop John Wordsworth. The book is a sacramentary, that is, it is simply a book of prayers, without explanations or directions for performing the rites. Its baptismal rite consists of seven prayers. The first five (numbered 7–11) deal with baptism. The last two (numbered 15 and 16) are separated from the others by the ordination prayers and are for oil and chrism. Wordsworth prints his translations of the thirty prayers which comprise the sacramentary in the order in which they appear in the manuscript (No. 149 of the Lavra on Mount Athos); Brightman, on the other hand, rearranges the prayers to form a liturgy.

[1] Lauchert, *Die Kanones der Wichtigsten Altkirchlichen Concilien*, p. 77.
[2] Duchesne, *The Early History of the Christian Church*, Vol. 2, p. 248, n. 1; Bright, *Notes on the Canons of the First Four General Councils*, p. 104.
[3] Lauchert, op. cit., pp. 77, 136.

The first prayer (no. 7) is entitled "Sanctification of Waters", and is, of course, the blessing of the font. The second is on behalf of those being baptized, and the third is entitled "After the renunciation—a prayer". This is presumably to follow the renunciation of the devil. Brightman places prayer 15, "A prayer for the anointing oil (ἄλειμμα) of those who are being baptized", next. The manuscript specifically ascribes it to Serapion, Bishop of Thmuis, and Wordsworth conjectures that he may have attached more importance to this pre-baptismal oil than his predecessors did.[1] Wordsworth calls this prayer a blessing of the oil, but Brightman considers it to be rather a prayer for its administration.[2] He believes that the oil was blessed at the Eucharist. Prayer 5 is a blessing of oil at the Eucharist, and although the oil mentioned in the prayer is the oil for the sick, as in the parallel prayer in *Ap. Trad.*, Brightman believes that other oils may have been consecrated at the same time.

The text of the prayer speaks of healing, forgiveness, and re-creation as the desired effects of the anointing, and quotes John 20.23 as the Scriptural warrant for what is being done.[3] The Lord Jesus Christ is invoked to work the effects, and after a reference to Eph. 4.23, the prayer closes with a petition for final victory and union with the flock of Christ.

The prayer which follows (no. 10) is entitled in the manuscript "After the taking up (ἀνάληψιν) a prayer", which Wordsworth interprets to mean a prayer after the acceptance of Christ, which customarily followed the rununciation of Satan. Brightman, on the other hand, emends ἀνάληψιν to ἄλειψιν, making it a prayer after the anointing. In either case, it is a prayer for one about to be baptized. The immersion presumably followed, as the next prayer is called, "After [he] has been baptized and has come up—a prayer". Brightman places prayer 16, "Prayer in regard to the Chrism (χρῖσμα) with which those who have been baptized are being anointed", after this, and assumes that the signing with chrism accompanied the recitation of the prayer. The text in Wordsworth's translation is:

God of Hosts, the helper of every soul that turns to thee and that cometh under the mighty hand of thy only-begotten, we invoke thee to work in this chrism (χρῖσμα) a divine and heavenly energy through the divine and unseen powers of our Lord and Saviour Jesus Christ, in order that they who have

---

[1] op. cit., p. 50.   [2] art. cit., p. 251.
[3] Brightman, p. 264; Wordsworth, p. 74.

been baptized, and are being anointed with it with the impress (ἐκτύπωμα) of the sign of the saving cross of the only-begotten, by which cross Satan and every opposing power was routed and triumphed over, they also as being regenerated and renewed through the washing of regeneration, may become partakers of the gift of the holy Spirit, and being made secure by this seal, may continue steadfast and unmovable, unhurt and inviolate, free from harsh treatment and intrigue, in the franchise of the faith and full knowledge of the truth, awaiting to the end the heavenly hopes of life and eternal promises of our Lord and Saviour Jesus Christ, through whom to thee [is] the glory and the strength both now and to all the ages of the ages. Amen.

The central section of this prayer corresponds to the prayer accompanying the laying on of the bishop's hands in the Oriental versions of *Ap. Trad.*, which accords well with Brightman's view of its purpose.

The prayers in Serapion's baptismal liturgy, as a whole, are not those of any surviving rite, and the entire question of their influence on baptismal practice outside their author's own diocese is doubtful. They do, nevertheless, show certain definite points of contact with other liturgies. There are two anointings, one before and one after baptism, performed with different types of oil. Brightman points out that the prayer for the pre-baptismal oil is really an exorcism, and that here we have a point of contact with Cyril of Jerusalem and *Ap. Trad.*[1] Certainly he is right that the effects expected from the two anointings are quite different: that before baptism is to cleanse and prepare; that after the laver to bestow the gift of the Holy Spirit. We have already noted the relation of the post-baptismal prayer to that in *Ap. Trad.*, while the emphasis upon the chrism bestowing the Spirit is reminiscent of Cyril. Serapion also describes the post-baptismal chrismation as a seal and a sign of the cross, leaving no doubt as to the theological congruity of this rite with the patristic testimony.

Unfortunately, we have no other Egyptian documents of a similar age to compare with the rite of Serapion.[2] There is, nevertheless, a basic structure of renunciation, anointing, baptism, and chrismation which runs through the non-Syrian rites. Certainly the ceremonies used in conjunction with these prayers must have been *similar* to those described by Cyril and *Ap. Trad.* It is impossible to ascertain exactly how the prayers were used. Certainly prayers 15 and 16 were used at the

---

[1] Brightman, art. cit., p. 251.

[2] Unless, of course, *Ap. Trad.* represents the practice of Alexandria rather than of Rome.

time of the anointings, but whether they are blessings of the oils, or formulas of administration, or perhaps prayers said by the bishop while the lesser clergy actually performed the anointings, we cannot tell with certainty.

THE CANONICAL RESPONSES OF TIMOTHY OF ALEXANDRIA

Two books of Canonical Responses, that is, questions and answers on various pastoral and liturgical questions, are attributed to Timothy of Alexandria (*fl.* 381). In the first book there are no questions regarding anointing, although the baptism of both adults and children is mentioned, and provision is made for conditional baptism, with the form, "If thou hast not been baptized, I baptize thee . . .".[1] From this we may conclude that the declarative formula in its Western, or active, form was regularly used at baptisms, as in the later Coptic rite.

The second book is of greater interest to us, but, unfortunately, it cannot be regarded as genuine. Brightman, in his previously cited article, states:

> This series cannot be authentic, since the eighteenth response deals with Christmas, which was not observed in Egypt until about 430. But it is Egyptian, and probably not later than of the fifth century.[2]

Whitaker, as preface to his translation of the relevant responses, says, "It is probable that the second book is wrongly attributed, and was written in the fifth century", presumably reflecting Brightman's view of sixty years before.

The second series of Canonical Responses gives us a different picture of baptismal customs from our earlier sources. First, baptism was not restricted to any one season of the year, and infants were normally baptized on the seventh day after birth.[3] Second, the presbyter was considered to be the normal minister of baptism, and the possibility of his performing the rite without additional clerics is foreseen.[4] The pre-baptismal unction is mentioned only because the questioner is uncertain how to follow the traditional order when he officiates without assistance:

> Ought he to perform the renunciation of the catechumen after consecrating

---

[1] J. B. Pitra, *Iuris Ecclesiastici Graecorum Historia et Monumenta*, Vol. I, p. 238; Whitaker, *Documents*, p. 77.

[2] *J.T.S.*, Vol. I (1899), p. 248.   [3] op. cit. 2.4.   [4] ibid. 2.8–11.

the water of the laver of regeneration, and then proceed to the unction of oil?[1]

It seems, at least to Brightman, that what the questioner here suggests was the customary practice. The answer given, however, is that the presbyter should first receive the renunciation, and then enter the baptistery and bless the water. The answer does not mention the anointing, but we may assume, on the basis of the wording of the question and the present practice of the Coptic and Ethiopic rites, that it immediately followed the renunciations of the devil, with which it is usually associated.

THE CANONS OF HIPPOLYTUS AND "TESTAMENTUM DOMINI"

The Canons of Hippolytus have received little study since their dependence on *Ap. Trad.* was generally accepted. They survive in an Arabic translation of a Coptic version of a lost Greek original. Easton places the work "almost certainly in the fifth century and beyond reasonable doubt in Egypt".[2]

The differences from *Ap. Trad.* are slight, except in regard to the baptismal formula and the post-baptismal anointing. There is no mention of deacons at the anointings, and it is assumed that a presbyter will fulfil the rôle of a deacon at the actual baptism.[3] This appears to reflect the same lack of lesser clergy noted in the Canonical Responses.

The Canons give the baptismal questions as in *Ap. Trad.*, but following them, the priest who baptizes is directed to say for each candidate, "I baptize thee, in the name of the Father ...".[4] The declarative formula has become an integral part of the rite.

The post-baptismal anointing is described thus:

When he comes up from the water the priest signs his forehead and mouth and breast with the oil of thanksgiving, which he holds, and anoints his whole body and his head and face, saying: I anoint thee in the name of the Father and of the Son and of the Holy Ghost.[5]

This is considerably expanded from the simple direction of *Ap. Trad.* that the presbyter is to anoint the neophyte who comes up out of the

[1] 2.8; Whitaker, p. 77.   [2] Easton, *Ap. Trad.*, p. 15.
[3] Canon 19.7–9; Haneberg, *Canones S. Hippolyti*, pp. 75f.
[4] Canon 19.11.   [5] Canon 19.12.

water, saying, "I anoint thee with holy oil in the name of Jesus Christ". Certainly, the anointing of the head and forehead, and the signing with the cross belong to the second anointing in *Ap. Trad.* Its transfer to this position in the Canons, and their complete omission of the second anointing, must indicate the influence of a practice with which the compiler was familiar. The pattern is similar to that in Cyril's *Mystagogical Catecheses*, although Cyril's catalogue of the parts of the body to be anointed differs slightly from those listed here.

The anointing is followed by the laying on of the bishop's hand. The accompanying prayer, which is different from that in *Ap. Trad.*, prays that those who have been born again may receive the Holy Ghost. It is in turn followed by a signing of the forehead made without chrism, and a kiss.[1] The second anointing from *Ap. Trad.* has disappeared, together with its formula.

The arrangement of the post-baptismal ceremonies in the Canons accords well with the thesis that the double chrismation after baptism is a Roman ceremony, unfamiliar to the Egyptian compiler of the Canons, who wished to conform his work more closely to the actual liturgical practice of his Church.

When we turn from the Canons to the *Testamentum Domini*, we find a different development. Little is known about the origin of this work. Easton dates it at the end of the fifth century and suggests Egypt as its place of origin, but it is usually believed to come from Syria. It was originally composed in Greek, but is known only in Syrian, Ethiopic, and Arabic versions. It purports to be the words of our Lord himself. The standard edition is the English version of Cooper and MacLean.

The baptismal section contains only minor differences from *Ap. Trad.* The formula for the pre-baptismal anointing with the oil of exorcism is, "I anoint thee with this oil of exorcism for a deliverance from every evil and unclean spirit, and for a deliverance from every evil."[2] The post-baptismal anointing is as in *Ap. Trad.*, with the same formula, but with this rubric following:

> But let the women be anointed by widows who sit in front, the presbyter saying over them [the words].[3]

We see here the same reluctance to allow a man to anoint the women which we saw in the *Didascalia*. Certainly this indicates that the custom

---

[1] Canon 19.13.   [2] *Test.* 2.8.   [3] *Test.* 2.9.

of having women anointed by women was known and practised in the area represented by *Test.*

Test. provides for the second, or episcopal anointing, as in *Ap. Trad.*, but the prayers have been considerably expanded. The bishop's prayer, accompanying the laying on of hands, has become a real *epiklēsis* of the Holy Spirit, while the formula of anointing is:

> Anointing I anoint thee in God Almighty, and in Jesus Christ, and in the Holy Ghost, that thou mayest be his soldier, having a perfect faith, and a vessel pleasing unto him.[1]

The anointing is followed by "sealing him on the forehead" and the kiss of peace.

Although the prayers of *Test.* have been considerably expanded from those in *Ap. Trad.*, this section of the later work contributes little to our study. The different practice of the Canons regarding post-baptismal anointing is more important, and represents a definite change in liturgical practice, or more probably, the different practice of a different area.

PSEUDO-DIONYSIUS THE AREOPAGITE

The second book of *On the Ecclesiastical Hierarchy* of Pseudo-Dionysius the Areopagite contains a description of the rites of baptism. This unknown author, who was identified with the Dionysius converted by St Paul (Acts 17.34), is believed to have flourished in Syria about the year 500.[2]

The minister of the sacrament is regularly described as the hierarch (ἱεράρχης), and is presumably the bishop. His assistants are described as λειτουργοί. The rite begins with the renunciation of Satan and adherence to Christ. The anointing follows. First the ministers (λειτουργοί) undress the candidate completely, then the priests bring the "holy oil of the anointing". The hierarch himself begins the anointing, then turns the catechumen over to the priests for them to anoint his whole body. The hierarch's own part in the anointing is described as a threefold seal.

While the priests continue the anointing, the hierarch consecrates the water. The blessing includes three cruciform effusions (χύσες) of chrism and the same number of injections (ἐπιβολή) of chrism. The actual baptism, with threefold immersions, follows, and, after the

---

[1] *Test.* 2.9.

[2] Greek text in J. Parker, *The Ecclesiastical Hierarchy by Dionysius the Areopagite*, London, 1899; trans. in Whitaker, *Documents*, pp. 48–50.

neophyte is dressed, he is brought to the hierarch, who seals him with chrism (μύρον), and admits him to the Eucharist.

The emphasis placed upon the pre-baptismal anointing by the hierarch in this description, coupled with the simplicity of its account of the post-baptismal sealing, indicate an affinity with the Syrian documents described in the last chapter, especially with the rite of *Ap. Con.*, 3.16, in which the post-baptismal anointing is overshadowed by that preceding baptism. The importance attached by the Monophysites to the writings of the Pseudo-Areopagite is reflected in the later West Syrian forms, which we shall discuss later in the chapter.

The use of chrism in the blessing of the font will find a place in the later rites of both East and West. Although its eventual elaboration may readily be dismissed as pure ceremoniousness, the mingling of the chrism with the baptismal water provided a continuing testimony to the essential unity of the baptismal rite in the face of the increasing tendency to separate baptism and confirmation.

A description of the consecration of the chrism is found in the fourth book. It gives us little precise information, save that it was consecrated at the altar by the hierarch after the dismissal of the catechumens. The consecration was preceded by the chanting of psalms and the reading of divine oracles "as at the synaxis". Probably, this means that the consecration of the chrism was a complete service parallel to the consecration of the eucharistic elements, and from which the catechumens were excluded after the *pro-anaphora*. This is, in fact, the practice of the present Coptic and Syrian rites.

THE BARBARINI EUCHOLOGION

We come now to the examination of the oldest of the Byzantine liturgical manuscripts, the Barbarini Euchologion, which we shall abbreviate as *Barb.* This manuscript is described by Conybeare as "a Greek Euchologion, written in uncials on vellum in the eighth century",[1] and is dated by Brightman, who edited its eucharistic liturgy in *Liturgies Eastern and Western*, between 788 and 797, on the basis of palaeographical evidence and the commemorations of the imperial family.[2]

The baptismal portions of this euchologion have been published by Conybeare in his *Rituale Armenorum*, pp. 389–442. It will be most convenient to describe the rites in *Barb.* in detail and to discuss other Eastern rites by reference to them.

[1] *Rituale Armenorum*, p. xxv. (This will be cited as *R.A.*)
[2] Brightman, op. cit., p. lxxxix.

There are two baptismal rites in the euchologion: one at folios 170ff, and one at folios 260ff. The second is unquestionably the older rite, since it refers to adult catechumens, but as it contains only the preliminary rites of renunciation, it will not be of particular use to us. The first is the text of a complete rite.

It is intended primarily for use with infants and begins with a prayer to be used on the eighth day after birth, when the child is signed with the cross and given his name. It is followed by a prayer for the fortieth day after birth, when the infant is brought into the church. The parallel to Jewish custom, as recorded in the case of our Lord in Luke 2, is obvious. *Barb.* next gives a prayer for making a catechumen and three exorcisms.[1]

The renunciation, which follows, begins with a prayer, the signing of the catechumen, and an exorcism. His clothes are then removed, and, facing west, he (or his sponsor) makes the threefold renunciation. Turning to the east he makes his adherence to Christ and recites the Nicene Creed. In the case of infants the replies are, of course, made by the sponsor. The priest concludes this preliminary rite with the prayer which stood in the same position in the older rite previously mentioned.[2]

Barb. begins its baptismal rite proper with the heading "The Diakonika of the Holy Sabbath at the Baptism". An eleventh-century manuscript collated by Conybeare inserts a rubric which reads in part:

> The prayers of the holy baptismal rite which the patriarch says when the foregoing prayers have been said: especially on the evening of the holy sabbath.[3]

In both of these texts we see the survival of the Holy Sabbath as the time even for infant baptism, although the later manuscript implies that baptism at other times was contemplated. The patriarch himself was expected to be the officiant at the solemn baptismal liturgy. On the other hand, the provision of special ceremonies to be performed at the eighth and fortieth days after the birth of the child mark an attempt to adapt the traditional practice to the new condition of infant baptism. The separation of the renunciation from the baptismal rites was also characteristic of the Western rites of the period.

The evening rites begin with a diaconal litany for the blessing of the

---

[1] *R.A.*, pp. 389–94.   [2] *R.A.*, p. 396, and p. 442.

[3] Codex Grotta Ferrata, *Γ*, *β*, 1; *R.A.*, p. 396n.; trans. in Whitaker, *Documents*, p. 69.

waters and those to be baptized therein. It is followed in the text by a prayer for the priest to say silently while the deacon is praying the litany. This prayer is an *apologia* in the first person singular, in which the priest expresses his own unworthiness. Such prayers are common in the Byzantine rite, but cannot be considered among its earlier strata. The priest recites the blessing of the font aloud at the conclusion of the diaconal litany. The prayer, "Great art thou, O Lord . . ." is interrupted for the priest to breathe upon the water and sign it with his finger. At its conclusion, the priest says, "Peace be to you all", and the deacon replies, "Let us bow our heads to the Lord". The priest then proceeds to the blessing of the oil, which is held in a vessel (ἀγγεῖον) by the deacon. He breathes upon it, and signs it thrice, apparently to exorcize it, and then says the prayer of blessing:

> Master, Lord God of our fathers, who didst send to those who were in Noah's ark a dove bearing a twig of olive in its mouth, to be a symbol of reconciliation and salvation from the flood, and thereby didst prefigure the mystery of grace: who hast furnished the fruit of the olive unto the fulfilment of thy holy mysteries, and thereby hast filled with the Holy Spirit those who are under the law, and hast perfected those who live in grace: do thou bless even this oil with the power and operation and indwelling of thy Holy Spirit, so that it may be a chrism of incorruption, a shield of righteousness, a renewal of soul and body, turning away every work of the devil, unto the deliverance from all evil of those that are anointed in faith and partake of it: unto thy glory, and the glory of thine Only-Begotten Son, and of thy holy and good and life-giving Spirit, now, etc.[1]

This prayer of blessing goes beyond the exorcism of which Cyril, *Ap. Trad.*, and Serapion speak, and anticipates positive benefits from the pre-baptismal anointing, although its identification of the oil with the dove of Noah's ark has been noted in various patristic testimonies to the anointing.

After the blessing of the oil, the priest makes three crosses with it in the water. Unlike the rite described by the Pseudo-Areopagite, it is the simple oil blessed by the priest, not chrism, which is mixed with the water.

Having blessed and anointed the water, the priest anoints the cate-chumens, making the sign of the cross upon their forehead, breast, and back. These are the places mentioned as anointed after baptism in the Canons of Hippolytus, while the anointing of the breast and back, though not of the forehead, occurs before baptism in the Roman rite.

[1] *R.A.*, p. 402; trans. in Whitaker, *Documents*, p. 72.

There is observable in rites having more than one anointing a tendency to transfer ceremonial, and even theological interpretation, from one anointing to another, and the pre-baptismal anointing of *Barb.* appears to have acquired certain features belonging more properly to the post-baptismal chrismation.

The form for this anointing is, "Such a one is anointed with the oil of gladness, in the Name of the Father and of the Son and of the Holy Ghost, etc". The later manuscripts collated in *R.A.* all add "the servant of God" before the name.[1] After this anointing by the priest, the deacon anoints the whole body. The priest then baptizes the candidate with the formula, "Such a one is baptized . . .". These passive forms for the anointing and baptism are also found in John Chrysostom, Theodore of Mopsuestia, and Narsai, and became the standard Eastern formulas, as the active forms became standard in the West.

After the baptism Psalm 32 is sung, or at least begun, and the deacon offers a prayer during which the priest prays, "Blessed art thou, O Lord God . . ." This prayer begins with a thanksgiving for the epiphany of the Only-Begotten, and for the cleansing of the holy water, and for the sanctification of the life-giving chrism ($\chi\rho\hat{\iota}\sigma\mu\alpha$). It goes on to speak of those "newly enlightened by water and Spirit". This phrase indicates *Barb.'s* agreement with the teaching of the confirmation prayer in *Ap. Trad.*, as Easton renders it, that is, the neophytes have already been regenerated by water and the Holy Ghost. The prayer continues:

> Master most benevolent, give to them also the seal of the gift of thy holy and all-powerful and worshipful Spirit, and the communion of the Holy Body and Precious Blood of thy Christ. Guard them in thy sanctification; strengthen them in the right ($\dot{o}\rho\theta o\delta\acute{o}\xi os$) faith . . .[2]

It ends with an *ekphōnēsis* and the recitation of Gal. 3.27, "As many as are baptized in Christ have put on Christ." The priest then anoints the neophytes with chrism, making the sign of the cross on their foreheads, their eyes, their nostrils, their mouth, and both ears, saying, "The seal of the gift of the Holy Spirit." This rite is identical with that described in Canon 7 of Constantinople, and in Canon 95 of the Trullan Synod of 692.

The rite concludes with the celebration of the Divine Liturgy.

Even a casual glance at the modern Orthodox rite as contained, for

[1] *R.A.*, p. 403.

[2] *R.A.*, p. 404; trans. in Whitaker, *Documents*, p. 73.

example, in Hapgood's *Service Book*[1] will show that this is substantially the rite which is presently used by those Christians who follow the Byzantine liturgy.

The oil used by the priest for the pre-baptismal anointing is blessed by him at the time of its use, while the chrism for the sealing after baptism is blessed by the patriarch at the Maundy Thursday liturgy, after the intercessions at the close of the *anaphora*.

The Byzantine prayer for the consecration of the chrism should also be briefly noted. It is similar to the Coptic prayers, but much more concise. It speaks of the chrism as a royal unction and a spiritual anointing, and asks the descent of the Holy Spirit upon it that it may be a robe of incorruptibility and "a perfect seal which imprints on those who receive the divine washing of baptism the right to bear thy Holy Name". It refers also to the anointing of prophets, priests, and kings, and to the anointing of Christian bishops and priests.[2]

The similarity of thought between this and the consecratory prayers of other Eastern rites, particularly those of the Churches not in communion with Constantinople, lends weight to the presumption of antiquity of at least the basic ideas and structure of the prayer for the blessing of chrism.

THE WEST SYRIAN RITE

In the previous chapter we discussed the ancient Syrian rite, in which there was no post-baptismal anointing. We saw also how such an anointing came to be introduced gradually into Syrian usage, particularly in the Western, Greek-speaking parts of Syria. The political situation in the fifth century and the Monophysite and Nestorian schisms divided Syria ecclesiastically into East and West, and their rites must be separately considered. A precise geographical line between the two regions is difficult to draw, and although Antioch is unquestionably the centre of West Syria, Edessa influenced both East and West.

The West Syrian rites are frequently called the Jacobite rites, but this designation is not completely accurate, for they are not only the rites of the Jacobites, or Monophysite Syrians, but also of the Syrian Uniats, and, until the fifteenth century, of the Maronites.

[1] I. F. Hapgood, *Service Book of the Holy Orthodox-Catholic Apostolic Church*, New York, 1906.
[2] Goar, *Euchologion*, Venice, 1730, p. 502.

Dom Bernard Botte, in an article in *L'Orient Syrien*,[1] sees the origin of these rites foreshadowed in such documents as the seventh book of *Ap. Con.*, and the *ordo* of Pseudo-Dionysius. To these early sources must be added a description of the rites attributed to James of Edessa,[2] a Monophysite scholar of the seventh century.

James divides the rite into two parts: the catechumenate, including the renunciations, and the actual baptism. His description of the second part is quite brief:

> Those who wish to receive baptism enter the baptistery and say, "We believe in one God", etc. Then the priest pronounces the Peace: he says a prayer and then signs them with holy oil, and they stand naked while another prayer is said, in which he breathes thrice upon the water in the form of a cross and says, "May the head of the dragon be beaten down." After that he pours the chrism thrice in the form of a cross while he says a prayer. Then he baptizes them in the Name of the Father and of the Son and of the Holy Ghost. Next he signs them with chrism saying: "And may they receive this sign in thy Name." Then he says a prayer of thanksgiving. Finally they go into the church and receive the holy mysteries.

The actual liturgical text of the West Syrian rite is known to us only in three recensions, printed in Latin in Denzinger's *Ritus Orientalium*.[3] Of the three, the first is anonymous, the second bears the name of James of Edessa, and the third that of Severus of Antioch. The critical situation is made clear by Dom Botte in his previously cited article. We do not, he affirms, have three different rituals, but three forms of the same ritual, and this is essentially that used by the Syrian Church at the present day. Furthermore, although the rite contains ancient elements, it must date from a time when the catechumenate had ceased to exist, except as a vestigial term for infants about to be baptized.

Botte concludes that the West Syrian rite contains a core of ancient

---

[1] "Le Baptême dans l'Église Syrienne", in *L'Orient Syrien*, Vol. 1 (1956), pp. 137-55.

[2] Latin trans. in Denzinger, *Ritus Orientalium*, Vol. 1, pp. 297f; English in Whitaker, *Documents*, p. 50.

[3] pp. 267-79, 280-301, 302-16. Henry Denzinger was professor of theology at Würzburg in the middle of the nineteenth century. *R.O.* is a collection of the texts of the rites for the administration of the sacraments among the Syrians, Copts, and Armenians. Although it is over one hundred years old it is an invaluable tool to the student of the Oriental liturgies, and has recently been reprinted by photographic reproduction. It is largely based upon the 13-volume *Codex Liturgicus Ecclesiae Universae* of Joseph A. Assemani, published one hundred years earlier, although it includes other material, and is much easier to use.

material which is common to it and to the Byzantine rite. The rite of James of Edessa is, as its most ancient manuscripts indicate, a translation from the Greek, but it is also an adaptation of the rite to the pastoral conditions of the seventh century, with new prayers added to the more ancient forms. The liturgy attributed to Severus of Antioch is, Botte is positive, much later than its reputed author, who was Monophysite Patriarch of Antioch about the year 500.

> That there are some parts which go back to his time is certain. Perhaps some are his. But he could not have composed such a ritual which corresponds to the needs of another time.[1]

With these considerations in mind, let us turn to the texts of the rites. For convenience in discussion, we shall call the anonymous recension *Syr.* 1, that bearing the name of James of Edessa *Syr.* 2, and that ascribed to Severus of Antioch *Syr.* 3. The pre-baptismal anointing in all three versions is practically identical. It occurs at the beginning of the second part of the rite as James of Edessa divided it. In *Syr.* 2 the second part begins with the Nicene Creed, followed by a ceremony of mixing hot and cold water in the font. After this the priest says:

> Holy Father, who through the hands of thine Apostles didst give the Holy Spirit to those who were baptized: even now, using the shadow of my hands, send thy Holy Spirit upon those who are to be baptized: that, filled with him and his divine gifts, they may bring forth fruit to thee, thirtyfold, sixtyfold, and an hundredfold. From thee, O Father of lights, is every good gift and every perfect service.

Then, raising his voice and extending his hands, the priest says:

> And form and fashion (*effinge et forma*) Christ in them, who through my weakness are to be regenerated. Confirm them upon the foundation of the prophets and apostles. Graft them as a true branch in the Holy Catholic Church: that when they advance in the fear of God thy glorious name may be praised before the ages, God the Father, and of thine only begotten Son and of thy Holy Spirit, now and ever . . .[2]

Both of these prayers occur in all three recensions, although with slight verbal changes, and not in the same order. Although they do not deal directly with the anointing, they show the persistence in the Syrian rites of the idea that the Spirit is given before baptism.

In *Syr.* 2 these prayers are immediately followed by the pre-baptismal

---

[1] art. cit., p. 154.   [2] *R.O.*, p. 284.

anointing. In *Syr.* 1 and 3 "Form and fashion them . . ." occurs before the renunciation of Satan, and "Holy Father . . ." is preceded by a prayer, "We give thee thanks . . ." which, after a reference to the preceding renunciation, prays:

> Vouchsafe, O Lord, to send upon them thy Holy Spirit, and descend, and search into (*scrutare*) every member and cleanse and sanctify them, that they may become worthy by holy unction and perfect faith, through Christ . . .[1]

The anointing which follows in all three versions is in the form of a triple signing of the cross on the forehead with olive oil. The form of the anointing (with only minor changes in word order in the three versions) is:

> N. is signed with the oil of gladness against every operation of the enemy that he may be grafted into the good olive tree in the Holy, Catholic, and Apostolic Church, in the Name . . .[2]

The anointing is followed by the blessing of the font, which includes a triple cruciform effusion of chrism (not simple oil) into the water, as in the description of the rite by James of Edessa and Pseudo-Dionysius. After the effusion of chrism into the font, the priest takes again the olive oil and anoints the entire body of the candidates. The rubric of *Syr.* 2 makes *totum corpus* more emphatic by mentioning specifically unction between the fingers and toes, and the loins. *Syr.* 1 and 3 provide no formula to be used by the priest at this anointing, but direct him to sing an anthem. *Syr.* 2, on the other hand, orders the deacons to sing the anthem, while the priest recites, "God has anointed thee above thy fellows with the oil of gladness, with myrrh and cassia."

The anthems sung after the anointing differ slightly in all three versions of the rite. They have in common a reference to the anointing of Aaron by Moses; *Syr.* 2 and 3 refer also to the anointing of David; *Syr.* 2 mentions the anointing of prophets, priests, and kings; and both *Syr.* 2 and *Syr.* 3 echo the refrain that in the Church the simple lambs who come to baptism are anointed with the holy oil.[3] *Syr.* 2 in its alternative form for the baptism of girls provides instead strophes from the third and fourth hymns on the Epiphany of Ephraem Syrus, including:

---

[1] *R.O.*, p. 273.   [2] ibid.   [3] *R.O.*, pp. 276, 286, 314.

Christ and chrism are conjoined. The hidden is mingled with the visible. The oil anoints openly; Christ secretly signs the new and spiritual lambs . . .[1]

It would be folly for the present writer to attempt any judgement as to which of these two anthems is "original" in this position. Certainly both present ancient ideas and make clear the importance which the West Syrian rite attaches to this pre-baptismal anointing. Mgr Khouri-Sarkis, commenting on this anointing in the present Syrian rite, identifies it with the pre-baptismal unction of the ancient Syrian rite, and with the attribution to it of the gift of the Holy Spirit in *Ap. Con.*, 3.15.[2]

The anointing is followed by baptism. The priest lays his right hand upon the candidate's head, and pours the water with his left hand. As the candidate goes down into the water *Syr.* 2 directs the singing of the opening strophe of Mar Ephraem's fourth Epiphany hymn, "Descend, my sealed brothers, put ye on the Lord." The baptismal formula is, "N. is baptized in the Name of the Father, and of the Son, and of the Holy Ghost, into the life of the ages of ages." An "Amen" follows the pronouncing of the name of each Divine Person.[3]

After the baptism, the priest takes the horn of chrism and prays silently:

> May these thy servants, who through the faith of baptism have made a beginning with thy soldiers, receive also this sign in thy name: that filled with every odour of spiritual sweetness through this chrism they may not be overcome by the adverse powers, and fearing nothing from the principalities and powers of darkness, but walking in light, they may be the sons of light: and thus will they walk by thee and come to thee. Thou indeed art the true light, and in thy light we see light, and thine is the glory . . .[4]

The rubrics directing the actual chrismation are quite complex. *Syr.* 1 and 3 speak of anointing the forehead and all the members with three signs of the cross. The formula is:

> With the holy chrism, the sweetness of the odour of Christ, the sign of true faith, the fulfilment (*complementum*) of the gift of the Holy Spirit, N. is signed, ✠ In the Name of the Father, Amen, ✠ and of the Son, Amen, ✠ and of the living and Holy Spirit, into the life of the ages of ages. Amen.[5]

[1] *R.O.* p. 294.
[2] "Prières et Cérémonies du Baptême", in *L'Orient Syrien*, Vol. 1 (1956), p. 177, n. 19.
[3] *R.O.*, pp. 277, 287, 314, There are minor verbal differences.
[4] *R.O.*, p. 277.   [5] *R.O.*, p. 278.

Syr. 2, on the other hand, directs this formula to be said while the priest pours the chrism over his thumbs. It then gives the following direction:

> And the priest pours the chrism into the hollow of his hand and anoints the persons baptized on the forehead, going down to his right ear, then his arm and shoulder, and between the fingers of his right hand and the toes of his right foot, and between his loins: then between the toes of his left foot, and he goes up to his left side, and between the fingers of his left hand, and arm, and shoulder, and ear, and returns to the forehead, both before and behind, perfectly, lest any part remain without anointing.[1]

After the anointing the neophytes are clothed in white, and the priest begins the prayer, "Blessed art thou, O Lord . . ." This is the same prayer which occurs before the chrismation in *Barb.* It is therefore one of the ancient features which the West Syrian rite has in common with the Byzantine.

As can be seen from this examination of the West Syrian rite, the tradition of the ancient Syrian rite has not been totally lost. The hymns of St Ephraem Syrus provide a continuing link, as do the references to the gift of the Spirit before baptism. On the other hand, the post-baptismal chrismation has become a definite and important feature.

Both the chrism and the holy oil were blessed by the bishop, the chrism on Maundy Thursday. James of Edessa describes the consecration of the chrism as a complete service parallel to the Eucharistic liturgy, as in the Pseudo-Areopagite.[2]

The Maronite rite attributed to Jacob of Serug provides for the blessing of the oil for the pre-baptismal unction during the baptism itself, as in *Barb.* As Narsai mentions the blessing of the oil during the service, the Maronites must here preserve an ancient Syrian custom. The prayer of blessing refers to the anointing of prophets, priests, and kings, and the signing of the lambs of Christ's flock which will be performed with the oil.[3]

Another ancient practice preserved in the Maronite rite is the assignment of the anointing of the whole body of the candidate to the deacons, as in the *Didascalia* and *Ap. Con.*, 3.16.[4] Of course, the Maronite practice is similar to that of the Byzantine rite, and, although

---

[1] R.O., p. 287. [2] R.O., pp. 262–3.
[3] R.O., p. 341. [4] R.O., p. 348.

these practices presumably belong to the ancient common core of both rites, the possibility of later Byzantine influence cannot be eliminated.

THE EAST SYRIAN RITE

The East Syrian rite is that of the Nestorian Church, of the Chaldean Uniats, and of the Syrian Uniats of Malabar. It is the descendant of the ancient Syrian rites described in the last chapter as they were revised by the Nestorian patriarch Icho-Yahb III in the seventh century. This rite, like its predecessors, is distinguished by the absence of a post-baptismal anointing with chrism.[1]

The Nestorian, or East Syrian, rite uses only one kind of oil. This is blessed by the priest during the baptismal service. The prayers for the blessing of the oil speak of it as conferring the *arrabōn* of the resurrection of the dead. It is described as fulfilling the type represented by the oil which anointed the temporal and transitory priests and kings of the Old Covenant, and as bestowing the circumcision not made with hands. These ideas, although not expressed in the same words, may be found in Ephraem Syrus. The identification of the baptismal anointing with circumcision is, as we have seen, a theme expounded by Lionel Thornton in *Confirmation, its Place in the Baptismal Mystery*. The prayer goes on to ask that the gift of the Holy Spirit may come into the oil and hallow it for the bestowing of the life-giving seal.[2] This use of the word *rushmâ* to apply to a pre-baptismal anointing is a link with the ancient Syrian rites.

At the beginning of the baptismal rite, before the priest enters the baptistery, the catechumen is signed with the cross with the form, "N. is signed in the name of the Father ..." The rubrics in *R.O.* do not mention the use of oil for this signing, but Timotheus II and the Pseudo-George of Arbeles (ninth or tenth century) direct this signing to be made with previously blessed oil, and Badger's edition of the modern rite directs the use of oil.[3] It seems strange, nevertheless, that the rite should include an anointing before the blessing of the oil, which would most logically precede its first use. If, on the other hand, the signing dates back to a period when the adult catechumenate still existed, it would not have been a part of the baptismal rite at all, but of a service held on a previous occasion, and its relative position becomes comprehensible.

[1] The only text readily available for study is that in *R.O.* (from Codex Vat. Syr. 16). The modern Nestorian rite has been published in English in G.P. Badger, *The Nestorians and their Rituals*, Vol. I.

[2] *R.O.*, p. 372.　　[3] *R.O.*, pp. 366, 372n.; Badger, p. 196.

The blessing of the oil does not occur until after the priest has entered the baptistery and immediately precedes the blessing of the water, after which the priest anoints the candidates "from top to bottom and from left to right", saying, "N. is anointed in the name of the Father, etc."[1] Having done this the priest anoints the whole body of the catechumen. The formula is that found in Chrysostom and Theodore of Mopsuestia, while the instruction that the oil is to be consecrated at this time is found in Narsai and, of course, in the Byzantine rite.

This second anointing is followed at once by the baptism. The usual Eastern formula is used. The controversial part of the rite is that which follows baptism. A procession is made from the baptistery to the sanctuary for the celebration of the Eucharist. Among the items carried in this procession is the horn of holy oil. A station is made before the doors of the sanctuary, and the priest lays his hand upon the head of each neophyte, praying:

> May the pledge of the Holy Spirit which you have received, may the mysteries of Christ which you have taken, may the living *rushmâ* which you have accepted, may the new life which you have acquired, may the armour of righteousness with which you have been clothed, guard you from the Evil One and from his forces, and sanctify your members in purity. And may this *rushmâ* with which you have been signed enable you to obtain those future blessings which shall not pass away when our Lord Jesus Christ shall appear, and in his new world, may he place you at his right hand, where you may render him praise and glory . . .[2]

This laying on of a hand is followed by a signing with the right thumb, "from bottom to top, and from right to left", with the formula:

> N. has been baptized and perfected, in the Name of the Father, and of the Son, and of the Holy Ghost.[3]

The rubrics do not mention the use of oil for this signing, and, according to T. Thompson,[4] the Nestorians do not customarily use oil. Denzinger quotes the Pseudo-George, affirming that this was an unction,[5] but it would in any case have been an anointing with simple oil, not with chrism. Furthermore, the prayer speaks of the *rushmâ* as already given, and the wording of the short formula makes it highly

---

[1] R.O., p. 374.
[2] R.O., p. 376; cf. L'Orient Syrien, Vol. 1 (1956), p. 249.
[3] R.O., p. 375; Badger, p. 210.
[4] *The Offices of Baptism and Confirmation*, p. 68.   [5] R.O., p. 375.

doubtful whether this rite can be intended as anything more than a final blessing of the neophytes. If an unction was once used at this point, it must have been in imitation of other rites. This is the view of Dom Connolly, who attributes it to the interest in things Byzantine of the patriarch Icho-Yahb III.[1]

It is worth noting that the Uniat patriarch John Sulaqa declared in 1552 that his Church did not possess the sacrament of confirmation, and the Chaldeans have subsequently modified their rite, substituting chrism consecrated annually by the bishop for the oil of the horn in the post-baptismal rite, and substituting the formulas of the Roman Ritual for the traditional East Syrian prayers in that rite.[2]

Even if the East Syrian rite has, or had, a post-baptismal unction, it is different from that in other rites, for it is performed with oil blessed by the priest himself. Certainly, it would be difficult to see in any form of this rite what the Western Church calls confirmation, and if we are looking for something in this baptismal liturgy with which to equate confirmation, we can do no better than to look at the ancient pre-baptismal anointing.[3]

THE COPTIC RITE

Two recensions of the Coptic rite are printed in *R.O.*, together with the Ethiopic rite, which is a variant of it. The present text has been translated into English by R. M. Woolley.[4]

Three different oils are used in the Coptic baptismal ritual: the oil of catechesis (which is exorcized oil), the *hagielaion* (or oil of gladness), and the chrism (or μύρον). The first oil is blessed by the priest. The other two are consecrated by the bishop.

The prayer for exorcizing the oil of catechesis prays:

> Make it to be free from demons and their magic and sorcery and all idolatry: and change it and manifest it as an oil for the anointing of catechumens, unto the making of the soul believing . . .[5]

This prayer is followed by another to the same effect, after which the

---

[1] *The Liturgical Homilies of Narsai*, p. lxix.
[2] A. Raes "La Confirmation dans le Rite Syro-Oriental", in *L'Orient Syrien*, Vol. 1 (1956), pp. 248, 253.
[3] cf. Raes, art. cit.; H. J. Lawlor, "Confirmation" in *Encyclopedia of Religion and Ethics*.
[4] Woolley, *Coptic Offices*. The important sections are reprinted in Whitaker, *Documents*, pp. 82–9.
[5] *R.O.*, p. 194.

catechumens are anointed. The priest first anoints the forehead and the shoulder blades with the formula, "We anoint thee in the name of the Father, and of the Son, and of the Holy Spirit, one God." Then he anoints the forehead saying, "We anoint thee, N., with the oil of catechesis in the One, Holy, Catholic, and Apostolic Church of God. Amen." Finally, he anoints the heart and hands and the *pars superior* saying, "May this oil destroy every power of the adversary."[1]

This blessing of oil and anointing take place at the first of a series of catecheses which precede the actual baptism. The renunciation and adherence follow the last catechesis, after which the catechumen is anointed with the *hagielaion* on the heart and the arms and the stomach and the back and between both hands. The anointings are in the form of a cross, and the formula recited is:

> I anoint thee, N., with the oil of gladness, as a defence against every work of the adversary, that thou mayest be grafted into the root of the sweet olive tree which is the Holy Catholic and Apostolic Church of God.[2]

The use of the active, rather than passive forms is characteristic of the Alexandrian rite, as we saw in the *Canonical Responses* of Timothy of Alexandria.

After this anointing the rite follows the same order as the Eucharist, on which it has unquestionably been modelled, with lections, psalmody, and intercessions. The blessing of the font takes the place of the eucharistic prayer, the infusion of chrism of the commixture, and the administration of baptism of the reception of Communion.

After the baptism, the priest takes the chrism and prays over it before the altar:

> Pour out the Holy Spirit through the anointing of the holy chrism, that it may be a living seal and strength, or confirmation to thy servant . . .[3]

The post-baptismal anointing takes the form of thirty-six signs of the cross, made on the forehead, the eyes, the nostrils, the mouth, the ears, the hands (inside and out), the heart, the knees, the soles of the feet, the back, the arms, the shoulders, and above the heart. The formulas are:

> In the Name of the Father, and of the Son, and of the Holy Ghost.
> The anointing of the grace of the Holy Ghost. Amen.

[1] *R.O.*, p. 195.   [2] *R.O.*, p. 200.   [3] *R.O.*, p. 209.

The anointing of the pledge (ἀρραβών) of the kingdom of heaven. Amen.
The anointing of participation in eternal and immortal life. Amen.
The perfection of the grace of the Holy Spirit, and the breastplate of faith and of righteousness. Amen.
I anoint thee, N. with holy oil: in the Name of the Father, and of the Son, and of the Holy Ghost. Amen.[1]

The anointing is followed by the laying on of the priest's hand. In one of the printed versions, the priest then blows in the neophyte's face, saying, "Receive the Holy Ghost and be a pure vessel."[2] This ceremony, however, is not in the second printed version, nor in the Ethiopic.

There can be no doubt that the Coptic rite intends to bestow the Holy Spirit by its post-baptismal rite. To the anointing are added the two Biblical ceremonies of laying on of hands and insufflation. The imperative formula at the insufflation presents a jarring note, and, as Thompson has observed,

It leaves it a little uncertain what the "matter" of confirmation is supposed to be in the Egyptian rite, whether unction, imposition of hand, or insufflation.[3]

The rite continues with the clothing of the neophytes in white, their crowning, and the administration of Communion. The Ethiopic, and one Egyptian manuscript, refer to the administration of milk and honey at this time.[4] This ceremony, although unconnected with the anointings, must be mentioned because of its presence in *Ap. Trad.* and in Roman baptismal rites. It provides one piece of evidence of the connection, not completely understood, between the Roman and Alexandrian liturgies.

Certainly there is nothing in the Coptic rite which we can connect with Serapion. The milk and honey provide a conspicuous link with *Ap. Trad.*, but the specifically baptismal formulas are not those of Hippolytus. The use of three types of oil shows influence both from the Roman use of oil of exorcism (found in the East also in Cyril of Jerusalem), and from the Eastern use of blessed olive oil.

The consecration of chrism took place at St Mark's Monastery on Maundy Thursday. It was performed by the patriarch and had the shape of a eucharistic liturgy. As in *Ap. Trad.* and the Roman rite the chrism

---

[1] R.O., p. 209.   [2] ibid.
[3] *The Offices of Baptism and Confirmation*, p. 97.
[4] R.O., pp. 221 n., 232.

is consecrated before the pre-baptismal oil. The rite is quite long, with many prayers and blessings and diaconal litanies. It is filled with references to the mystical seal and the royal anointing ($\chi\rho\hat{\iota}\sigma\mu\alpha$). It refers repeatedly to the anointing of prophets, priests, and kings, and particularly to the anointing of Aaron. Most pertinent to our purpose is this prayer:

> Send thy Holy Spirit upon this chrism ($\mu\acute{\upsilon}\rho\upsilon$) that it may be an incorruptible robe and an holy anointing to the honour and glory of thy holy blessed Name, and of thine only-begotten Son, and of the Holy Ghost. In this are anointed Apostles and all holy infants who are reborn in the Name of Christ that they may come to the anointing of regeneration. From this also are anointed bishops and other presbyters even to this day. We beseech thee, O our Lord, that it may be a glorious unction, a firm seal ($\sigma\phi\rho\alpha\gamma\acute{\iota}s$) of those who are presented before thy sight to be baptized in the baptism of regeneration. . . .[1]

The blessing of the *hagielaion*, which follows, is much shorter. There are three prayers which might be called prayers of blessing.[2] The first speaks of the oil of gladness "with which priests and martyrs have been anointed", and asks that the Holy Ghost descend into it to destroy the worship of idols, and magic, and sorcery, and for the safety and health of the faithful. The second invokes the Name of God to much the same end, and the third again asks that the Holy Spirit be sent into the oil, "that it may be to all who receive it from thy faithful and orthodox servants a guard to our souls, bodies, and spirits, a joy to our hearts, glory and honour to thy holy Name".

The great complexity of these blessings is in marked contrast to the simplicity of the Byzantine and Western blessings of the chrism, although the ideas expressed are common to the several rites. The consecration of the oils in the reverse order of their intended use is particularly noteworthy.

THE ARMENIAN RITE

The text we shall use is that printed in Conybeare's *Rituale Armenorum*, which is a translation of uncial codex no. 457, viii, 6 of the library of San Lazaro in Venice. Conybeare dates this manuscript from the ninth or tenth century.[3]

---

[1] R.O., p. 256. [2] R.O., pp. 264-5.
[3] R.A., pp. ix-xii. His translation of the rite is reprinted in Whitaker, *Documents*, pp. 52-9.

The Armenian rite has no pre-baptismal anointing, although Thompson is certain that it must have had such an anointing anciently. The rite contains a prayer for the blessing of oil, before the blessing of the water, and Thompson affirms that, although it is now said over already consecrated chrism, it is clearly a prayer of blessing.

> As of old thou didst anoint priests and kings and prophets with such all-holy oil, so now also, we pray thee, beneficent Lord, send the grace of thy holy Spirit into this oil; to the end that it shall be for him that is anointed therewith unto holiness of spiritual wisdom, that he may manfully fight and triumph over the adversary . . .

The only use which the rite makes of the "holy oil" over which this prayer is said is to pour it into the font at the blessing of the water. The universal custom of Armenians in modern times, however, is to use the chrism consecrated by the catholicos at Etchmiatiadzin. This is borne out by a thirteenth-century (?) Armenian treatise on baptism, which speaks of dropping the myrrh into the water.[1]

The baptism follows the blessing of the font, and after it the Gospel account of Christ's baptism in Matt. 3.13-16 is read. Then follows a prayer for those who have become the sons of God "through the regeneration of water and spirit", that they may be replenished with the grace of the Holy Spirit and become a temple in which God's Name may dwell. The priest then anoints the neophytes on the forehead, eyes, ears, nostrils, mouth, palms, heart, backbone, and feet. The formulas are appropriate to the sense which is anointed.[2] After he has been anointed, the neophyte is reclothed, led before the altar, and communicated.

Denzinger quotes a canon of Sion, an Armenian patriarch of the eighth century, that bishops did not dare to consecrate the chrism, but only the catholicos consecrated it, once a year, "according to the canonical precepts of the holy fathers".[3] As we have already seen, Thompson is certain that the existence of a form for blessing oil in the Armenian rite is evidence that it was once used for a pre-baptismal anointing. Unquestionably the prayer of blessing expects people to be anointed with that oil. There is, nevertheless, another possible interpretation of the evidence. The rite in *R.A.* never speaks of chrism or myrrh, but always of "holy oil", both in the blessing of the oil and of the water, and in the anointing. Perhaps the blessing in the rite is a vestige of the

---

[1] *R.A.*, p. 107.   [2] *R.A.*, p. 98.   [3] *R.O.*, p. 55.

administration of baptism at the solemn seasons by the bishop, who consecrated the chrism with this prayer, and the subsequent reservation of the consecration of chrism to the catholicos and delegation of baptism to the parish priest have produced the phenomena described by Thompson of having the prayer said over the already consecrated chrism. Another possibility is that Armenian presbyters were once permitted to bless the oil. In favour of these explanations is the lack of evidence for the use of more than one kind of liturgical oil by the Armenians. *R.A.* speaks of oil, and other sources of myrrh, but none seems to presuppose the use of two different oils in the baptismal rite.

CONCLUSION

This concludes our study of the Eastern rites of baptismal anointing. From the fifth century we have seen the general acceptance of a rite of post-baptismal unction, which, whatever the actual formula used at its administration might be, could be fairly described in the words of the Byzantine rite as "the seal of the gift of the Holy Spirit". Over against this general pattern we must place those rites derived from the ancient Syrian rite, in which the *rushmâ* preceded baptism. The East Syrian rite does not know a post-baptismal chrismation to this day, although it has introduced a laying on of hands and signing, which has included in some places an anointing with the oil of gladness. The text of the accompanying prayer and the failure to use chrism, however, make it impossible to identify this rite with a gift of the Holy Spirit. The West Syrian rite has a post-baptismal chrismation, but it has retained much ancient Syrian language in its formularies which speak of the giving of the Holy Spirit before baptism. Although it uses the Byzantine term "oil of gladness" rather than the Syrian *rushmâ* of the pre-baptismal anointing, it has not completely lost the traditional Syrian idea that the Spirit is given by this first anointing.

We have traced the identification of the chrismation with the gift of the Spirit as far back as Origen, and although he also knew a christological interpretation of the anointing, identifying it with the blood of the Paschal lamb which anointed the doorposts of the Israelites, this latter meaning does not seem to have survived. The anointing with chrism in the East is the anointing of the Holy Spirit.

There is considerable variation in practice concerning the pre-baptismal anointing. We have already mentioned the Syrian tendency to identify the pre-baptismal anointing with the gift of the Holy Spirit, following the tradition of Mar Ephraem Syrus. The Byzantine rite has an anointing with the oil of gladness, blessed by the priest during the rite. It immediately precedes baptism, as did the similar anointing in *Ap. Trad.*, but it seems to have acquired some of the characteristics of the post-baptismal anointing in Hippolytus. The oil is blessed, not exorcized as in *Ap. Trad.*, Cyril, and Serapion. This relative increase in dignity in the pre-baptismal oil in the Byzantine usage is not surprising in the light of the ancient Syrian evidence. We noted in chapter III that St John Chrysostom himself, whose name the Church of Constantinople attached to its normal eucharistic liturgy, spoke of the pre-baptismal anointing as the seal and the anointing of God himself. The teaching of its greatest patriarch can hardly have failed to influence the Church of the imperial City.

The later Alexandrian rite has two pre-baptismal anointings, one parallel to the Roman anointing with exorcized oil, and the other parallel to the Byzantine anointing. The Armenians have no pre-baptismal anointing whatever.

We are now ready to turn our attention to the West, where the availability of liturgical texts and the great amount of scholarly research which has already gone into their identification will make possible a more detailed consideration.

V

The Western Rites

THE AFRICAN FATHERS

The great African Church, which by the time of St Cyprian numbered fully a hundred bishops in the territory of the Roman province of Africa, perished without leaving a single liturgical book. We are therefore compelled to turn to the sermons, tractates, and other writings of the African Fathers for information about their liturgy. Unfortunately, none of their writings contains such a detailed description of the baptismal rites as we find in St Ambrose of Milan, or in St Cyril of Jerusalem. Yet they do tell us a great deal.

The evidence of Tertullian has already been discussed in chapter II. From *de Baptismo* and *de Resurrectione Carnis* we learn of an anointing with chrism after baptism, which Tertullian connects with the priestly anointing of Aaron and the Messianic anointing of Christ. The anointing was followed by a signing and the laying on of hands for the bestowal of the Holy Ghost.[1]

St Cyprian, Bishop of Carthage, was martyred on 14 September 258. A great part of his episcopate was concerned with the rebaptism controversy stemming from the Novatianist schism. Writing against the validity of schismatic baptism, he said:

> He who has been baptized must also be anointed, that having received the chrism, that is the unction, he may be anointed of God and have the grace of Christ in him. Further it is the Eucharist from which the baptized are anointed with oil sanctified on the altar (*oleum in altari sanctificatum*). They cannot then sanctify the creature of oil who have neither altar nor church. For which cause there can be no spiritual unction among the heretics, for it is true that they can in no way consecrate the oil nor celebrate the Eucharist.[2]

[1] *de Baptismo*, 7, 8; *de Resurrectione Carnis* 8.
[2] Ep. 70.2 (*C.S.E.L.*, Vol. 3, p. 768).

From this passage we learn that St Cyprian considered the unction to be so immediately bound up with the baptism itself that he was prepared to deny the validity of the baptism if the chrism had not been properly consecrated. This consecration took place at the Eucharist. St Cyprian follows Tertullian in associating the effect of the anointing with incorporation into Christ. He does not mention the Holy Spirit in the context of the anointing. His phrase is *unctio spiritalis* not *Spiritus*.

Cyprian's reference to the consecration of the chrism at the Eucharist leads to the assumption that the custom of consecrating the oil on Maundy Thursday had already become established by his time, since this would be the last Eucharist at which it could be consecrated before the Easter baptisms. At least it implies a different custom from that of *Ap. Trad.*, in which the oil was consecrated at the beginning of the baptismal rites.

St Cyprian does speak of the gift of the Holy Spirit in baptism, but, like Tertullian, he connects it with the laying on of hands.

> Those who are baptized in the Church ... receive the Holy Spirit and are completed with the seal of the Lord (*signaculo dominico consummentur*) through our prayer and the imposition of a hand.[1]

The *signaculum* to which Cyprian refers is the sign of the cross, which he, like Tertullian, identifies with the *taw* of Ezek. 9.4, "That in this sign of the cross salvation may be to all who are marked on the forehead".[2] He does not state that the cross was made with oil, and there is no evidence that it was. The christological anointing immediately following baptism is the only anointing mentioned by St Cyprian.

Professor Lampe discusses the theology of St Cyprian in some detail and praises his attempt to maintain the unity of the baptismal rite, including the laying on of hands. His conclusion is worth quoting:

> It is with the laying on of hands that Cyprian, following the African tradition of Tertullian, and finding Scriptural authority in the Acts of the Apostles, has to associate the gift of the Spirit. About unction with chrism he says comparatively little. Like his second-century predecessors, he regards it as a subsidiary ceremony which follows Baptism with the object of demonstrating to the newly baptized that he has become a member of Christ, a sharer in the Messianic character of the Lord, and a partaker of the grace of Christ.[3]

Although the facts asserted by Professor Lampe are beyond question,

[1] *Ep.* 73.9 (*C.S.E.L.*, Vol. 3, p. 785).
[2] *Testimonia* 2.22 (*C.S.E.L.*, Vol. 3, p. 90).
[3] *The Seal of the Spirit*, pp. 176f.

the use of the word "subsidiary" connotes a rite of little importance, which is hardly a fair description of St Cyprian's view. Lampe is right that Cyprian does not anywhere associate the anointing with the gift of the Spirit, but he does believe it to be of great importance as a christological baptismal rite.

This is shown more clearly when we move on from Cyprian to St Optatus of Milevis, who flourished about 370. We find Optatus speaking of three mysteries, including with baptism the *sacramentum olei* and the *sacramentum impositionis manuum*. His view is made clear in his description of the baptism of Christ:

> The heaven is open. When God anoints him the spiritual oil at once comes down under the form of a dove and sits upon his head and pours over him; the oil is spread asunder (*digestum est*); whence he began to be called Christ, for he was anointed by God the Father; and lest he should seem to lack the imposition of a hand, the voice of God was heard from the cloud, saying . . .[1]

We find here the same rite described by Tertullian and St Cyprian. The baptism, anointing, and laying on of hands are considered to be three co-ordinate elements (*tria mysteria*), and all must be found in the baptism of Christ, which is the model of Christian baptism. In another passage Optatus speaks of the oil as preparing a throne for the Holy Ghost,[2] making it clear that he is not ascribing the gift of the Spirit to the oil.

Mason, in his classic study, makes this comment:

> Optatus' language reads here as if he had Tertullian's treatise *de Baptismo* open before him . . . Certainly the doctrine is Tertullian's. The water does not convey the Spirit; the oil does not convey it. The Unction is a preparatory rite. It makes the newly-cleansed soul ready to receive the Spirit so that he may be invoked to take up his abode through the Laying on of Hands.[3]

The figure of St Augustine must necessarily dominate any discussion of the African Church. Both in the extent of his writings and in the influence they have wielded, the great Bishop of Hippo is the pre-eminent figure of the African, if not of the Western Church. Augustine has much to say about Christian initiation, and we are indebted to Dom Benedict Busch for an extensive study of the Augustinian material relating to the catechumenate and baptism.[4]

---

[1] *Contra Parmenianum Donatistam*, 4.7 (*P.L.*, 11, 1040).   [2] ibid., 7.4.

[3] *The Relation of Confirmation to Baptism*, p. 81.

[4] "De Initiatione Christiana secundum Sanctum Augustinum", in *Ephemerides Liturgicae*, Vol. 52 (1938), pp. 159–78, 385–481.

There is no direct evidence in St Augustine of a pre-baptismal unction. W. C. Bishop, nevertheless, has cited a passage from Augustine commenting upon John 9.6 as indirect evidence that anointing was a part of the ceremonies for making a catechumen.[1] In this passage Augustine compares the washing of the blind man in the pool of Siloam to baptism, and the anointing of his eyes with spittle to the catechumenate. The distinction, says Augustine, between the catechumen and the faithful is, "The catechumen is anointed, but not yet washed." But he goes on to add that if you ask "When were you anointed?", he will reply that he has believed in Christ, the Anointed One. Busch believes that this passage is to be understood symbolically, and not of an actual anointing,[2] and there does not seem to be any need to interpret it literally, because of the highly allegorical setting in which it is placed. The Johannine passage is, nevertheless, one of those which has had a profound influence on the development of baptismal rites.

The unction following baptism was certainly known to Augustine, and he discussed it at much greater length than his predecessors. Chrism is a sacrament like baptism itself.[3] It is associated with the person of Christ and is a sign of our participation in him. It is also a royal and priestly anointing.[4] We are anointed as wrestlers (luctatores) against the devil, an idea found also in Ambrose and in John Chrysostom.[5]

This is not, however, the totality of the teaching of Augustine concerning the anointing. He expounds the mystery beginning with the baptism of Christ:

> It is written that God anointed him with the Holy Spirit, not indeed with visible oil, but with the gift of grace, which is signified by the visible unguent with which the Church anoints the baptized. Nor indeed was Christ anointed with the Holy Spirit when at his baptism he descended upon him as a dove—then indeed his body was anointed, which he deigned to prefigure his Church: but it is to be understood of that mystic and invisible anointing by which the Word of God was made flesh ... By this we confess him to be born of the Holy Spirit from the Virgin Mary.[6]

[1] Tract. in Ioan. Ev. 44.2, cited by W. C. Bishop, "The African Rite", in J.T.S., Vol. 13 (1911), p. 265.

[2] Busch, art. cit., p. 398.

[3] contra Litteras Petiliani, 2.104, 239 (P.L., 43, 342).

[4] de Civitate Dei, 17.49; Sermo 351, 5.12; Enarratio in Psalmum 44, 19.

[5] Enarratio in Psalmum 26, II, 2 (P.L., 36, 200).

[6] de Trinitate, XV, 46 (P.L., 42, 1093).

In another place Augustine says, "The spiritual unction is the Holy Spirit himself, whose sacrament is in the visible anointing",[1] or again, "The oil indeed is the sacrament of the fire of our Holy Spirit.[2] He distinguishes between the gift of the Spirit to our Lord in the Incarnation, which he compares with the gift we receive in baptism, and the gift in the Messianic anointing, which he compares with that received in the post-baptismal rites. "It is one thing", he says, "to be born of the Holy Spirit, another to be nourished (*pasci*) by the Spirit."[3] He therefore goes on to explain:

> The Holy Spirit is signified whether through the water for cleansing and washing, or through the oil for exultation and the inflaming of charity; nor indeed, although the signs are different, does he differ from himself.[4]

The effect of the teaching of St Augustine is described by Joseph Coppens in his comprehensive study *L'Imposition des Mains et les Rites Connexes*:

> St Augustine contributed greatly to the acceptance of a new interpretation of the post-baptismal unction, and this was the grouping henceforth of the chrismation and the imposition of hands, which were in the eyes of the later African Church the sacrament of confirmation; the unction soon became the principal rite and the only one of which the sacramental value was upheld in the controversies with the Donatists.[5]

St Augustine was careful to distinguish between the external anointing with oil and the internal unction of the Holy Ghost. "The visible oil is in the sign, the invisible oil is in the sacrament, the spiritual oil is inward (*intus*)."[6] The visible oil all receive equally, but the invisible *unctio caritatis* is received only by the good.

Concerning the manner of performing the post-baptismal rites, Augustine tells us very little. He rarely speaks openly about the details of Christian rites, and the post-baptismal ceremonies were particularly a subject for reticence. It is not clear whether a separate consignation followed the anointing. The signing of the brow with a cross was a prominent ceremony at the making of a catechumen, and it is therefore difficult to know whether Augustine's references to the *signum* refer to this or to a post-baptismal signing. In any case, there is no evidence of

---

[1] *Tract. in I Ep.*, Ioan. 3.5 (*P.L.*, 37, 1443).
[2] *Sermo 227 ad infantes* (*P.L.*, 38, 1100).
[3] *Sermo 71*, 12.19 (*P.L.*, 38, 454).
[4] *Enarratio in Psalmum 108*, 26 (*P.L.*, 37, 1443).   [5] op. cit., p. 302.
[6] *Enarratio in Psalmum 44*, 19 (*P.L.*, 36, 505).

more than one post-baptismal anointing, and Augustine associates that both with the participation in Christ and the gift of the Spirit. Busch says that the sign of the cross was made on the forehead, perhaps with oil, at the time of the laying on of hands, but the question must remain open.

In *Sermo* 324 Augustine speaks of *presbyteri* as the ministers of the total rite of initiation, including the imposition of hands. The third Council of Carthage in 397 decreed that the presbyter was never to consecrate the chrism (*chrisma conficere*), but that this was reserved to the bishop.[1] The passage of such a canon leads us to believe that presbyters were in fact consecrating the chrism, as we know that they did at a later period.[2] This makes it seem likely that presbyters did at least administer the chrism at baptism.

The conclusion of any particular scholar on these uncertain points will probably be influenced by whether he believes the African rite to have been of the Roman or Gallican type, that is, whether he tries to fit the statements of Augustine into the framework of a rite having two anointings and an episcopal laying on of hands, or into that of a rite having a single post-baptismal anointing. In one case the laying on of hands can be stressed and the unity with Rome emphasized, while in the other, the mention of presbyters as possible ministers of the total rite and its similarity to the rites of Gaul and Milan are brought to the fore.

The total eclipse of the African Church under the shadow, first of Vandal invaders, and later of the Arabs, made the further development of its rite impossible, and we are left with an incomplete picture. Certainly the theological reversal accomplished by Augustine in making the anointing the sacramental rite of the Holy Spirit is the outstanding feature of the available evidence.

ST AMBROSE OF MILAN

We are indeed fortunate in possessing a detailed description of the baptismal rites of the Church of Milan from the hand of its greatest bishop. Although the authorship of *de Sacramentis* has been sharply questioned since the sixteenth century, it is generally accepted to-day as being the work of St Ambrose.[3] The principal works vindicating the

---

[1] Canons 32 and 36 (Mansi, *Conciliorum Omnium Amplissima Collectio*, III, 885).
[2] cf. John the Deacon, *Ep. ad Senarium*, 8 (ed. Wilmart, p. 175).
[3] A summary of the critical controversy will be found in the introduction to Botte's edition of *de Sacramentis* (pp. 1–24) and in J. H. Srawley's introduction to T. Thompson's translation (pp. 1–13).

Ambrosian authorship were published by Fr Otto Faller and Dom R. Hugh Connolly.[1]

On the basis of these discussions we shall assume that the *de Sacramentis* represents the actual text of mystagogical lectures given by St Ambrose at Milan, and that the related *de Mysteriis* represents a treatise prepared by Ambrose for publication.[2]

Ambrose describes the baptismal rites as taking place on the sabbath. From other references we know that the Holy Sabbath is meant.[3] The opening ceremony is the *effeta*, or *aperitio*. This ceremony, based upon our Lord's healing miracle in Mark 7.32f, is performed by the bishop, who touches the ears and nostrils of the candidate. There is no mention of the use of either oil or saliva. Dom Botte connects the ceremony with the direction in *Ap. Trad.* to "seal their foreheads, ears, and noses" on Saturday.[4] The formula is given as simply, "Effeta, that is be opened".[5]

After the *effeta* the *competentes* are led into the baptistery where they are anointed by a presbyter and a deacon (*levita*) "as athletes of Christ". No formula for the anointing is given. It is particularly worthy of note that the anointing here precedes the renunciation of the devil, whereas in *Ap. Trad.* and the Eastern sources we have considered, it follows.

The rite continues after the anointing with the renunciation and the consecration of the font. The actual baptism corresponds closely to the form in *Ap. Trad.*, save that the second credal question seems to have been abbreviated to the form, "Dost thou believe in our Lord Jesus Christ, and in his cross?"[6]

The baptism is followed at once by the anointing. Ambrose describes it as being performed with *myron*, which he translates *unguentum*.[7] The minister is called *sacerdos*, which unquestionably means the bishop, since he has previously referred to the *presbyter et levita*. The place anointed is *supra caput*.[8] He quotes the formula as,

[1] "Ambrosius, der Verfasser von *De Sacramentis*", in *Zeitschrift für Katholische Theologie*, Vol. 64 (1940), pp. 1–14, 81–101; *The De Sacramentis a work of St Ambrose. Two Papers*, Oxford, 1942. (The Second World War prevented them from reading each other's work.)

[2] Botte's Latin text and Thompson's translation will be used. *de Sacramentis* is cited as *S* and *de Mysteriis* as *M*.

[3] For example, *Ep.* 20.4.

[4] Botte, *Des Sacrements*, p. 54, n. 2; *Ap. Trad.*, 20.

[5] *S.*, I, 1, 2–3; *M.*, I, 3–4: "Effeta, quod est adperire."

[6] *S.*, II, 7, 20.   [7] *S.*, III, 1, 1.   [8] *S.*, II, 7, 24; III, 1, 1.

God the Father Almighty, who hath regenerated thee by water and the Holy Ghost, and hath forgiven thee thy sins, himself anoint thee (*ipse te unguet*) unto eternal life.

This prayer, with only slight verbal changes, will occur again in the medieval Ambrosian liturgical books, and in those of the Roman and Gallican rites. We shall refer to it as the chrismal prayer.

It seems apparent that St Ambrose is describing an actual anointing of the head, not simply a signing with the holy oil. In *de Mysteriis* he quotes Ps. 133.2, with its reference to the flowing of the oil, and comments:

> Understand why this is done, because the wise man's eyes are in his head. It flowed down unto the beard—that is, unto the grace of youth—even unto Aaron's beard, for this purpose, that thou mayest become a chosen generation, priestly, precious; for we are all anointed with spiritual grace unto the kingdom of God and the priesthood (*consacerdotium*).[1]

It also seems clear that the meaning of this post-baptismal unction is christological, as in Tertullian, for he speaks of us as fellow-priests (*consacerdotes*) with Christ, and in the parallel passage in *de Sacramentis* he describes the rite of baptism and chrismation together as *regeneratio*, quoting with reference to the baptism of Christ Ps. 2 and Acts 13.33.[2]

The chrismation was followed by the reading of John 13 and the foot-washing, a distinctively non-Roman ceremony,[3] and the clothing in white robes. The *spiritale signaculum* followed. This is described in *de Sacramentis*:

> There follows the spiritual seal (*spiritale signaculum*), which you have heard mentioned in the lesson today. For after the font it remains for the perfecting (*perfectio*) to take place, when, at the invocation of the priest (*sacerdos*), the Holy Spirit is bestowed, the spirit of wisdom and understanding, the spirit of counsel and strength, the spirit of knowledge and godliness, the spirit of holy fear, as it were seven virtues of the Spirit . . . These are the seven virtues when thou art sealed (*quando consignaris*).[4]

A parallel description occurs in *de Mysteriis*:

> Wherefore recollect that thou hast received the spiritual seal, the spirit of wisdom and . . . holy fear, and preserve what thou hast received. God the

[1] M., VI, 30.   [2] S., III, 1, 1–2.
[3] cf. my "Ambrosian Baptismal Rites", in *Studia Liturgica*, Vol. 1 (1962), p. 249.
[4] S., III, 2, 8–10.

Father hath sealed (*signavit*) thee, Christ the Lord hath confirmed (*confirmavit*) thee, and hath given thee the earnest (*pignus*) of the Spirit in thy heart, as thou hast learned from the apostolic lesson.[1]

From these descriptions there can be little doubt that St Ambrose identified the *spiritale signaculum* with the bestowal of the sevenfold gift of the Holy Ghost. He was willing to use the verbs *consignare*, *signare*, and *confirmare*, and the noun *perfectio* to describe it. He uses *infundere* to describe the pouring out of the Spirit, and says specifically that it occurs at the invocation of the *sacerdos*. The parallel between this rite and that described in *Ap. Trad.* for the laying on of the bishop's hand is quite clear. It is, in fact, what we are accustomed to call confirmation. It is less clear exactly what external ceremony accompanied the seal.

Lejay, writing in *D.A.C.L.*, is perfectly sure that it was the imposition of hands.[2] Galtier is of the same view. He also denies that an anointing, or signing with chrism, was a part of this rite.[3] On the other hand, Dom Benedict Busch, a more recent commentator, believes the external rite to have been a second anointing, "by which he is sealed with the sign of the cross unto the spiritual priesthood and kingdom and through which he receives as it were the seven virtues of the Spirit."[4] All of these commentators are attempting to fit the work of St Ambrose into a pattern with other rites, and their conclusions must be accepted with serious reservations. It is Galtier's belief, for example, that the double anointing found in the Roman rite was exclusively Roman, and he is anxious to show that St Ambrose, like Tertullian and the Canons of Hippolytus, did not know a second anointing.

If we return to the actual text, there is no indication in the two passages cited what the external ceremony was which accompanied the prayer of the bishop. The use of terms common to other liturgical books, nevertheless, suggests certain ceremonies. In the sixth book of *de Sacramentis* St Ambrose defends the working of the mystery of the Trinity in the sacraments against the Arians. In this context he speaks again of the *spiritale signaculum* as revealing not only the distinction of persons, "but that the whole mystery of the Trinity is bound up together".

---

[1] *M.*, VII, 42.   [2] "Ambrosien (rit)", in *D.A.C.L.*, I, 1432.

[3] "La Consignation dans les Églises d'Occident", in *Revue d'Histoire Ecclésiastique*, Vol. 13 (1912), pp. 261–70.

[4] "De Initiatione Christiana secundum Sanctum Augustinum", in *Ephemerides Liturgicae*, Vol. 52 (1938), p. 177.

It is God who anointed (*unxit*) thee, and the Lord signed (*signavit*) thee, and put the Holy Spirit in thy heart. Thou therefore hast received the Holy Spirit in thy heart. How? Thou hast Christ saying this to his Church in Canticles: Set me a seal (*signaculum*) in thy heart, as a seal upon thy arms. Therefore God anointed thee, the Lord signed thee. How? Because thou wast signed with the image of the cross itself (*ad crucis ipsius signatus es formam*) unto his passion, thou receivedst a seal unto his likeness (*similitudo*), that thou mayest rise unto his image (*forma*), and live after his pattern (*figura*), who was crucified to sin, and liveth to God. And thy old man plunged into the font was crucified to sin, but rose again unto God.[1]

In this passage we have a masterful summary of the theology of Christian baptism. It is God who acts in and through the rite, placing his Spirit as a seal in our hearts, that we may be conformed to the cross of Christ, crucified and raised with him in the holy font. Clearly, St Ambrose is describing a single rite, of which the washing, anointing, and signing with the cross are all parts. There is no question here of baptism followed by another sacrament. There is a single sacramental rite in which we are brought into the life of the Trinity.

Looking at this passage along with the two previously quoted, we can begin to obtain a picture of the rite itself. The two verbs *unxit* and *signavit* are here brought into correlation, raising the possibility that the signing was an anointing. The sign of the cross is definitely used, and it is most logical, therefore, to assume that "*quando consignaris*" refers to the marking of the sign of the cross on the neophyte's brow by the bishop, while he invoked the sevenfold Spirit. That such a signing was all but universal makes this inference almost certain. In spite of the opinions of Galtier and Lejay, there is no evidence for an imposition of hands at this point in the rite.[2]

It does not appear possible to state definitely whether or not the signing was performed with oil. In *de Spiritu Sancto* St Ambrose says, "The anointing (*unguentum*) of Christ is the Holy Spirit", but his reference is to the Messianic anointing of Jesus,[3] and in *de Salomone*, commenting upon Deut. 32.13, "He made them to suck honey out of the rock, and oil out of the flinty rock", he applies the words to our Lord giving the sweetness of the Gospel and the Holy Spirit "through the anointing of chrism".[4] These passages, together with the use of the

[1] S., VI, 2. 6–7.
[2] The absence of any laying on of hands in the medieval Milanese rite, even when the bishop himself baptizes, is an important piece of negative evidence.
[3] op. cit. I, 9, 100–3. [4] op. cit., 3.

verb *ungere*, tend to support the view that oil was used, for Ambrose no-where associates the anointing of the head immediately after baptism with the Holy Spirit. If this *spiritale signaculum* was accompanied by an anointing, then the rite described by St Ambrose is similar to that of *Ap. Trad.* Certainly Fr Galtier's opposite opinion must be taken seriously, but he is not primarily interested in St Ambrose, but rather in showing that only the pure Roman rite had a second anointing at the consignation. He believes that Africa, Milan, and Gaul had an imposition of hands, and a signing made without oil.

One other piece of ancient evidence must be considered as bearing on this question. Fragment seven of the Mai fragments of an Arian sermon[1] quotes several orthodox prayers in defence of Arian doctrine. Among these are the interrogative form of the creed used in baptism, and immediately after it, this, described as used *in benedictionibus suis*:

> God and Father of our Lord Jesus Christ, who has regenerated thee by water, himself anoint (*linet*) thee with the Holy Spirit.

The relationship of this form to that quoted by St Ambrose for the post-baptismal unction is obvious. The anointing which this form is intended to convey is pneumatological, however, like the Eastern "seal of the gift of the Holy Spirit". The alteration of the Biblical "by water and the Holy Ghost" is in accordance with the Oriental versions of *Ap. Trad.* and implies a doctrine of the bestowal of the Spirit by the anointing. This purports, nevertheless, to be a recognizably orthodox liturgical form identified with North Italy. It is my belief that this formula is later than *de Sacramentis* and shows the effects of the confusion and conflation of the two post-baptismal rites which are reflected in the *ordo* of Beroldus and the *Manuale Ambrosianum* of the Middle Ages. The words *et cetera* appear following the formula as quoted, and so it is possible that it went on to enumerate the sevenfold gifts of the Spirit, but any attempt to complete the formula would be mere conjecture.

H. M. Bannister, in a letter to Giovanni Mercati, raised the question of whether the Arian author is accurately quoting liturgical formulas, or simply giving the sense of them. Bannister believes that this formula was intended to accompany an imposition of hands (*in manupositionibus*)

---

[1] *Scriptorum Veterum Nova Collectio*, ed. Mai, Vol. 3, Pt. 2, pp. 222–3; cf. G. Mercati, *Antiche Reliquie Liturgiche Ambrosiani e Romani* (Studi e Testi, Vol. 7), pp. 44–56.

and would, therefore, be a variant of the "confirmation" prayer in a rite which used chrism at the episcopal benediction.[1]

A further problem presented by the *spiritale signaculum* in St Ambrose is the form of words which accompanied the seal. The enumeration of the sevenfold gifts of the Holy Spirit in both *de Sacramentis* and *de Mysteriis* naturally leads to the presumption that they were a part of the form. We might envisage a prayer similar to that in the Gelasian Sacramentary, or the *Book of Common Prayer*. On the other hand, St Ambrose does not say that these phrases were used as a formula, and in *de Mysteriis* he generally avoids quoting liturgical forms. The text, however, which is the same in both accounts, is different from that of the Vulgate, and the difference may result from the quotation of a liturgical text. The case cannot be regarded as proven, but the probability is great that a form mentioning the seven gifts of the Spirit was used.[2]

The writings of St Ambrose are a major source for our knowledge of Western baptismal rites in the fourth century. Unfortunately, we do not possess comparable descriptions of the rites of Rome, Africa, and Gaul, so it is impossible to state precisely which of the ceremonies described by Ambrose were peculiar to his own Church, and which were common to Latin rites, but we have his assurance that Milan follows the Roman Church, whose "type and form we follow in all things".[3] While this statement need not be taken literally, and indeed cannot be, we may assume that the rites he describes were at least generally similar to those of other Latin Churches.

The rites described by St Ambrose follow the general pattern of *Ap. Trad.* and Tertullian. There is a pre-baptismal anointing of a preparatory nature, a post-baptismal anointing with *myron*, or chrism, followed by an episcopal signing, probably also with chrism. The sevenfold gift of the Holy Spirit is connected with the episcopal consignation. There are slight differences of detail, but the separation of the christological baptismal unction from the *spiritale signaculum* and the gift of the Spirit speaks of a Western liturgical tradition to which, in spite of local differences, *Ap. Trad.*, Tertullian, and St Ambrose bear witness.

[1] Mercati, op. cit., pp. 54–6.
[2] cf. G. Morin, "Pour l'Authenticité du *De Sacramentis*", in *Jahrbuch für Liturgiewissenschaft*, Vol. 8 (1928), p. 100, and R. H. Connolly, *The De Sacramentis a Work of St Ambrose*, pp. 11f.
[3] S., III, 1, 5. Ambrose, nevertheless, defends the foot-washing as an ancient local usage.

THE EARLY ROMAN EVIDENCE

In chapter II we considered the work of Justin Martyr, the earliest Roman author to discuss the baptismal rites. The *Apostolic Tradition* of Hippolytus, with which we began this study, must also be assigned to the Roman Church. It will therefore be with Hippolytus that we resume our study of the early Roman evidence.

Two passages in works of Hippolytus other than *Ap. Trad.* relate to our inquiry. In his *Commentary on Daniel*, he says, speaking of the bath of Susanna:

> What is the oil (ἔλαιον) but the power of the Holy Ghost? As after the washing (λουτρόν) those who believe are anointed with chrism (μύρον).[1]

The use of the word μύρον which does not occur in *Ap. Trad.*, to designate the "oil of thanksgiving" provides an immediate point of contact with later usage, while the association of the oil with the Holy Spirit indicates that the reference here is to the second anointing of *Ap. Trad.*

The second passage is in *de Christo et Antichristo*:

> The heavenly Spirit by whom those who believe in God are sealed (σφραγίζονται).[2]

We may see in this passage a reference to the Roman use of the term *consignatio* to designate the rite by which the Spirit is conferred. The reference is presumably to the sealing of the foreheads of the neophytes, as described in *Ap. Trad.*, 22. It need not mean that the Spirit is given by the signing, apart from the laying on of hands, with which *Ap. Trad.* so closely associates it.

In the following generation we have the testimony of Cornelius, Bishop of Rome, writing to Fabian of Antioch concerning the case of the heresiarch Novatian, who had been baptized clinically, that is *in extremis*, without the addition of the customary post-baptismal rites. He complained that Novatian, after his recovery, did not do what was necessary according to the rule (κανῶν) of the Church, namely: to be sealed (σφραγισθῆναι) by the bishop (ἐπίσκοπος), of which he said,

> Since he has not done this, how has he come by (ἔτυχεν) the Holy Ghost?[3]

---

[1] op. cit., 1.16 (Bonwetsch and Achelis, *Hippolytus Werke*, Vol. 1, p. 26).
[2] op. cit., 49 (ibid., Vol. 2, p. 40).
[3] Eusebius, *Hist. Eccl.* VI, 43, 15 (ed. Schwartz, Vol. 2, p. 620).

Again it is the seal, or σφραγίς, to which the receiving of the Spirit is attached.

The *Liber Pontificalis* ascribes the Roman rule of chrismation to St Silvester, who was bishop of that city from 314 to 325. The first edition said:

> He ordered the chrism to be consecrated (*confici*) by the bishop and the bishops to have the privilege of signing (*ut consignent*) the baptized.[1]

To this the second edition added:

> And he also ordered that the presbyter should anoint (*lineret*) the baptized with chrism when they come up from the water, on account of the danger of death.[2]

Obviously we cannot accept this statement as true in its entirety, unless we are prepared to deny that *Ap. Trad.* was known in Rome, for it clearly provides that the presbyter should anoint the neophyte when he comes up from the water. It is possible, nevertheless, to make sense of the *Liber Pontificalis* without discarding *Ap. Trad.* Hippolytus assumes the situation of solemn baptism at Easter, conferred by the bishop, with the assistance of a great body of presbyters and deacons. *Liber Pontificalis* seems concerned rather with the situation of a local presbyter administering the sacrament to children. He is directed to anoint (*lineret*) the neophyte immediately, as a part of the baptismal rite, but he is forbidden to consecrate the chrism, or to perform the episcopal rite of consignation. We learn from Jerome, later in the same century, that the bishops were accustomed to visit those baptized by presbyters and deacons in the remote villages and to lay hands on them, invoking the Holy Ghost.[3] If this custom already existed at the time of Silvester, the situation becomes comprehensible. He is concerned to maintain the prerogative of the bishop, while ensuring that all who are baptized are anointed, lest they die without receiving the chrism.

An inscription found at Spoleto, dating from the pontificate of Liberius (352-6), mentions a woman as "*consignata a Liberio papa*".[4] The use of *consignata* rather than *baptizata* may indicate that she was "confirmed" at a time other than at her baptism, and that even then the solemn sealing by the bishop, rather than the baptism administered by the parish priest, was the rite worthy of mention.

---

[1] Duchesne, *Liber Pontificalis*, Vol. 1, pp. 76–7.   [2] ibid., p. 171.
[3] *contra Luciferanos*. 9.
[4] H. Leclercq, "Confirmation", *D.A.C.L.*, III, 1, 2545.

Another inscription which appears to relate to the consignation is a third-century epitaph from the catacombs of Callixtus in Rome. It

shows a dove holding an object resembling a paint-brush in its foot and marking the monogram *chi-rho*. Cyril Pocknee, who illustrated the inscription in his *Cross and Crucifix*,[1] comments that it indicates that the departed person was a Christian who had received the gift of the Holy Spirit through the anointing of the forehead with the chrism in the form of the *chi-rho* cross. It is difficult to see what other interpretation can be attached to the picture, and if it is correct, it provides corroboration for the explanation of the anointing in Hippolytus' *Commentary on Daniel* as an unction of the Holy Spirit. The signing of the cross on the forehead is, of course, the ceremony of the second, or episcopal, post-baptismal chrismation in *Ap. Trad.*

St Jerome, although a priest of the Roman Church, lived so much of his life away from Rome that his testimony is of value for a much wider area than the local Roman Church. In his *Dialogue against the Luciferians* he replies to the question of his opponent with the statement already cited:

I do not deny this to be the custom of the churches that the bishop runs about (*excurrat*) to those who, far from larger cities, have been baptized by

[1] *Alcuin Club Tracts*, No. 32, Plate I, pp. 17, 33.

presbyters and deacons, to lay on a hand for the calling down (*ad invocationem*) of the Holy Spirit.[1]

Here is definite evidence of a rite of laying on of hands by the bishop, separated from baptism. Here is evidence also of the breakdown of the restriction of baptism to the bishop. Both Jerome and his opponent recognize this rite of imposition of hands as universal, and restricted to the bishop. Jerome, nevertheless, has an interesting explanation of the restriction:

In many places we find the same practice, rather for the honour of the episcopate (*sacerdotium*) than by the pressure of necessity (*ad legem necessitatis*).

He is also unwilling to restrict the gift of the Spirit to the episcopally performed rite:

If indeed the Holy Ghost flows down (*defluit*) at the invocation (*imprecatio*) of the bishop only, they are most unfortunate who in farms, or hamlets, or more remote places have been baptized by presbyters and deacons, and die before they are discovered (*inviserentur*) by the bishops.

He concludes:

From thence it happened that neither presbyter nor deacon has the right (*ius*) to baptize without chrism and the command of the bishop. But we know that this is frequently permitted even to laymen, if necessity requires.

Apparently the bishop was still the normal minister of baptism for Jerome, and it was only in the remoter areas, and in case of necessity, that others baptized, and then as the bishop's deputy and with chrism consecrated by him. The anointing with chrism by the presbyter, the first anointing of *Ap. Trad.*, was, it seems, the invariable accompaniment of baptism. The episcopal sealing, whether it included a signing with chrism or not, had become a detachable rite, to be supplied later when the bishop himself did not baptize. Certainly some such explanation as this lies behind the "*consignata a Liberio papa*" inscription.

Canon 8 of the *Canones ad Gallos*, the reply of a Roman synod about the year 400 to certain questions asked by Gallic bishops, sheds some light on the question of the pre-baptismal anointing. The exorcized oil is directed to be used at the third scrutiny, although the council does not consider it important how frequently the oil is administered.[2] The

---

[1] *contra Luciferanos*, 9 (P.L., 23, 172f).
[2] Mansi, III, 1137; Whitaker, *Documents*, pp. 217f.

scrutinies were examinations, or more properly exorcisms of the candidates conducted at intervals before baptism. John the Deacon tells us
that there were three scrutinies at Rome, preparing the candidates for
baptism at Easter. The anointing with the oil of exorcism would then
have taken place at the final scrutiny. One further scrap of liturgical
information is provided by this canon: the chrismation was an anointing of the head only, and no longer of the whole body.

> For if the chrism poured (*infusum*) upon the head imparts its grace to the
> whole body, in the same way also, if he who is scrutinized at the third
> scrutiny is touched with the oil only once and not many times, God [never-
> theless] acts upon his [whole] life.

To this same period belongs the testimony of Innocent I, in his
famous letter to Decentius, Bishop of Gubbio, dated 19 March 416.

> Concerning the consignation (*de consignandis*) of infants, it is clear that this
> should not be done by any but the bishop. For presbyters, although they are
> priests (*secundi sint sacerdotes*), have not attained the highest rank (*apex*) of the
> pontificate. The right of bishops alone to seal (*ut consignent*) and to deliver
> (*tradant*) the Spirit the Paraclete is proved not only by the custom of the
> Church, but also by that reading in the Acts of the Apostles which tells how
> Peter and John were directed to deliver the Holy Spirit to people who were
> already baptized. For it is permissible (*licet*) for presbyters, either in the
> absence of a bishop, or when they baptize in his presence to anoint (*ungere*)
> the baptized with chrism, but only with such as has been consecrated by the
> bishop: and even then they are not to sign the brow (*frontem signare*) with that
> oil, for this is reserved to bishops alone when they deliver the Holy Spirit
> (*cum tradunt Spiritum sanctum*).[1]

This letter makes explicit certain things which we have had to infer
from evidence previously considered. First, the chrism must be consecrated by the bishop. As we noted above, this regulation is ascribed by
the *Liber Pontificalis* to St Silvester, and certainly the ceremony envisaged by Innocent is that which the *Liber Pontificalis* implies. The
consignatio is to be performed only by bishops, but the post-baptismal
anointing is to be administered by the baptizing presbyter, whether the
bishop be present or not. The association by Innocent of the *consignatio*
with the lesson from Acts 8 shows that this signing of the forehead was
identified with the apostolic laying on of hands.

The picture which we obtain from these documents seems to accord
with that in *Ap. Trad.* The baptism is followed at once by an anointing

---

[1] *Ep.* 25 (P.L., 20, 554–5); trans. in Whitaker, *Documents*, p. 218.

performed by the presbyter and, either immediately, if the bishop were present, or later, if he were not, by the sealing of the forehead by the bishop with chrism. At this second anointing the bishop was said to deliver (*tradere*) the Holy Spirit. Jerome speaks of the laying on of hands as a ceremony of the consignation, but none of the other Roman authors does. Whether or not the rite was known, it was certainly not considered to be the essential act.

The important difference between the rites to which these authors refer and that of *Ap. Trad.* lies in the possibility that the bishop's part of the rite might be held separately. This separability, under certain circumstances, can be traced back as far as Cornelius, who clearly expected that those clinically baptized would, upon their recovery, be sealed, as a matter of course, by the bishop.

Our most extensive source for the early history of the Roman baptismal liturgy is the letter of John the Deacon to Senarius, written in the early sixth century. First printed by Dom Jean Mabillon in his *Museum Italicum*, it has been edited most recently by Dom André Wilmart in his *Analecta Reginensia*.[1] The letter was written in answer to a question concerning the scrutinies and their meaning. It gives us our most complete description of the Roman rites of the catechumenate and baptism at this early period.

Catēchēsis, says John, is the Greek word for instruction, and he describes the rites of the catechumenate as instruction. They consist of the laying on of hands, exsufflation, exorcism, the giving of blessed salt, the renunciation of the devil, and the *traditio symboli*. The *catechumenus* now becomes a *competens* and the scrutinies begin.

> We scrutinize their hearts through faith, to ascertain whether since the renunciation of the devil the sacred words have fastened themselves on his mind ... And when by their replies it becomes clear that it is so, according as it is written: With the heart man believeth unto righteousness, but with the mouth confession is made unto salvation: their ears are touched with the oil of sanctification, and their nostrils also are touched.

Taking this text together with the reference to an anointing at the third scrutiny in the *Canones ad Gallos* would lead us to assume that John intends this ceremony to follow the last scrutiny. The later rite has this anointing on Holy Saturday. This anointing of the ears and nostrils is the *effeta*. It is based upon our Lord's healing miracle in Mark 7.

---

[1] Studi e Testi, Vol. 59 (1933), pp. 170–9; partial translation in Whitaker, *Documents*, pp. 144–8.

We encountered the same ceremony in *de Sacramentis*, although St Ambrose made no mention of the use of oil.

John explains these anointings as a protection against all that hinders holiness.

> The ears [are anointed] because through them faith enters the mind ... so that, the ears being as it were fortified by a kind of wall of sanctification, may permit entrance to nothing harmful, nothing which might entice them back. When their nostrils are touched, they are thus without doubt admonished that for as long as they draw the breath of life through their nostrils they must abide in the commandments of God ..., that since the oil is blessed in the name of the Saviour, they may be led unto his spiritual odour by the inner perception of a certain ineffable sweetness ... And so the nostrils, being fortified by this mystery, can give no admittance to the pleasures of this world, nor anything which might weaken their minds.

From the anointing of the ears and nostrils John passes at once to the anointing of the breast, "so that they may understand that they promise with a firm mind (*firma conscientia*) and a pure heart eagerly to follow after the commandments of Christ, now that the devil has been driven out". This completes the pre-baptismal anointings. Although the details are different from those in *Ap. Trad.* the anointings remain exorcisms. John claims these baptismal rites to have been established "with watchful care over many years, although the old books may not show traces of them (*quamvis horum vestigia vetus pagina non ostendat*)". It sounds as if, even in the time of John the Deacon, old liturgical texts were difficult to find, and the history of rites veiled in obscurity.

John next describes the baptism itself, and the subsequent clothing in white robes. He does not mention an anointing immediately following baptism, but says:

> He is next arrayed in white vesture, and his head anointed with the unction of the sacred chrism.

He explains this anointing in terms of a royal and priestly mystery, into which the neophyte now enters.

The only other baptismal ceremony described by John is the cup of milk and honey administered at the Paschal Eucharist. This ceremony is found in *Ap. Trad.* and in the Leonine Sacramentary, but not otherwise in the pure Roman rite. He also speaks of the consecration of chrism, which is confined to the *pontifex*, and not performed by the presbyters. He recognizes that African presbyters are said to consecrate chrism, and explains that bishops have the right to permit the lower order to consecrate chrism in case of necessity.

John does not assign any specific function to the bishop in the baptismal rites, other than the consecrating of the chrism. He does tell us, nevertheless, that those baptized by heretics who enter the Church are not to be baptized again "but are to be incorporated into the bowels (*viscera*) of Mother Church by receiving the blessing of the pontiff", and later in the letter he undertakes to answer the question,

> If someone baptized without the unction of chrism or the blessing of the pontiff departs from this life, is he hindered (*obsit*), or not?

Unfortunately, the manuscript breaks off before he can complete the answer to the question, and what he does say throws no light on the nature and meaning of the customary rites. It does show, nevertheless, that he considered the question difficult, for he begins, "Concerning this thing, I would rather hear more from the learned than say anything myself", a sentiment shared by many theologians since.

It would seem from this question, and from the custom in the reception of heretics, that some form of episcopal benediction was intended to follow baptism. In this case, the unction described by John would be the first, or presbyteral, anointing of *Ap. Trad.*, removed to a place following the clothing. Since this anointing was now confined to the head, it would be reasonable to clothe the neophyte before anointing him. John also tells us that a linen covering was placed on the neophyte's head after the anointing, which would, in a symbolic manner, retain the ancient order.

If our interpretation is correct, it means that John the Deacon omits all reference to the episcopal consignation from his description of the baptismal rites. In the light of the separation we have seen developing between the consignation and the rest of the baptismal rite, we can account for this by saying that John did not expect the bishop to be present for the solemn Easter baptism in his church. His question about the child who dies baptized, but without the anointing with chrism or episcopal blessing, would then be quite meaningful and practical.

Almost in an aside John tells us that the baptismal rites in their entirety are performed even for *parvuli*, showing the increasing importance of infant baptism. This would be an additional factor tending to separate the episcopal consignation from the rest of the rite. It must have been impossible at Rome for the pope to have been present at the baptism of all children, and the consignation could easily have been added at a convenient time.

Two letters of Gregory the Great to Januarius, Bishop of Cagliari in Sardinia, provide further evidence concerning the anointings. The crucial passage in the first reads:

> Let the bishops not presume to seal (*signare*) the baptized children (*baptizatos infantes*) twice on the forehead, but let the presbyters anoint those to be baptized (*baptizandos*) on the breast, that the bishops may anoint them afterward on the forehead.[1]

It is not clear exactly what St Gregory means by this. Does he, for example, mean that if the presbyter, contrary to Innocent's direction, has sealed the infant on the forehead, then the bishop is not to do it again, or that the bishop is not to repeat the ceremony himself? It would seem that the first alternative was the only one possible, in spite of the theological difficulty of accepting presbyteral confirmation as identical with episcopal.

Another problem raised by Gregory's letter is the unction *in pectore*. The only unction of the breast described in John the Deacon is that before baptism, and the use of the gerundive *baptizandi* rather than the past participle *baptizati* would be consistent with a reference to a pre-baptismal anointing. Gregory, however, in his second letter to Januarius also uses the gerundive when he is clearly talking about those already baptized. Innocent had specifically authorized presbyters to anoint with chrism, and *Ap. Trad.* had also assigned the first anointing after baptism to the presbyter. The letter is in many respects a puzzle, not only to us, but also to those who received it, for it was followed by a second letter to Januarius, which says:

> It has happened also that certain ones have been scandalized by us, that we have forbidden presbyters to touch (*tangere*) with chrism those who have been baptized. And we indeed followed the ancient use (*usum veterum*) of our Church.[2]

Certainly the presbyters of Sardinia must have been accustomed to anoint with chrism, but the reference to the *usum veterum Ecclesiae nostrae* is more difficult to understand, unless Gregory is referring, not to the post-baptismal anointing, but to the anointing of the consignation, which Roman use had always reserved to the bishop. If we accept

---

[1] *Ep.* 4.9 (P.L., 77, 677A).
[2] *Ep.* 4.26 (P.L., 77, 696B).

this hypothesis, the letter can be made to fit into the existing evidence. We would assume that the presbyters of Sardinia were accustomed to sign the foreheads of the baptized with chrism, perhaps in the Eastern fashion. Gregory's first letter would then refer to this. The signing, he would then be saying, should be reserved to the bishop, although, if it had been administered by the presbyter at baptism, it should not be repeated. In the event, Gregory capitulated completely in the face of local opposition and wrote:

> But if any are made completely sad by this thing, we concede that, where bishops are wanting, presbyters ought to touch with chrism the baptized (*baptizandos*) even on the foreheads.

This concession seems to have been intended only for Sardinia, as we read in other letters that Gregory expected the bishops to make visits for consignation, even directing one infirm bishop to visit those churches which he can, so that those baptized there may not have to go *inconsignati*.[1]

We have seen in these early Roman sources how, with some slight changes and development, the basic structure of *Ap. Trad.* was preserved at Rome. The *consignatio* by the bishop, however, had become detached from the other ceremonies, through force of necessity, and was supplied by the bishops, who made visits to the churches in their care to do this. Although in some remote places like Sardinia, and in Africa after the expulsion of the Catholic bishops by Hunneric, the Roman Church authorized consignation by presbyters, and even, in case of necessity, the consecration of chrism by them, the normal practice was for the bishop himself to confirm. The Roman rite also retained the pre-baptismal anointing as an exorcism, rather than attaching to it the fuller meaning found in Eastern rites.

The picture is not as clear as we might wish, and there is inevitably a certain interpretation of the evidence in the light of later sources. It is my belief that *Ap. Trad.* provides us with the main line of development for the Roman rite, and that, when we come to discuss the Gelasian Sacramentary in the next section, we shall find there a rite clearly related to that in *Ap. Trad.* It is in this light that I have examined the early Roman sources, and although it is possible to interpret them differently,[2] I believe the evidence here presented to be thoroughly

---

[1] cf. *Ep.* 10.45; 13.18; and 14.17.
[2] cf. Fr Hanssens, *La Liturgie d'Hippolyte*, for a different view.

consistent with the view that *Ap. Trad.* is the earliest liturgical document of the Roman rite.

THE GELASIAN SACRAMENTARY

The principal key with which we shall attempt to unlock the door to the baptismal liturgy of the Latin Church is the Gelasian Sacramentary, hereafter cited as *Gel.* This sacramentary exhibits the Roman rite in substantially the form in which it entered Gaul in the eighth century, to influence the local Gallican uses and to be influenced by them in turn. It will therefore be of considerable assistance in understanding, not only the Roman baptismal liturgy, but also the Gallican rites, to have the baptismal rite of *Gel.* clearly fixed in mind.

By *Gel.* we mean the text of the manuscript known as Vat. Reg. 316, a codex written in uncials on parchment, customarily dated from the middle of the eighth century. Its first printed edition was that of Tomasi in 1680, while the most useful editions for the modern student are that of L. C. Mohlberg, to which we shall normally refer, and that of H. A. Wilson. Eminent scholars hold divergent views as to the place of origin of *Gel.* Emmanuel Bourque, the noted Canadian scholar, in his remarkable *Étude sur les Sacramentaires Romains*, defends the view that *Gel.* is the oldest Roman sacramentary, having received only a few minor additions in northern Europe.[1] Baumstark, on the other hand, believes that it is a northern book containing a large number of Roman forms.[2] A similar view is adopted by Hanssens, who assigns the sacramentary "not to Rome, but to Provence or Lombardy, in the neighbourhood of the three great non-Roman Latin liturgies".[3] Antoine Chavasse, by contrast, in his study published in 1958, calls it "a presbyteral sacramentary in use in the Roman *tituli* in the seventh century".[4]

The study by Chavasse is the most extensive, and most recently published. His general thesis is that the actual manuscript Vat. Reg. 316 was written in the vicinity of Paris, probably at St Denis, about 750. The materials which comprise it, he believes, derive from a sixth-century "Gelasian type" presbyteral sacramentary, and the papal liturgy of which the Sacramentary of Hadrian is the direct descendant.

[1] op. cit., Vol. 1, pp. 171–298.
[2] A. Baumstark, *Die älteste erreichbare Gestalt des Liber Sacramentorum Anni Circuli der römischen Kirche*, pp. 43*–45*.
[3] *La Liturgie d'Hippolyte*, p. 518.   [4] *Le Sacramentaire gélasien.*

Gel. is, in his view, a complex compilation deriving from the marriage of these two rites as the papal liturgy reached out from the Lateran into the presbyteral *tituli* in the first half of the seventh century. This presbyteral sacramentary, he believes, entered Gaul at the end of the seventh century, or at the beginning of the eighth century, where certain forms necessary for its adaptation to episcopal use were added to it, such as the ordination rites. Also added were certain Gallican forms, such as those for funerals. This state of development, Chavasse believes, is represented by Vat. Reg. 316.[1]

Bourque agrees with Chavasse in dating the composition of the original Gelasian at the beginning of the sixth century, but he believes that it is a papal sacramentary. Writing in 1947, he naturally did not know the work of Chavasse, but he did consider and reject a similar theory of Dom de Puniet, distinguishing between the liturgies of the basilicas and the *tituli*.[2]

An answer to Chavasse's arguments by Dom Charles Coeburgh, published in *Archiv für Liturgiewissenschaft*,[3] does not appear to affect the baptismal portions of *Gel.*, even if it be accepted as refuting Chavasse's main thesis.

The baptismal rites of *Gel.* begin with the scrutinies, for which *Gel.* provides extensive material, beginning with a mass *quae pro scrutiniis electorum celebratur*, for the Third Sunday in Lent.[4] At this mass the names of the godparents presenting children for baptism were recited in the *Memento, Domine* in the canon, while the names of the *electi*, that is of the candidates themselves, were recited after the *Hanc igitur*. The prayers of the mass also refer to those seeking baptism.

The mass for the Fourth Sunday, entitled *Pro Scrutinio II*, repeats the direction to recite the names, as does the mass *quae pro scrutinio celebratur* assigned to the Fifth Sunday.[5] It is reasonable to assume that these are the original dates of the three Roman scrutinies mentioned by John the Deacon. *Gel.* also directs that the names be read on the Monday following the Third Sunday in Lent, for which day it also provides a *denuntiatio*, announcing the first scrutiny for later in that week, and directing that the names of the children be inscribed that day.[6] Clearly

---

[1] op. cit., pp. 685–9. [2] Bourque, op. cit., Vol. 1, pp. 292–7.
[3] "Le Sacramentaire Gélasien Ancien, une compilation de clercs romanisants du VIIe siècle" in *Archiv*, Vol. 7 (1961), pp. 45–88.
[4] *Gel.* (ed. Mohlberg), pp. 32–3, nn. 193–9.
[5] *Gel.*, pp. 36, 39, nn. 225–8, 254–7.
[6] *Gel.*, p. 42, nn. 283–4.

there is some confusion, for it makes no sense to announce the coming of the scrutinies when they have already begun the day before.

Dean Andrieu explains this confusion by saying that the Section XXVIIII in *Gel.* (*Denuntiatio pro Scrutinio quod Tertia Hebdomada in Quadragesima Secunda Feria Initiarum*) is interpolated from *Ordo XI*, which has a different sequence of scrutinies.[1] Although this explanation is quite generally accepted, it is specifically rejected by Chavasse, who believes that a detailed examination of the texts requires the opposite conclusion, namely: *Ordo XI* is an expansion of the material in *Gel.* He accounts for the confusion in this section as occasioned by a liturgical reform, which consisted in moving the scrutinies from the Lenten Sundays to weekdays. The propers of the Sunday masses, he believes, belong to the earliest stratum of material in *Gel.*, while the forms provided for the rites of the catechumenate are part of a later redaction, but none the less earlier than *Ordo XI*.[2]

Gel. provides a series of rites for making a catechumen, for blessing and giving salt, for exorcising the elect, and for the *traditio* of the Gospel, the Creed, and the Lord's Prayer, in a continuous sequence, with no indication as to when the rites were to be used.[3] It seems that a diversity of practice existed as to the occasions of the scrutinies. With the end of the adult catechumenate, the pre-baptismal ceremonies tended to be conflated and compressed,[4] and it is possible that in some places all the rites were performed in a single scrutiny.

There is no anointing prescribed in any of the scrutinies in *Gel.* The third scrutiny is called *aurium apertio*, but the *effeta*, which presumably was placed here by John the Deacon, is performed on Holy Saturday morning. The ceremonies of the *aurium apertio* consisted in the solemn reading of the opening words of the four gospels to the *electi*, followed by the *traditio symboli* (the delivery of the creed), and the *traditio* of the

---

[1] Andrieu, *Les Ordines Romani du Haut Moyen Âge*, Vol. 2, p. 387.

[2] Chavasse, op. cit., pp. 159, 167f.

[3] *Gel.* pp. 42–53, nn. 285–328.

[4] Following Chavasse, we may assign the *Orationes super electos ad Catechumenum Faciendum* (nn. 285–6), the blessing of the salt (n. 288), and the blessing *post datum sale* (n. 290) to the ancient admission to the catechumenate. The *denuntiatio pro scrutinio* (nn. 283–4), which ends with the direction, "And let the presbyter give a prayer over them", would then be followed by the prayer *Deus qui humani generis* (n. 287), and would be the form used at the giving of the names which made *electi*, or *competentes* out of the *catechumeni*. The prayers entitled *Item exorcismi super electos* (nn. 291–8) would then be the formulas of the scrutiny cf. Chavasse, op. cit., pp. 161f.

Lord's Prayer. The ears of the elect were opened to hear the mysteries of faith.[1]

The *traditio symboli* presents certain unique features. The creed used is the Nicene rather than the Apostles' Creed, although the opening address of the celebrant speaks of it as "instituted by the apostles". The creed is recited first in Greek, then in Latin, by an acolyte holding a child in his arms. The Greek text is spelled out in Latin letters with an interlinear translation provided, apparently for the benefit of non-Greek-speaking clergy. Unquestionably this custom must date from a period when the Roman Church was bilingual, that is, after the Byzantine expansion in the middle of the sixth century.

The delivery of the gospels is a distinctly Roman feature. The phrase *aurium apertio* used to describe the ceremony, coupled with the earlier Roman association of an anointing of the ears with the scrutiny, suggests that the *effeta*, performed, as in John the Deacon, with exorcized oil, once formed a part of this solemn ceremony of the Fifth Sunday in Lent.

Palm Sunday in *Gel.* is *Dominica in Palmas de Passione Domini*. There are none of the baptismal ceremonies associated with this day in Milan, in Gaul, and in Spain, nor are any forms given for blessing palms. As in the Anglican Prayer Books, the joyous Gallican ceremonies are suggested only by the name Palm Sunday, while the text of the liturgy speaks of the *passio Domini*.

Maundy Thursday in *Gel.* has three masses, for the reconciliation of penitents, the *missa chrismalis*, and an evening mass commemorating the Last Supper. It is with the *missa chrismalis* that we are concerned. It contains a preface relating to the chrism, and forms for blessing the oil for the sick, the oil for the catechumens, and the chrism as well as alternative forms. Antoine Chavasse has pointed out[2] that the preface to the chrismal mass and the alternative forms headed *Item olei exorcizati confectio* are actually Gallican in origin.[3] The Roman forms are those for the blessing of the oil of the sick, the oil of the catechumens, and the chrism.[4] Even here some non-Roman influence must be noted, for the traditional Roman order is to consecrate the chrism before exorcizing the oil of the catechumens.[5]

[1] *Gel.*, pp. 46–53, nn. 299–328.
[2] "La Bénédiction du Chrême en Gaule", in *Revue du Moyen Âge Latin*, Vol. I (1948), pp. 109–28.
[3] *Gel.*, pp. 60, 63, nn. 378, 389–90.   [4] *Gel.*, nn. 381–8.
[5] This is the order of *Ap. Trad.*, *Greg.*, and the *ordines Romani*.

The preface of the *missa chrismalis* is of great beauty, and it has been again assigned by the Roman Catholic Church to the chrismal mass in the "restored" Holy Week rites of 1955. It prays for those to be made new in the spiritual laver of baptism that they may be freed from the corruption of their first birth by the infusion of the sacred anointing, that they may give forth the innocent odour of an acceptable life, and that, flooded with royal, priestly, and prophetic honour, they may put on an incorruptible robe.

This preface expects the chrism to be poured upon those anointed, using the words *infusa* and *perfusi*. This, as we shall see, is the Gallican manner of anointing with chrism. It also speaks of the chrism as a *vestimentum incorrupti muneris*, a typically Gallican idea.[1] The association of the anointing with that of prophets, priests, and kings is found in *Ap. Trad.* and is the classical reference for all baptismal anointings.

The *Gel.* form for exorcizing the oil of the catechumens follows the fraction of the mass. It consists of a single prayer, "Deus incrementorum et profectuum spiritalium munerator . . .". The same prayer, although without the initial phrase, occurs in the Gregorian Sacramentary, which we shall hereafter abbreviate as *Greg.*,[2] for the exorcism of the oil, and it may be considered the Roman form. It is a proper exorcism, praying for those who come to baptism "that if any trace of adverse spirits remain in them, they may depart at the touch of this holy (*sanctificatum*) oil". This exorcism is followed by the consecration of the chrism, cast in the form of a Eucharistic preface. This form, also in *Greg.*, is of great length. It begins by thanking God for his gift of the olive tree, from which the sacred chrism is derived, and continues with a reference to the joy of being anointed with oil from Ps. 104.15 and to the return of the dove bearing the olive branch to Noah. It passes on to describe the anointing of Aaron by Moses, making him a priest first by the washing of water and then by the infusion of this ointment. All this is brought to a climax in the *amplior honor* done to the chrism by our Lord Jesus Christ, who at his baptism was anointed with the oil of gladness above his fellows, when the Holy Ghost descended upon him in the form of a dove, and he heard the voice of the Father.

This thanksgiving for chrism ends in a petition introduced by the words "Te igitur deprecamur, domine, sancte pater, omnipotens

---

[1] cf. Chavasse, art. cit., pp. 109f. The phrase is found also in the Byzantine and Coptic rites.

[2] *Greg.* (*The Gregorian Sacramentary under Charles the Great*, ed. H. A. Wilson, H.B.S., Vol. 49), p. 50.

aeternae deus." The analogy to the *canon missae* appears obvious. The actual petition is:

> Mix in the power of the Holy Spirit through the might of thy Christ, from whose holy name chrism received its name, with which thou didst anoint thy priests, kings, prophets and martyrs, that it may be to those who shall be born again of water and the Holy Spirit a chrism of salvation, and make them to be partakers of eternal life and sharers in the heavenly glory.[1]

Several phrases in this petition are similar to phrases in the prayer for the blessing of the oil for the sick, which appears in turn to be derived from the blessing of oil and olives in *Ap. Trad.* This prayer was apparently already archaic when it was included in *Gel.*, for it speaks of the anointing of the sick as *chrisma tuum perfectum*, and of the oil as that with which priests, kings, prophets, and martyrs were anointed.[2] The inclusion of martyrs among those anointed is found also in the Coptic forms for the blessing of the *hagielaion*. Although there are many interesting points of similarity between the Coptic and Roman rites, it is not immediately evident that there is any direct relationship between these forms of blessing oil.

From its blessing we see that the chrism was associated with the Messianic anointing of Christ at his baptism, and with the royal, priestly, and prophetic anointings of the Old Testament, and also that the Holy Spirit was invoked upon it, so that its use might reasonably be called the anointing of the Holy Spirit.

The forms which follow this in *Gel.* are a source of almost unbounded confusion. The first form is an exorcism, and is so titled, but it is preceded by a rubric directing the mixing of oil and balsam. Chavasse considers this form to have been a Gallican addition, intended for use with the following *vere dignum* as a form for consecrating chrism. He believes it was added to the *missa chrismalis* of *Gel.* prior to the inclusion of the Roman blessing of chrism. The rubric for the mixing of the balsam and oil would date from this first addition, while the title *Item olei exorcizati confectio* would have been added when the Roman form (*Gel.*, nn. 386–8) was included.[3]

The chrismal preface which follows this exorcism is quite brief,

---

[1] *Gel.*, p. 62, n. 388.

[2] Professor H. B. Porter, in his unpublished thesis, *The Reform of Holy Baptism and the Other Sacraments under Charles the Great* (Oxford, 1954), offers evidence that this blessing was not, in fact, used in Frankland in the eighth century. op. cit., pp. 344–6.

[3] Chavasse, *Le Sacramentaire Gélasien*, pp. 133f.

referring to the dove sent forth by Noah, but not containing any actual petition. It is also of Gallican origin and is linguistically related to a *contestatio* for the Rogations in *Missale Gothicum*.[1]

The baptismal rites of *Gel.* are resumed on the morning of Holy Saturday.[2] The *competentes* gather in the church to recite the creed committed to them in the ceremonies of the third scrutiny. This is known as the *redditio symboli*. They are catechized and exorcized, with the laying on of a hand. The *effeta* follows, performed not with oil, but with spittle. In view of the evidence that this was once an anointing at Rome, we can only conclude that the ceremonial has been "corrected" to conform literally to our Lord's action in the gospel. Immediately following the *effeta*, however, the candidates are anointed on the chest and between the shoulders with the exorcized oil. No formula is given, but the renunciation of the devil follows immediately. Undoubtedly the absence of a formula has resulted from the disassociation of the anointing from the *effeta*, which provided the formula to accompany the pre-baptismal anointing.

The baptism proper took place on the evening of the Holy Sabbath, during the Easter Vigil. *Gel.* has the forms for blessing the font following the collects which accompanied the reading of the lessons. A rubric following the last collect directs them to proceed to the font with the litany for the baptism. It concludes:

> When baptism is completed the children (*infantes*) are sealed (*consignantur*) by the bishop, while they receive the seven gifts of grace of the Holy Ghost, and he places (*mittit*) chrism on their foreheads.[3]

The blessing of the font is followed by the baptism, which is performed in response to the three credal questions, as in *Ap. Trad.*, and not with a declarative formula. When the child comes up out of the font, he is signed (*signatur*) by the presbyter on the head (*in cerebro*) with chrism. The prayer which he uses is:

> Almighty God, Father of our Lord Jesus Christ, who has regenerated thee by water and the Holy Ghost, and who has given thee remission of all thy sins, himself anoint thee (*ipse te linit*) with the chrism of salvation in Christ Jesus our Lord unto eternal life.[4]

This prayer is a variant of that quoted by St Ambrose in *de Sacra-*

---

[1] *Goth.* (ed. Mohlberg), p. 84, n. 336.   [2] *Gel.*, pp. 67f, nn. 419–24.
[3] *Gel.*, p. 72, n. 443.
[4] *Gel.*, p. 74, n. 450; see also Diagram on p. 122 below.

mentis, and will be found in almost all Roman, Ambrosian, and Gallican sources, and in the First English Prayer Book of Edward VI. It is here provided for the first of two post-baptismal chrismations, an anointing of the head by the presbyter.

This presbyteral chrismation is followed by a second, the anointing by the bishop to which the previously quoted rubric refers.

Then the sevenfold Spirit is given to them by the bishop. For the sealing (*ad consignandum*) he places his hands upon them with these words . . .

The words which follow are a prayer for the sevenfold gifts of the Holy Spirit, commonly referred to as the "confirmation prayer". It occurs in substantially the same form in *Greg.*, but with a different *incipit*.[1] In *Gel.* this prayer and that for the preceding presbyteral chrismation have the same *incipit*. The "confirmation prayer" is immediately followed by a rubric, "Afterward let him sign (*signat*) them on the forehead with chrism . . .". The formula is, "The sign (*signum*) of Christ unto eternal life."[2]

The Easter mass and the communion of the neophytes complete the initiatory rites.

Before Pentecost, the other solemn season for the administration of baptism, *Gel.* provides additional baptismal material, namely: the forms for the baptism of the sick. Those of immediate concern to us are sections 72, 75, and 76, entitled *Item ad Succurrendum Infirmum Caticuminum, Item Alia Benedictio,* and *Ad Succurrendum. Benedictio Olei Exorcizato.*[3]

Chavasse has pointed out, undoubtedly correctly, that the entire section of forms for baptism of the sick, sections 66–76, has been inserted into *Gel.* The opening rubric of section 66, "On the sabbath of Pentecost thou shalt celebrate baptism as on the night of the Holy Pascha", originally was followed by "Prayers for the Individual Lessons of the Sabbath of Pentecost" (section 77).[4] By a comparison of the texts of the forms given in these sections with those provided for Easter baptism, Chavasse concludes that these formulas represent a version of the Gelasian text later than that provided at Easter, but older than the text of *Greg.*[5] The principle upon which he bases this conclusion is that the rubrics in the second person singular are older than those in the third person.

---

[1] *Greg.*, pp. 57f.   [2] *Gel.*, p. 74, n. 451.
[3] *Gel.*, pp. 94–7, nn. 602, 607–17.   [4] *Gel.*, pp. 91, 97, nn. 591b, 618.
[5] *le Sacramentaire Gélasian*, p. 176.

Section 72, *Item ad Succurrendum Infirmum Caticuminum*, consists of the exorcism of the sick catechumen, the delivery to him of the creed and the Lord's Prayer, and the exorcism "Nec te lateat, satanas ..." as provided, the rubric says, *in nocte sancta*. This error, perhaps, reflects the abandonment of the rites of Saturday morning and the attaching of them to the liturgy of the vigil. This exorcism is followed by the *effeta* and the anointing of the chest and shoulders, with the renunciation of the devil. The text is identical with that for Holy Saturday, except that the rubrics have been changed to the third person.

Section 75 begins with a brief exorcism of the water, followed by the baptism and post-baptismal anointing exactly as in the Easter rite. After the anointing the neophyte is communicated, either at a celebration of the Eucharist, or from the reserved sacrament. Two prayers follow the reception of Communion, and last of all the consignation by the bishop is directed, accompanied by the "confirmation prayer" in the singular number, and with the addition of a phrase after the catalogue of the seven gifts of the Spirit:

> And order them to be sealed (*consignari*) with the sign of the cross unto eternal life ...

Immediately after this prayer the rubric directing the signing of the forehead with the formula "The sign of Christ ..." is given exactly as at Easter.

The differences between the two orders, although slight, are significant. There is no mention here of an *impositio manuum*, and the addition of the new phrase to the "confirmation prayer" makes it clear that the signing with chrism is the significant rite. The change from the plural to the singular number is simply an adaptation to the case of the baptism of a single candidate, although the use of the plural at Easter lends itself readily to the assumption that the bishop did not actually lay hands on anyone, but recited the prayer with hands extended towards the candidates, and then signed them individually with the short formula, "The sign of Christ ...". The removal of the *consignatio* from its place following the presbyteral chrismation to the end of the rite probably reflects the realities of the situation. It would have been quite unlikely that the bishop would be present at the baptism of a sick catechumen, and the presbyter presumably would have performed his part of the rite, admitting the neophyte to Communion immediately after the first chrismation. The episcopal consignation would then have

been added later, when possible. This would conform to the tradition
expounded in the third century by Pope Cornelius.

The rites for baptism of the sick conclude with a blessing for exorcized oil, apparently intended for use by the priest as needed. Chavasse
is convinced that this is a purely Roman form, but H. B. Porter, who
has made a detailed study of it and found extensive parallels in Gallican
and Celtic liturgical books, questions this.[1]

The form itself exorcizes the *exercitus diaboli* from the oil, and prays
"that it may be to all who shall be anointed with it for the adoption of
sons through the Holy Spirit".

Section 85, which follows the prayers of the Pentecost octave,
provides a "Blessing upon those who Return to Catholic Unity from
Arianism".[2] This is, in fact, a variant of the "confirmation prayer"
asking the sevenfold gifts of the Spirit. A subsequent prayer for those
coming from diverse heresies has the same structure. No directions are
given for their use, but we may reasonably assume that they were
accompanied by the same ceremonies as the consignation, that is, the
signing with chrism and imposition of hands.

The baptismal rites of *Gel.* contain unquestionably ancient elements,
such as the lack of a declarative baptismal formula, as well as elements
of a later date, such as the use of the Nicene Creed for the *traditio
symboli*. Chavasse dates the first compilation of the Gelasian rites, those
parts with rubrics in the second person singular, not earlier than the
almost exclusive predominance of infant baptism in the sixth century.[3]
The rites are unquestionably intended for use with children. This is
obvious from the ceremonial of the *redditio symboli*. The priest is
directed to say the creed himself, placing his hand upon the young
electi.

The second form of the baptismal rites Chavasse would place no
earlier than 550, the beginning of the Byzantine period in Rome. He
believes that this is the earliest date at which the Nicene Creed could
have been substituted for the Apostles' Creed in the *traditio symboli*.

If Chavasse is correct, the forms for the pre-baptismal anointing and
for the chrismation and consignation at Easter belong to the earlier
stratum, while the forms for the baptism of the sick are of the later. In
any case, he believes that the Roman baptismal rites of *Gel.* achieved

[1] "La Bénédiction du Chrême", p. 128; Porter, op. cit., pp. 227–31, 338–9.
[2] *Gel.*, p. 105, n. 683.
[3] Chavasse, op. cit., p. 168.

9

the form found in Vat. Reg. 316 no later than the early seventh century, and are earlier than the forms of *Ordo XI* and *Greg.*

Looking at the baptismal rites of *Gel.* in their totality, we find a liturgy markedly similar to that in *Ap. Trad.* A single anointing with the oil of exorcism precedes baptism. The interrogative form of the creed is the baptismal formula. An unction with chrism by the presbyter immediately follows baptism, and there is a second anointing by the bishop, accompanying the laying on of hands and the signing of the neophyte's forehead with the cross. The "confirmation prayer" is similar in thought to that in *Ap. Trad.*

I believe that we see in *Gel.* the main line of development of the Roman baptismal liturgy from *Ap. Trad.*, and that we shall see in our consideration of the rites of *Greg.*, the *ordines Romani*, and the "Eighth-Century Gelasian" the preservation in Rome of certain distinctive features throughout its liturgical history. The most important of these is the double anointing with chrism, preserved in the Roman rite to the present day.

THE GALLICAN AND CELTIC RITES

The great Louis Duchesne began his discussion of the Gallican baptismal rites by saying, "It is somewhat difficult to reconstruct the baptismal ritual of the Gallican Church."[1] The principal Gallican liturgical books are fragmentary, and there is considerable local variation. I believe that we shall find, nevertheless, that there is a Gallican tradition of baptismal anointing, and that it is related to that of the Mozarabic and Ambrosian rites.

Missale Gallicanum Vetus, which we shall cite as *Gal. Vet.*, is MS. no. 493 of the Palatine collection in the Vatican Library. The manuscript dates from the early eighth century. It appears to be composed of parts of two sacramentaries, with considerable lacunas. *Missale Gothicum*, hereafter cited as *Goth.*, is of approximately the same date. It is MS. Vat. Reg. Lat. 317. It was formerly believed to come from Autun, and its Burgundian origin is still generally accepted. The *Missale Bobbiense*, hereafter abbreviated *Bob.*, presents a considerable puzzle. The manuscript, Paris. Lat. 13246, was found by Mabillon at Bobbio, in northern Italy. It is a mixture of North Italian, Gallican, Roman, Spanish, and Celtic material which defies attempts to determine its place of origin. The *Expositio Antiquae Liturgiae Gallicanae*, which we shall cite as *Ger.*,

---

[1] *Christian Worship* (5th edition), p. 316.

in the form of two letters ascribed to St Germanus of Paris, was originally believed to be a genuine work of the sixth-century bishop. It has been shown, however, to contain quotations from the seventh-century writer, St Isidore of Seville, and should be assigned to the South of France, about 700.[1]

Because of the fragmentary state of the Gallican evidence, we shall consider the rites in their normal order, referring in each case to the available material.

In Gallican use the order *ad Christianum faciendum* corresponds to the Roman *ad catechumenum faciendum*, and is the first of the baptismal rites. A lacuna has deprived us of all but a few lines of the order from *Gal. Vet.*[2]

The order in *Goth.*[3] begins with a prayer that the children (*infantes*) may be signed with the cross before they know good from evil. The collect which follows reads:

Receive the sign (*signaculum*) of Christ, accept the divine words, be enlightened with the Word of the Lord, since to-day thou art confessed by Christ...

This is followed by the signing of the eyes, ears, nostrils, tongue, and heart. Although *Goth.* does not direct that oil be used for these signings, I believe that they were made with oil in the sixth century.

The Council of Mâcon in 585 directed:

We require all men to attend the church with their children (*infantes*) from the First Sunday of Lent (*a die quadragesimo*) that they may receive the laying on of hands on certain days and be anointed with the liquid of the holy oil.[4]

The order of *Goth.* appears to be a conflation of the ancient forms for making adult catechumens with the pre-baptismal unction to which the council refers. *Ger.* speaks of blessing oil and chrism on Palm Sunday, apparently for the anointing of the catechumens.[5] It would seem reasonable to assume, therefore, that the normal Gallican time for performing the *ordo ad Christianum faciendum* was at the mass *in symboli traditione* on Palm Sunday, where we find the *ordo* in *Gal. Vet.*

---

[1] A. Wilmart, "Germain de Paris" in *D.A.C.L.*, Vol. 1, Pt. 1, col. 1042–1102.
[2] *Gal. Vet.* (ed. Mohlberg), p. 16, n. 60.
[3] *Goth.* (ed. Mohlberg), pp. 65f, nn. 252–4.
[4] F. Maassen, *Concilia Aevi Merov.* (*M.G.H.*, *leg. sect.* III, *conc.* Vol. 1) p. 166 (Canon 3).
[5] *Ger.* (ed. Quasten), p. 25.

In the life of the illustrious sixth-century Gallican prelate, St Caesarius of Arles, we read:

> Now to bless the oil for the *competentes* he would go each year into the baptistery. And going into the *cucumula*, when he sat down to sign the children (*ad consignandos infantes*) . . .[1]

Eminent scholars have contended that this passage describes the bishop coming into the *cucumula* (the meaning of which is uncertain) for the purpose of administering consignation in the Roman sense, that is to those already baptized.[2] I have, nevertheless, been unable to find any evidence requiring me to explain away the clear words of the text that the annual visit was to the baptistery in the cathedral *ad oleum benedicendum competentibus*. If we read this account in connection with the forms for making a Christian from *Goth.*, we shall, I believe, see that it is this rite of making a Christian which is here described.

In the Roman rite, *ad consignandos infantes* would undoubtedly mean the episcopal rite described in *Gel.* and *Greg.* as following the baptism proper. Objection is therefore raised to the interpretation I have suggested on the grounds that *consignatio* is a technical term for the post-baptismal signing of the forehead by the bishop, and *infantes* is a technical term for the newly-baptized.[3] When we look at the afore-mentioned *ordo* in *Goth.*, however, we see *signo* and *signaculum crucis* used repeatedly, and also the word *infantes* applied to those not yet baptized. The words of our Lord, quoted in the opening prayer of the rite, are given as, "Nolite prohibere infantes . . .", even though the text of the Vulgate calls them *parvulos*. It would therefore appear that in Gaul *infantes* meant children, and was not always a technical term for neophytes, and the passage from the *Vita S. Caesarii* gives us a picture of the bishop's visit to his own cathedral to anoint the *competentes* and to sign them with the cross.[4]

Bob.[5] also directs the signing of the catechumens with the cross, although the forms given are different from those in *Goth.* After four prayers, a rubric directs:

---

[1] *Vita S. Caesarii* 2.14 (*P.L.*, 67, 1032).

[2] Coppens, *L'Imposition des Mains*, p. 338, n. 4; G. Morin, "Une particularité arlésienne de la liturgie du Samedi-saint", in *Ephemerides Liturgicae*, Vol. 49 (1935), pp. 146–9.

[3] M. Beck, *Pastoral Care in South-East France*, pp. 180–1.

[4] cf. Chavasse, "La Bénédiction du Chrême".

[5] *Bob.* (ed. E. A. Lowe), pp. 71f, nn. 228–33.

Make the sign of the cross and say the creed.

The accompanying form, "Receive the sign of the Cross", speaks of the signing of the forehead and the heart. The form itself is a shorter variant of that in *Gel.* for a converted catechumen.[1] The rite concludes with a triple insufflation, with the form "N., receive the Holy Spirit, mayest thou keep him in thy heart."

In the light of the whole of the Gallican evidence, it is a reasonable hypothesis that in many places the *ordo ad Christianum faciendum* was the first of the rites of Palm Sunday, and that in the tradition represented by *Goth.* and St Caesarius of Arles it was accompanied by the anointing of various parts of the body.

We do not possess any complete Gallican description of the rites of Palm Sunday, and so we do not know definitely the order in which the various ceremonies assigned to that day were performed. *Ger.* assigns to it the blessing of oil and chrism, the *traditio symboli*, and probably the anointing of the catechumens.[2] *Bob.* has the blessing of palms and olives, the *traditio* of the gospels, and the *traditio symboli*.[3] *Gal. Vet.* supplies (possibly the admission of catechumens) two forms for the *traditio symboli*, the delivery of the gospels, and the delivery of the Lord's Prayer, as well as an exorcism and a form entitled *praemissiones ad scrutamen*.[4] In *Goth.* we find only the forms for the mass *in symboli traditione*, with no provision for any special ceremony.[5]

Unquestionably the great ceremony of the day was the *traditio symboli*, which gave its name to the day. None of the surviving liturgical books provides for the blessing of the oils on this day, although *Ger.* definitely states that it was done on this occasion. *Gal. Vet.* provides a part of a chrismal mass for Maundy Thursday.

The Council of Vaison in 442 directed that in each area the presbyters should seek the chrism from their own bishops "at the approach of the Paschal solemnity".[6] The *Statuta Ecclesiae Antiqua* from the beginning of the sixth century similarly directs presbyters to seek the chrism "before the solemnity of Easter".[7] At the end of the sixth century the Council of Auxerre directed them to seek the chrism *ad media quadragesima*,[8] that is on the Fourth Sunday in Lent, indicating that it must

[1] *Gel.*, p. 93, n. 598.   [2] *Ger.*, pp. 25–7.
[3] *Bob.*, p. 170, n. 558; pp. 54–8, nn. 174–85.
[4] *Gal. Vet.*, p. 9, n. 25; pp. 17–23, nn. 61–80.
[5] *Goth.*, pp. 53ff, nn. 196–204.   [6] Mansi, VI, 453C (Canon 3).
[7] op. cit., 87 (ed. Munier, p. 94).   [8] Maassen, op. cit., p. 180.

have been consecrated no later than that day. Long distances and poor communications in Gaul would have required that chrism be available earlier than Maundy Thursday. These canons, however, refer only to the chrism, and no mention is made of the oil of the catechumens. If the priest were permitted to bless the oil himself, as was undoubtedly the case, there would be no need for it to be blessed ahead of time, and, as the *Vita S. Caesarii* indicates, it would normally be done when it was to be used.[1] This was certainly Palm Sunday in some places.

With the testimony of *Ger.* already cited may be read the form in *Bob.* entitled "Blessing of Palms and Olives upon the Altar",[2] and given among the blessings at the end of the book. Its text makes it clear that it is intended for use on Palm Sunday, and also, surprisingly enough, that the olives were not olive branches, but olive oil. The gospel appointed in *Bob.* is John 12.1–15, describing the anointing of Christ at Bethany and the triumphal entry.[3] From this gospel lesson we may see the reason for associating olive oil with palm branches and include *Bob.* among our witnesses to a blessing of oil on Palm Sunday.

The chrism was therefore blessed sometime in Lent, on or before Palm Sunday. There was presumably some local variation. The transfer of the blessing of the chrism to Maundy Thursday, to which *Gal. Vet.* bears witness, took place in the seventh and eighth centuries under the influence of the Roman rite, which entered Gaul at this period. There is no reason to dissent from the conclusion of Chavasse:

> But before adopting the formulae and order of the Roman liturgy for Holy Thursday, there was provided for that day a mass for the blessing of the chrism, in which the preface was a chrismal preface.
>
> The *Missale Gallicanum Vetus* and the Gelasian Vat. Reg. 316 are witnesses to this intermediate step between the old and the new discipline.[4]

From *Ger.* we obtain an explanation of the meaning of the oils, and a rather confusing account of their use. *Ger.* speaks of two oils, *oleum* and *chrisma*, which are blessed together. To the *oleum* he refers the words of Ps. 45.8, "God anointed thee with the oil of gladness above they fellows", and of Ps. 89.21, "With my holy oil have I anointed him." He concludes, "First the ancients were anointed with oil, then thy were moistened with ointment."[5] However faulty his exegesis of the Psalter may be, the Pseudo-Germanus obviously intends to show that

---

[1] cf. Chavasse, art. cit., pp. 123–6.   [2] *Bob.*, p. 170, n. 558.
[3] *Bob.*, p. 58, n. 188; also *Le Lectionaire de Luxeuil*, ed. P. Salmon, p. 80.
[4] Chavasse, art. cit., p. 115.   [5] *Ger.*, p. 25.

this is parallel to the Christian custom of anointing first with *oleum*, and then with *unguentum*, or chrism. The oil (*oleum*) represents the grace of the Holy Spirit, and is consecrated for the making of ointments (*unguenta*), the preparation of lights, and the healing of the wound of sin.[1] The references appear to be to its use in the preparation of chrism, to the burning of oil in the lamps before the altar, and to the anointing of catechumens.

The chrism, he says, is made from balsam, which is in turn derived from a tree called *lentiseus* which tradition says was used for the cross-piece of the cross to which our Lord's hands were nailed.[2]

Ger.'s description of the use of the oil is confusing. He speaks of the blessing of the oil and chrism on the first day of the week, at the time of the *traditio symboli*. He then says:

> The seventh day he blessed and sanctified in rest: and so on this day (*hac die*) the faith of the people is strengthened and nourished with creed and the milk of chrism (*lac chrismatis*), since on the seventh day the rest of Christ in the sepulchre is celebrated, and at the end of the day (*declinante in die*) the triumph of his resurrection is observed.[3]

The meaning of this passage seems perfectly clear: on the Holy Sabbath, when we celebrate the burial of Christ and, as the vigil proceeds, his resurrection, the faithful are nourished with the creed (in the *redditio symboli* at the beginning of the vigil) and with the anointing of chrism.[4] E. C. Whitaker, in his English translation in *Documents of the Baptismal Liturgy*, makes what I believe to be a wholly gratuitous addition to the text:

> The seventh day he blessed and hallowed with rest, and so upon the first day the faith of the people . . .[5]

The mention of the creed has undoubtedly led Whitaker to refer the events back to the *traditio symboli*, but to translate *hac die* as *on the first day* is not only to do violence to the Latin text, but also to create the additional difficulty of having to explain a totally unprecedented anointing of catechumens with chrism on Palm Sunday. The evidence of *Ger.* is sufficiently confusing by itself without creating fresh problems in translation.

---

[1] *Ger.*, p. 25.   [2] *Ger.*, p. 27.   [3] *Ger.*, p. 26.
[4] *Ger.* expounds *lac chrismatis* as, "The child is nourished with milk, and the catechumen is anointed with chrism". It may possibly be a reminiscence of the cup of milk and honey.
[5] op. cit., p. 154.

Ger., then, assigns to Palm Sunday the blessing of the oils, the *traditio symboli*, apparently the *traditio* of the gospels, and (by implication) the anointing of the catechumens with the exorcized oil, and to Holy Saturday the *redditio symboli* and the anointing with chrism (presumably after the baptism proper, which *Ger.* does not mention).

About the actual blessing *Ger.* tells us little. The oil and chrism are poured into chalices, "because all the sacraments of baptism are founded (*firmantur*) on the passion of Christ". The glass or crystal vessels of chrism signify the brightness of baptism.[1] This ceremonial corresponds to that in the Mozarabic Antiphonary of León.

We may now return to the chrismal preface of *Gal. Vet.* to examine the content of the blessing of chrism. The first part of the preface is missing from the manuscript, and we do not know how it began, but in the fragment which is preserved, reference is made to an unguent made from spices (*ex aromatibus*) with which prophets, priests, and kings were anointed (*perfusus*). The sweetness of its fragrance is compared to the perpetual flowers of paradise. The concluding petition is:

> ... that when we anoint from this a new family to thee, that coming upon them, by the co-operation of thy Holy Spirit, He (*sic*) may breathe into them the breath of heavenly grace, that they also may be made thy Christs and by thy Son and the infused power of the Holy Spirit may always be fellow-heirs of that Name.[2]

As we have already seen, *Gel.* contains a Gallican chrismal preface, and two other forms for blessing oil which are probably of Gallican origin.[3] Chavasse believes that these forms, together with those of *Gal. Vet.*, represent an intermediate step between the ancient Gallican custom of consecrating chrism earlier in Lent and the adoption of the Roman *ordo* for Maundy Thursday, that is, the construction of a Gallican chrismal mass for the day. Roman influence on the chrismal mass in *Gal. Vet.* is clearly shown by the provision of *Te igitur* as a *post-sanctus*.[4]

The three forms which *Bob.* provides for the exorcism and blessing of oil[5] are general blessings of oil for a variety of purposes. They may, of course, be similar to the forms for blessing the oil of the catechumens, but this is not certain.

The actual baptismal rites took place during the Easter vigil. There

---

[1] *Ger.*, pp. 26f.   [2] *Gal. Vet.*, p. 26, n. 82.
[3] *Gel.*, pp. 60, 63, nn. 378, 389, 390.
[4] *Gal. Vet.*, p. 26, nn. 83ff.   [5] *Bob.*, p. 178, nn. 574–6.

were no Saturday morning ceremonies, as at Rome, presumably
because the rites corresponding to the *effeta* had already been held.
Baptism followed the *Exultet* and solemn prayers of the vigil rite.
Bob. and *Goth.* place the *ordo ad Christianum faciendum* first among
the baptismal ceremonies, and it is possible that in some places
there was no advance preparation for baptism, and these forms were
used here. This would be most likely to be true of baptisms performed outside the solemn seasons, or perhaps even at Pentecost.
Certainly it was not originally a part of the rite of solemn baptism at
Easter.

The baptismal ceremonies begin with the exorcism and blessing of
the font. The forms differ in all three sacramentaries. The *contestatio
fontis*, modelled after the preface of the mass and introduced by *Sursum
corda*, was the principal feature of the blessing. That in *Goth.* is noteworthy in the context of this study for its beginning:

> It is meet and right, O Lord, Holy Father, Almighty, Everlasting God,
> Source of holiness (*iniciatur sanctorum*), Father of chrisms . . .[1]

In all three rites a sign of the cross was made in the water with chrism
at the end of the *contestatio*. *Bob.* provides the formula:

> The infusion of the chrism of salvation of our Lord Jesus Christ that this may
> be a font of living water springing up for all who come unto eternal life.[2]

Goth. provides substantially the same formula,[3] but for a second signing
of the font with chrism. The first signing, at the end of the *contestatio*,
is followed by the exorcism of the font, at the end of which the priest
breathes thrice into the water and signs it again with the form quoted
above. The signing of the font with three signs of the cross in *Gal. Vet.*
is followed by a prayer for those to be baptized which contains no
direct reference to the chrism.

In *Bob.* a series of ceremonies corresponding to the Saturday morning
rites in *Gel.* follow. After an exorcism the *effeta* is performed. The use
of oil is not prescribed, and the rubric mentions only the touching of
the nose. After the *effeta Bob.* says:

> *You anoint him with holy oil saying,* "I anoint thee with holy oil as Samuel
> anointed David as king and prophet."[4]

---

[1] *Goth.*, p. 66, n. 257.   [2] *Bob.*, p. 73, n. 238.
[3] *Goth.*, p. 67, n. 259. The ending here is ". . . to all who go down . . .".
[4] *Bob.*, p. 74, n. 242.

This amazing formula, which recurs as an anointing formula at ordinations, sick unctions, and the anointing of kings, seems to be more appropriate to use with a post-baptismal chrismation than the pre-baptismal unction.[1] It is followed in the text of *Bob.* by a rubric, "You touch his nose, ears, and breast", and a formula of exorcism beginning, "*Operare creatura olei* . . .". It appears that some confusion has taken place, as the second formula is most appropriate to a pre-baptismal anointing with exorcized oil. It asks that the unclean spirit depart and the power of Christ and the Holy Ghost work upon the anointed. The two formulas, however, tend to occur together in other documents, and there is undoubtedly some connection between them which is not apparent to the modern student.

This apparent doubling of the anointing points to some confusion in the rubrics of *Bob.*, presumably caused by the wish of the compiler to adapt his Gallican material to the Roman model. If we were better informed as to the origin of *Bob.*, we might be able to explain the difficulty more readily.

Gal. Vet. places the renunciation of the devil immediately after the blessing of the font,[2] and in *Bob.* it follows the anointing we have been discussing.[3] The actual baptism does not take place as the candidate answers the credal questions, but is accompanied in all three sacramentaries by a declarative formula, the actual wording of which varies slightly in each.[4] The baptism is followed by the anointing with chrism. *Gal. Vet.* calls it an *infusio chrismae*. *Bob.* says, "Superfundes crisma in fronte eius", and places a cross in the text of the formula. *Goth.* says simply, "Chrisma eum tangis."[5] Both *Bob.* and *Gal. Vet.* have the chrismal prayer from *Gel.*, with a few minor verbal changes. The diagram on p. 122 shows this prayer as it appears in various sources. *Goth.* has a different form:

> I anoint thee with the chrism of holiness, the tunic of immortality, which our Lord Jesus Christ first received from the Father, that thou mayest bear it

---

[1] It is used for the sick in the Sacramentary of St Eloy, for anointing the priest's hands at ordination in *Missale Francorum*, and for anointing the king in the Freising Benedictional.

[2] *Gal. Vet.*, p. 41, nn. 140ff.   [3] *Bob.*, p. 74, nn. 244ff.

[4] The credal questions in *Gal. Vet.* and the baptismal formula in *Bob.* show evidence of definite anti-Arian feeling. All three questions in *Gal. Vet.* name all three Persons of the Trinity, and *Bob.* adds, "being of one substance" to the Names in the baptismal formula.

[5] *Gal. Vet.*, p. 42, n. 175; *Bob.*, p. 75, n. 249; *Goth.*, p. 67, n. 260.

whole and undefiled before the tribunal of Christ and live unto the Age of Ages.[1]

Mohlberg has inserted the words *indua te* (put on) in brackets before *tonicam immortalitatis* in printing the form, but this appears to be a mistake. We have seen that chrism is referred to as a *vestimentum incorrupti muneris* in the Gallican chrismal preface in *Gel.*'s mass for Maundy Thursday,[2] and as an "incorruptible robe" in the Coptic and Byzantine rites. Undoubtedly the *tonica immortalitatis* is the chrism itself, and not a garment. The form in *Goth.* must then be a native Gallican form which has been replaced by the Roman form in the other books.

As to the method of applying the chrism, *infusio* and *superfundes* imply that the chrism was poured over the forehead, or head of the neophyte, while *tangis* and the cross-mark in *Bob.* seem to indicate that the custom was to sign the forehead.

The *Historia Francorum* of Gregory of Tours describes the signing of the cross with chrism at the baptism of Clovis:

> The king, having confessed the Almighty God in Trinity, was baptized in the name of the Father, and of the Son, and of the Holy Ghost, and anointed (*delibutus*) with the holy chrism with the sign (*signaculum*) of the cross of Christ.[3]

This same source speaks of the reconciliation of Arians to the Catholic Church, "when they have received the sign of the blessed cross with the anointing of chrism".[4] And in the *Liber in Gloria Martyrum* Gregory speaks of those whose brow is signed with the mark of chrism (*inscriptio chrismae*).[5] It would appear that the signing of the forehead with chrism was a Gallican practice in the days of Gregory of Tours, and that *Bob.* bears witness to its continuance. This does not necessarily imply any contradiction of the idea of the *infusio chrismae*. *Ap. Trad.* spoke of the bishop as pouring (*infundens*) the holy oil from his hand and signing the brow.

The Gallican sacramentaries have only one anointing with chrism after baptism, and no laying on of hands. Gregory of Tours likewise knows only chrismation as a post-baptismal ceremony and for the reconciliation of heretics. There is possible evidence of a laying on of hands in the fourth century in Gaul. Hilary of Poitiers spoke of the bestowal

---

[1] *Goth.*, p. 67, n. 261.   [2] *Gel.*, p. 60, n. 378.
[3] op. cit., 2.31 (*P. L.*, 71, 227).   [4] ibid., 9.15 (*P.L.*, 71, 493).
[5] op. cit., 40 (*P.L.*, 71, 742).

THE CHRISMAL PRAYER

Gel., nn. 450 & 610
Deus omnipotens, pater domini nostri Iesu Christi qui te regeneravit ex aqua et spiritu sancti quique dedit tibi remissionem omnium peccatorum, ipse te linit chrisma salutis in Christo Iesu domino nostro in vitam aeternam.

Greg., p. 57

. . . ipse te linit chrismate salutis in vitam aeternam.

Gal. Vet., n. 175

. . . quique tibi dedit

. . . ipsi te lenet chrismate suo sancto, ut habes vitam aeternam in saecula saeculorum.

Bob., n. 249
Deus pater domini Iesu Christi qui te regeneravit per aqua et spiritu sancto quicquid tibi dedit remissione peccatorum per lavacrum regeneracionis et sanguine ✝ ipse te liniat crisma suo sancto in vitam aeternam.

Berg., n. 537
(as in *Gel.*)

North, p. 34
Deus pater omnipotens . . .
(as in *Gel.*)

Man, Amb., p. 209
Deus pater omnipotens . . .
(as in *Gel.*, but in plural)

Stowe, p. 31
(as in *Gel.*, ending)
. . . in Christo.

---

de Sacramentis 2.7.24
Deus, pater omnipotens, qui te regeneravit ex aqua et spiritu sancto tibi peccata tua, ipse te unguet in vitam aeternam.

Mai fragment
Deus et pater domini nostri Iesu Christi, qui te regeneravit ex aqua, ipse te linet spiritu sancto.

Edward VI
Almighty God, the Father of our Lord Jesus Christ, who hath regenerated thee by water and the Holy Ghost, and hath given unto thee remission of all thy sins: he vouchsafe to anoint thee with the unction of his Holy Spirit and bring thee to the inheritance of everlasting life.

of the gift of the Holy Spirit upon the Gentiles "through the imposition of hands and prayers".[1] It is not clear whether Hilary is referring to a rite with which he is familiar, or simply expounding the text of Matt. 19.14, in which he saw a figure of the blessing of the Gentiles. He describes the actual sequence of baptismal rites by comparing them to the baptism of Christ:

> For in this the order of the heavenly secret is portrayed. For when he was baptized, when he had heard the opening of the heavens, the Holy Ghost was sent forth, and was known in the visible form of a dove, and in this manner he was anointed with the unction of the Father's favour. Then the voice spoke thus from heaven: Thou art my son, to-day have I begotten thee . . . likewise . . . after the washing with water, the Holy Ghost came down upon us from the gates of heaven, we were anointed with the unction of the heavenly glory, and by the adoption of the voice of the Father we became sons of God.[2]

And in another place he speaks of the sacraments of baptism and of the Spirit.[3] It would therefore appear that even if Hilary did know the laying on of hands as a present rite of the Church, it was the unction of the Holy Ghost to which he attached the greater importance.[4]

Earlier in the fourth century, the eighth canon of the first Council of Arles directs that, in the case of the reception of baptized heretics, they should be asked to reply to the questions of the *symbolum*:

> . . . and if they find him to have been baptized in [the Name of] the Father and the Son and the Holy Ghost, only a hand shall be laid upon him, that he may receive the Holy Ghost. And if, when he is asked, he shall not reply [correctly] let him be baptized in [the Name of] the Trinity.[5]

Since we have the testimony of Gregory of Tours in the sixth century that heretics were received by the anointing with chrism, and with no mention of the laying on of hands, we are led to conclude that the laying on of hands dropped out of the Gallican rite between the

---

[1] *Commenta in Matt.*, 19.3 (P.L. 9, 1024).

[2] ibid., 2.6 (*P.L.*, 9, 927).   [3] ibid., 4.27 (*P.L.*, 9, 942C).

[4] Wirgman, *Doctrine of Confirmation*, p. 232, states that Hilary knew a *gratia augmenti* in "the perfecting gifts of the Holy Ghost, which were given, after Baptism, by a distinct rite". and quotes *Tract. in Ps.* 118, Gimel, 5, "The cleansing which gives that perfect purity is reserved for us even after the waters of baptism to sanctify us by the coming of the Holy Ghost." An examination of the passage in *C.S.E.L.*, Vol. 22, p. 380, reveals the further "rite" is the martyrs' baptism of blood, not confirmation.

[5] Lauchert, op. cit., p. 27.

fourth and sixth centuries, certainly in the reception of heretics, and probably also in the normal course of Christian initiation. We may also note the geographical proximity of Arles to Italy, and the consequent possibility of Italian influence upon the early practice of that region.

In the fifth century we have the evidence of the second Council of Arles that the Bosonian heretics were to be received "with chrism and the imposition of the hand",[1] and of Gennadius of Marseilles concerning children received from heresy:

> If they are children (*parvuli*) . . . let those who present them answer for them, as is the custom at baptism, and thus fortified (*communiti*) by the imposition of the hand and chrism, let them be admitted to the mysteries of the eucharist.[2]

The passage from Gennadius is of particular interest, since, immediately before the portion quoted, he speaks of the reception of adult converts with the imposition of a hand. The comment of A. J. Mason is still relevant:

> From the ritual point of view this passage is of value, as it shows how the Imposition of the Hand and the Chrism were coming to be two names for one and the same rite . . . The "Imposition of the Hand" in the first case is equivalent to the "Imposition of the Hand and Chrism" in the second. It means that the Unction upon the brow at the time of the Laying on of Hands was becoming increasingly "the Chrism".[3]

Gennadius also provides us with actual testimony to the laying on of hands at baptism:

> He who is to be baptized confesses his faith before the priest, and when he is questioned he replies: this also the martyr does before the persecutor, who also confesses his faith, and when he is questioned he replies. The former after his confession is either sprinkled with water, or dipped in it; the martyr is either sprinkled with blood, or placed in the fire. The former receives the Holy Spirit by the imposition of the hands of the bishop; the latter is made a habitation of the Holy Spirit, for it is not he who speaks, but the Spirit of the Father who speaks in him. The former communicates at the Eucharist in commemoration of the death of Christ: the latter himself dies with Christ.[4]

This magnificent passage has an archaic ring. There could certainly have

---

[1] Canon 17, Mansi, VII, 800.
[2] de Ecclesiasticis Dogmatibus, 52 (P.L., 58, 993).
[3] The Relation of Confirmation to Baptism, p. 194.
[4] Gennadius, op. cit., 47 (P.L., 58, 997).

been no martyrdoms in southern France in the last decade of the fifth century, and it is possible that Gennadius is quoting, or paraphrasing an earlier author. We must therefore accept his account of the sequence of baptismal rites with some reservation. It may not have been the actual sequence customary in Gaul, but an ideal description based upon the data of an earlier period.

In sum, none of the Gallican sacramentaries includes a rite of episcopal confirmation, nor have we any evidence requiring us to assume that such a rite was customarily added to the extant baptismal rites, nor that the administration of the single Gallican post-baptismal anointing was confined to bishops.

A most confusing canon of the Council of Orange led to a debate among Roman Catholic scholars in the early seventeenth century as to the meaning of the Gallican anointing. The controversy was not settled then, and in our own century Fr Paul Galtier and Dom Paul de Puniet have conducted a learned argument through the pages of various scholarly journals as to the meaning of the rite.[1] Briefly, Galtier identifies the Gallican anointing with the single post-baptismal anointing in Tertullian, and with the first Roman anointing (*unctio capitis*). He believes that the baptismal rites were followed by a separate episcopal confirmation, consisting of the imposition of hands and a signing without oil. De Puniet believes that anointing was a part of the Gallican rite of consignation, and that Gallican and Roman practice was similar.

The canon in question, Canon 2 of the Council of Orange (A.D. 441), reads:

> No minister who has the office of baptizing shall begin without chrism: for that it was agreed among us that there shall be one chrismation (*semel chrismari*). When anyone for any reason does not receive chrism in baptism, the priest (*sacerdos*) shall be advised of this at his Confirmation (*in confirmatione*). For chrism can only confer its blessing once (*Nam inter quoslibet chrismatis ipsius nonnisi una benedictio sit.*): and we say this not to any man's prejudice, but that the repetition of chrismation should not be thought necessary.[2]

Dom de Puniet believes that the proper clue to the interpretation of

---

[1] *Revue des Questions Historiques*, Vol. 72 (1902), pp. 382–423 (de Puniet, "La Liturgie Baptismale en Gaule avant Charlemagne"); *Recherches de Science Religieuse*, Vol. 2 (1911), pp. 350–83 (Galtier, "La Consignation à Carthage et à Rome"); *Revue d'Histoire Ecclésiastique*, Vol. 13 (1912), pp. 257–301 (Galtier, "La Consignation dans les Églises d'Occident"), pp. 450–66 (de Puniet, "Onction et Confirmation"), pp. 467–76 (Galtier, "Onction et Confirmation").

[2] Mansi, VI, 435; trans in Whitaker, *Documents*, p. 216.

this canon is found in examining it in its context. The first canon of Orange provided:

> If the Bishop is lacking, heretics in danger of death, if they desire to be-come Catholics may be signed (*consignari*) by presbyters with chrism and and the blessing.[1]

This established the right of presbyters to reconcile dying heretics. The third canon also refers to the dying. De Puniet interprets Canon 2 to mean that since there is but one blessing of the chrism, the anointing by a presbyter of the person clinically baptized is to be considered the equivalent of the episcopal anointing at confirmation. If, on the other hand, for some reason the baptismal anointing has been omitted, the anointing by the bishop (*sacerdos*) will supply the lack, since it is not necessary for the anointing to be repeated. Galtier, for his part, placing the stress upon the phrase *placuit non semel chrismari*, interprets this to mean that an anointing took place at confirmation only when it had been omitted at baptism.

No matter which interpretation we accept, the rite of episcopal consignation does not appear to have survived in Gaul into the sixth century, and, as we saw foreshadowed in Gennadius, the anointing with chrism appears to have replaced it. It is possible that in an earlier period a second anointing with oil accompanied the laying on of hands, but when we enter the period represented by Gregory of Tours and the liturgical books, there is no evidence of any rite beyond baptism as described in the sacramentaries.

Whatever the original intention of the Gallican Fathers, the rite of anointing after baptism, the only anointing in the surviving Gallican liturgical books, like the presbyteral anointing in the East, or that permitted by Gregory the Great in Sardinia, was regarded by those who used it as conferring the Holy Spirit. It was only with the introduction of the Roman rite in the eighth century that a separate rite of episcopal confirmation was introduced, or reintroduced into Gaul.

The baptismal rites of the Gallican sacramentaries, to which we shall now return, continue after the anointing with the washing of the feet,[2] a non-Roman ceremony which we first encountered in St Ambrose. It is found also in *Stowe* and the Ambrosian liturgical books, and is one of the chief links between the baptismal rites of the Gallican, Celtic, and Ambrosian types.

---

[1] Mansi, loc. cit.
[2] *Gal. Vet.*, p. 42, n. 176; *Goth.*, p. 67, n. 262; *Bob.*, p. 75, n. 251.

The clothing with white robes and the celebration of the vigil mass, at which the neophytes were undoubtedly communicated, concluded the solemn rites. Among the additional prayers provided for after baptism, we may particularly note this from *Goth.*:

> For those who are baptized, who seek the chrism, who are crowned in Christ, to whom our Lord has been pleased to grant a new birth, let us beseech Almighty God that they may bear the baptism which they have received spotless unto the end . . .[1]

We may, perhaps, now be prepared to look at the complex provisions of the Stowe Missal. This is our only source of information concerning the baptismal rites of the Irish Church. Even a cursory examination of the material in the Henry Bradshaw Society edition, or in the English translation of E. C. Whitaker,[2] will convince the reader that Thompson is not exaggerating when he says, "The book is in almost complete confusion."[3] Many strata of Roman and non-Roman forms are mixed together in an all but unintelligible jumble. Thompson has undertaken a study of the material common to *Stowe* and *Bob.*,[4] and concludes that they have a common source, now lost, which was formed by combining Irish and Gelasian books, and that the missionary activity of Irish monks brought *Bob.*, which he considers to be Irish, to North Italy. Dom Wilmart, although admitting that *Bob.* contains Irish material, denies that it is an Irish book.[5]

We are therefore left with *Stowe* and parts of *Bob.* as witnesses to the Celtic baptismal liturgy. From the structure of *Bob.*, we are almost forced to conclude that the Celtic rites were similar to the Gallican, and we shall proceed on this basis. *Stowe* contains more Roman elements than *Bob.*, and we must admit that the Celtic rites were under severe pressure from the Roman rite imported to Britain by St Augustine of Canterbury in the seventh century.

Stowe itself is a small book of sixty-seven leaves, measuring $5\frac{5}{8}$ by $4\frac{1}{2}$ inches. It contains extracts from the Gospel of St John, the ordinary and canon of the mass, with a few sets of propers, the section on baptism, forms for unction and Communion of the sick, a treatise on the mass in Gaelic, and three short Gaelic spells. It seems to have been intended

---

[1] *Goth.*, p. 68, n. 265; trans in Whitaker, *Documents*, p. 152.
[2] *The Stowe Missal*, ed. G. F. Warner (H.B.S., Vol. 32); Whitaker, *Documents*, pp. 203–11.
[3] *Offices of Baptism and Confirmation*, p. 157.   [4] ibid., pp. 157–9.
[5] *The Bobbio Missal, Notes and Studies* (H.B.S., Vol. 61), pp. 4–58.

for use by a Gaelic monk on his journeys, providing him with the forms he would need on the road.

The *ordo babtismi* in *Stowe* is a single long section,[1] and would presumably have been used as a single rite if the book was really intended for use by a travelling missionary monk. It is quite disjointed, and parts that appear to belong together are separated by seemingly unrelated material.

After the opening prayers, the rite begins with the blessing of salt, but the salt is not administered until after the renunciation of the devil and the recitation of several prayers derived from the forms in *Gel.* for sick catechumens. This disarrangement is typical. The renunciation of the devil is followed by the three credal questions and the rubric:

> You make an exsufflation and touch him: then you touch his breast and back with oil and chrism, saying: I anoint thee with sanctified oil, in the Name of the Father and of the Son and of the Holy Ghost.

The description of the pre-baptismal anointing as *de oleo et chrismate* is all but unique in Western rites of this period.[2] We can only assume that the careful distinction between the pre-baptismal oil of exorcism and the chrism was foreign to the Celtic Church, where olive oil of any form must have been exceedingly scarce.

After the anointing there is a second renunciation of the devil and the previously mentioned prayers. Then the *effeta* appears. Neither spittle nor oil is mentioned, but the rubric, which is in Irish, directs that salt be here placed in the child's mouth.

After two more prayers, a rubric directs:

> Up to this point he has been a catechumen. He now begins to be anointed with oil and chrism (*oleari oleo et chrismate*) upon the breast and between the shoulder blades, before he is baptized.

Bob. had a double pre-baptismal anointing, and it may be that a second anointing is intended here. If this is so, then the first would be that associated with entry into the catechumenate, and this, as the rubric declares, would be strictly pre-baptismal. The confusion of the text of *Stowe*, however, makes it difficult to see what was originally planned. Certainly, as the rite must have been performed by someone using *Stowe*, this would have been a second anointing.

---

[1] *Stowe*, pp. 24–33.
[2] The same phrase occurs in the anointing of the hands of a priest in *Missale Francorum*, with the Samuel–David formula.

Several prayers for the exorcism and blessing of the font follow, at the end of which the priest pours chrism into the font in the form of a cross. The baptism itself is in threefold form. No declarative formula is given, but the credal questions are asked.

The post-baptismal anointing follows, but the rubric is confused. It directs:

> After he has been baptized, let him be anointed with chrism (*oleatur crismate*) on his head and brow (*in cerebro in fronte*); and the deacon puts the white robe over his head upon his brow (*super caput eius in fronte*) and the presbyter says...

The deacon is directed to give the white robe again after the anointing, and it appears that two forms have been unskilfully joined to produce the text. The anointing is to be performed by the presbyter, although whether *in cerebro* or *in fronte* is not quite clear. This may represent an attempt to adapt the Roman practice of presbyteral anointing of the head to the native custom of signing the brow. The form given is the chrismal prayer as in *Gel*.[1]

This form is followed by a rubric in Irish, "It is here that the anointing is done", and two formulas. The first is:

> I anoint thee with the oil and the chrism of salvation and sanctification in the Name of the Father, and of the Son, and of the Holy Ghost, now and throughout all ages of ages.

The second is *operare creatura olei*, used in *Bob*. at the pre-baptismal anointing.[2] It is after this that the rubric concerning the white robe reappears.

The Irish rubric and the undeniably non-Roman nature of the second set of anointing prayers indicate that these are the original Celtic forms with which the presbyter anointed the brow of those whom he had baptized. The form from *Gel*. and the confusing phrases in the preceding rubric have resulted from the unskilful introduction of the Roman forms into the native rite, a practice which did not cease in the eighth century. This post-baptismal anointing is also said to be *de oleo et chrismate*, further evidence of the confusion of the holy oils in the Celtic Church.

The giving of the white robe is followed by the signing of the cross on the right hand of the neophyte and the foot washing. The communicating of the newly baptized was the final ceremony.

---

[1] See Diagram on p. 122 above.   [2] *Bob*., p. 74, n. 244; see p. 120 above.

We may now look back on the complex of Gallican and Celtic rites of baptism. In Gaul the Roman rite was formally adopted by Charlemagne. The Celtic rites were also superseded by that of Rome, and their service books have almost all perished. As in all conquests, however, the victor was not given undisputed possession of the spoils, and Gallican elements entered the Roman rite and found a permanent place therein. This interaction of Roman and Gallican rites has produced a measure of confusion in the surviving liturgical books, which, with few exceptions, contain material from both sources.

The Gallican rites of baptism centred around two great occasions: Palm Sunday, with its *traditio symboli*, and the Easter vigil, at which the baptisms were actually performed. The Gallican evidence concerning pre-baptismal anointing is confusing, and there appears to have been some local variation. I believe that we have shown that at least a single pre-baptismal anointing, probably on Palm Sunday, was common. There is some evidence of a rite of post-baptismal episcopal consignation, at least in certain cases, in the fourth and fifth centuries, but from the sixth century until the introduction of the Roman rite into Gaul in the eighth century there is a single post-baptismal anointing, the *infusio chrismae*. It appears to have been performed by the officiating priest, whether bishop or presbyter. It is possible that the oil was poured upon the head and a cross traced in it upon the brow, as in *Ap. Trad.*, or the signing which Gregory of Tours mentions may simply have been abandoned.

Concerning the Celtic rite we can say little, except that any distinction between pre-baptismal oil and chrism seems to have been unknown and the terms were either considered synonymous, or both oils were used for both anointings.

The long-standing argument among Roman Catholic scholars concerning the meaning of the Gallican anointing will have to remain unsettled on the basis of our study, although there is no reason for the assumption made by both sides that episcopal confirmation continued in Gaul in the sixth, seventh, and eighth centuries. If, as I believe, there was no rite practised beyond those described in the Gallican sacramentaries, the question of the original meaning of the rite loses its urgency. As the second canon of Orange makes clear, there is but one blessing of chrism, and it was immediately following baptism that the faithful of Gaul received it. When we add to the Gallican evidence that of the Spanish and North Italian Churches, which we shall consider in the next two sections, the conclusion becomes almost inescapable that episcopal confirmation separate from episcopally-conferred baptism was a Roman usage, unknown after the fourth or fifth century. except where the Roman rite was followed.

THE MOZARABIC RITE

According to Dom Marius Férotin the Visigothic or Mozarabic liturgy is the totality of formulas and rites used in the Church of Spain from the conversion of the country to Christianity until the introduction of the Roman rite in the eleventh century.[1] We shall therefore examine under this title the baptismal liturgies of the Spanish Church, as found in its liturgical books, and in the testimony of its councils and Fathers.

The surviving rites are published by Férotin in the *Liber Ordinum*, hereafter referred to as *L.O.*, together with the related forms for the reconciliation of heretics,[2] while the general framework into which the rites fit is found in Cardinal Ximenes' *Missale Mixtum*.[3] An additional source for the rites of solemn baptism is the antiphonary of the cathedral of León, preserved in a tenth-century manuscript.[4] In addition to the material proper to an antiphonary it contains an *ordo* for the performance of the solemn rites of Palm Sunday, including the texts of several prayers. Our study must begin, however, with the literary writings of the earlier Spanish Fathers.

The fourth-century bishop, St Pacian of Barcelona, in his epistle which contains the oft-quoted phrase, "My name is Christian, and my surname (*cognomen*) Catholic", discusses the power of binding and loosing given by our Lord to his apostles and asks whether this was given to the apostles alone. For if it was, he argues, "Therefore they alone are permitted to baptize and to give the Holy Ghost ...". His conclusion is that the *lavacri et chrismatis potestas* has come down from them to the bishops.[5] From our point of view the importance of the passage is the parallel which it draws between *Spiritum sanctum dare* and *chrismatis potestas*. In both cases the phrase is conjoined to the mention of baptism, and we have here our earliest evidence for the baptismal anointing in the Spanish Church, together with an explanation of its meaning as "to give the Holy Spirit".

A sermon of St Pacian on baptism has also been preserved, which gives us a fuller picture of his understanding of the sacrament.

---

[1] *Liber Ordinum*, p. xi.
[2] *L.O.*, Ordines IV, XXXVII–XL, LXXXI, LXXXVI.
[3] *P.L.*, 85.   [4] *Antifonario Visigótico*, ed. Brou and Vives.
[5] *Ep.* I. 4, 6 (*P.L.* 13, 1055A, 1057B).

Commenting upon the passage, "But as many as received him, to them gave he power to become the sons of God (John 1.12)", he tells us:

> These things cannot be accomplished except by the sacrament of washing (*lavacri*), chrism, and the high priest (*antistitis*): by washing sins are cleansed; by chrism the Holy Ghost is poured upon him; and both these things are effected by the hand and mouth of the high priest; and thus the whole man is reborn and renewed in Christ.[1]

The familiar three liturgical acts of washing, anointing, and laying on hands, constitute baptism, the sacrament in which man is reborn in Christ by the power of the Holy Ghost.

Along with the testimony of St Pacian we must examine the canons of the Spanish Council of Elvira, which met in 306 under the presidency of Hosius of Cordova. Canon 38 deals with the case of a man baptized *in extremis* at sea, or far from a church. It affirms the right of the faithful layman to baptize in case of necessity, but, "If he survives, let him bring him to the bishop, that he may be perfected through the laying on of hands."[2]

Canon 77 of the same council speaks of catechumens baptized by a deacon in charge of a congregation (*diaconus regens plebem*) without bishop or presbyter. The bishop ought to perfect them with the blessing (*per benedictionem*), but if they should die before receiving it, they are considered *fideles*, that is baptized Christians.[3] It seems clear that the *benedictio* of Canon 77 should be identified with the *manus impositio* of Canon 38. No mention is made of chrismation in these canons, but this does not mean it was not contemplated. If, as I believe we shall see, the Spanish Church closely identified the anointing with the laying on of hands, the mention of the one ceremony might have implied the other. It should be noted that these canons do not apply to baptisms by presbyters, but only to baptisms by laymen or deacons. They do not prove that any additional ceremony was required, or even desired, in the case of those baptized by a priest. The Council of Toledo (A.D. 400) in its twentieth canon provided that, in spite of rumours to the contrary, none but bishops was permitted to consecrate the chrism, and that each local church should send a deacon or sub-deacon to the bishop before Easter to bring chrism back in time for the Easter baptism. It continues:

> While the bishops have the undoubted right to bless chrism at any time,

---

[1] *Sermo de Baptismo*, 6 (P.L., 13, 1993).   [2] Mansi, VI, 12; Lauchert, p. 19.
[3] Mansi, VI, 18; Lauchert, p. 25.

presbyters may do nothing without the knowledge of the bishop: it is decreed that the deacon may not give the chrism but the presbyter may do so in the absence of the bishop, or in his presence if he commands.[1]

The same language is used in the *Capitulary of Martin of Braga*, dating from about 580:

> The presbyter, in the presence of the bishop, may not sign infants, unless he is ordered by the bishop.[2]

The right of the presbyter to administer the episcopally consecrated chrism was further expounded by the second canon of the Council of Barcelona in 599, which states that the chrism is to be given to the presbyters of the diocese *pro neophytis confirmandis*, leaving little doubt that the Council, at least, considered the presbyteral chrismation to be confirmation.[3]

An additional glimpse into the sixth century is provided for us by letters exchanged by Eugene, Bishop of Toledo, and St Braulion, Bishop of Saragossa. The answer of St Braulion to Eugene's questions is a short treatise on the post-baptismal unction.

> Your wisdom has recognized that the ancient rule of the canons is that a presbyter may not presume to chrismate, which we know both the East and all Italy to keep until now; but later it was decided that a presbyter might chrismate, but with chrism blessed by bishops, that this should not seem to be a privilege of presbyters to sanctify the people of God with this holy anointing, but that with the blessing and permission of their bishops they perform this office as if by the hand of the bishop.[4]

The right to anoint is inherent in the episcopal office, and it is by licence of the bishop that presbyters exercise it. The true and holy chrism is that which has been consecrated by the bishop and administered by his permission. Chrism consecrated by a presbyter he does not even consider to be chrism.

Braulion's insistence on the close connection of chrismation to the *ius episcoporum* is further shown by his providing that those who are received from heresy should be anointed. Since they had been baptized without the consent of the legitimate bishop, it follows that they have not received true Catholic chrism, and should receive it upon their entry into the communion of the Church.

---

[1] Lauchert, p. 121; trans. in Whitaker, *Documents*, p. 213.
[2] op. cit., 52; Mansi, IX, 856.   [3] Mansi, X, 482.
[4] *Ep. ad Eugenum Toletanum*, 4 (*P.L.*, 87, 407).

The picture presented by the early Spanish evidence is of baptism regularly performed at Easter by the bishop in his cathedral, and by the presbyters in the remote parish churches. In both cases the neophyte was anointed with chrism blessed by the bishop *pro neophytis confirmandis*. The anointing might be performed only by a priest, that is by a presbyter or bishop. If the bishop were present he was expected to perform the rite himself, although he might delegate it to one of his presbyters.

In case of necessity deacons, or even laymen, might baptize, but they were forbidden to administer the chrism, and if those who were baptized lived, they were to be brought to the bishop to be blessed and perfected by the laying on of hands.

The writings of St Isidore of Seville (c. 560–636) are a principal source of information about the Mozarabic rite, and it is to them we now turn.

St Isidore, after giving his definition of a sacrament, states, "These moreover are sacraments: baptism and chrism, body and blood."[1] From this we may be sure that Isidore considered both the washing and the anointing to be sacramental acts, but we should be hard pressed to maintain that he considered them separate sacraments, since the parallel to the Body and Blood of Christ would more naturally lead us to consider them a single sacrament.

In the same book he also defines *chrisma* as Greek for the Latin *unctio*, "from the name of which Christ is called, and man is sanctified after the washings".[2] The anointing is described as the sanctification of the Spirit, and identified with the royal and priestly anointings of the Old Covenant.[3] The imposition of hands is also mentioned as calling down the Holy Spirit *per benedictionem*.[4]

With this as background we may turn to the *de Ecclesiasticis Officiis*, in which he describes the actual rites of baptism. Isidore divides Christians into three classes: catechumens, *competentes*, and baptized. The rites of the catechumenate are threefold: "First they are exorcized, then they receive the salt, and are anointed."[5] Although Isidore expounds the meaning of the exorcism and salt, he does not say more about this first anointing. From Ildephonsus and *L.O.* we shall be able to learn more, although in the later books the anointing is administered to *competentes*. Isidore speaks of the *competentes* as learning the mysteries

---

[1] *Etymologiarum Libri* VI, 39 (P.L., 82, 255).   [2] ibid., 50.   [3] ibid., 51.
[4] ibid., 54.   [5] op. cit., 2.21 (P.L., 83, 814).

of faith, and follows his chapter *de competentibus* with chapters *de symbulo* and *de regula fidei*, presumably referring to the *traditio symboli*.

After his description of the baptism itself, he writes *de chrismate* and *de manuum impositione*. He identifies the chrism with the unguent prepared by Moses in Exodus, and he explains that under the New Covenant not only *pontifices* and kings, "but the whole Church is consecrated with the anointing of chrism, because it is a member of the eternal king and priest. Therefore since we are a priestly and royal race (*genus*), we anoint after the washing, that we may be consecrated by the name of Christ."[1] Isidore follows this statement immediately by saying: "After baptism the Holy Spirit is given by the bishops with the laying on of hands."[2] Apparently nothing could be clearer. The anointing is described in purely christological terms, and the gift of the Spirit is associated with the imposition of hands, as in Acts 19, and 8, which Isidore quotes. He concludes the passage by repeating the caution of St Augustine, "We can receive the Holy Spirit, we cannot give him, but we call upon the Lord, that he may be given",[3] and by quoting the letter of Innocent I to Decentius restricting the signing of the forehead to bishops.

The difficulty with Isidore's interpretation, which is obviously based upon St Augustine, is that it was not the customary interpretation of the Spanish Church, nor was the injunction of Innocent which he quotes observed in the Mozarabic rite. Isidore is here reproducing what he believes to be the ancient tradition of the Western Church on the basis of the writings of its acknowledged doctors. In other places he himself associates the gift of the Spirit with the anointing, and his Augustinian theories left no trace even in the works of St Ildephonsus, on whom he exercised a profound influence.

St Ildephonsus of Toledo, who died in 669, summarizes the baptismal rites as "the exorcism by word, the declaration of the commandment, the anointing with oil, the receiving of the creed, the sacrament of baptism, the chrism of the Holy Spirit, the participation of the Body and Blood of Christ".[4] These rites he explains in detail in *de Cognitione Baptismi*, hereafter cited as *Ild*.[5]

Although Ildephonsus follows Isidore in distinguishing between

---

[1] ibid., 2.26.   [2] ibid., 2.27.

[3] Augustine, *de Baptismo contra Donatum*, 5.28.

[4] *de Itinere Deserti*, 76 (P.L., 96, 188).

[5] The text is in *P.L.*, 96, and translations of portions in Whitaker, *Documents*, pp. 101–5.

catechumens and *competentes*, it appears from his description that the ceremonies of the catechumenate and the scrutinies have actually disappeared, and that a single rite of exorcism on Palm Sunday in preparation for baptism is envisaged. The exorcism described by *Ild.* in chapter 22 is practically identical with that in *L.O.* for the exorcism of an unclean spirit,[1] and we may read the two accounts together for a description of the rite.[2] *Ild.* describes the children (for his catechumens are expected to be children) as led over a carpet of goatskin to the anointing, as a token of penitence. This same ceremony is found in the Ambrosian rite. Isidore mentioned the anointing as the last of the three ceremonies of the catechumenate. *Ild.* also associates the anointing with exorcism, but apparently with the anointing of the *effeta* on Palm Sunday. The most reasonable explanation for this would be that the original rites performed with adult catechumens had had an anointing at their entrance into the catechumenate, while, with the disappearance of the adult catechumenate, the rites were compressed and all held on Palm Sunday.

The anointing follows the exorcism[3] and is performed with oil blessed by the priest, following the example of our Lord in Mark 7.32, that is the *effeta*.[4] *Ild.* describes the anointing as of the ears and mouth, as in the gospel account, not of the ears and nostrils, as in John the Deacon and St Ambrose. It was considered a preparation for the delivery of the creed which took place on the same day.[5]

The *ordo* for Palm Sunday in *L.O.* does not preserve the rite of the *effeta*. The previously mentioned order for the exorcism of an unclean spirit, however, directs the clergy to form in two choirs "as is the custom at the *effeta* on Palm Sunday". The *ordo* for baptism *quolibet tempore* provides the following form:

> Effeta, effeta, with the Holy Spirit unto an odour of sweetness, effeta. He hath done all things well: he maketh the deaf to hear and the dumb to speak.[6]

The anointing of the *effeta* is described in the Palm Sunday rites of the *Antifonario Visigótico* of León,[7] hereafter cited as *Ant.* The rite begins after the second antiphon of mattins with the blessing of the oil

---

[1] *L.O.*, col. 73.

[2] *Ild.* mentions the giving of the salt, but it was apparently not the custom of his own Church. He allows it as an ancient custom, but without Scriptural basis (*Ild.*, 26).

[3] *Ild.*, 21.   [4] *Ild.*, 27.   [5] *Ild.*, 29, 34.

[6] *L.O.*, col. 28; trans. in Whitaker, *Documents*, p. 108.   [7] *Ant.*, pp. 243f.

of the catechumens. The bishop breathes thrice on the oil and says the exorcism, "I exorcize thee, creature of oil." This is probably the form preserved in *Gel.* under the title *Item olei exorcizati confectio*.[1] This form is closely related to that given in *Ordo* III of *L.O.*, apparently intended to serve as a blessing for both oil of the catechumens and oil of the sick.[2]

The exorcism of the oil is followed by the blessing "Almighty God who createst", presumably parallel to the *benedictio* in *L.O.* which follows the aforementioned exorcism in *Ordo* III. An antiphon is then sung praising the unguent of olive oil with which the tabernacle and all the sacred vessels of the Lord were anointed. At the end of the antiphon the candidates are exorcized. They are then signed by various clerics and brought to the bishop *ad oleandum*. He performs the *effeta*, making the sign of the cross on their ears and mouths, and using the formula quoted above from *L.O.* The bishop sings the "Effeta, effeta . . ." over each child, and the choir responds, "He hath done all things well . . .".

According to *L.O.* the anointing is followed by a laying on of hands, accompanied by a long cento of Luke 1.17, 68–78, concluding with a prayer in which we find this petition:

> Thou who art anointed by the Father with the oil of gladness above thy fellows. O Lord, pour upon these people the blessing of thy grace . . .[3]

After this prayer the *traditio symboli* takes place. According to *Ild.* there is also a *redditio symboli*, on Maundy Thursday. The text is found in *L.O.*, col. 184–7.

The *Orational Visigótico*, believed by its editor to derive from the Church of Tarragona earlier than the year 711, includes among the prayers for Palm Sunday three with baptismal references. The last of these prays:

> Behold, O Lord Jesus, great and good high priest, thy people . . . that anointed with the sacred ointment (*unguine sacro linita*) they may become a royal priesthood, an holy nation . . .[4]

The *illatio* for Palm Sunday in the *Liber Mozarabicus Sacramentorum*[5] also contains baptismal references, but makes no mention of the specific rites of that day.

Ant. tells us that at the offertory of the mass chrism was placed upon

[1] *Gel.*, p. 63, n. 389.   [2] *L.O.*, col. 22–3.
[3] *L.O.*, col. 28, trans. in Whitaker, p. 108.
[4] op. cit. (ed. José Vives), p. 245, n. 764.
[5] op. cit. (ed. Férotin), 224–5, n. 541.

the altar, "and that whole mass said over the vessel".[1] Nothing is said about consecrating the chrism, and no Mozarabic form for the purpose survives. This has given rise to various speculations, such as that the placing of the chrism upon the altar during mass sufficed to consecrate it, or that the same blessing was used for the oil of the catechumens. These theories are discussed by H. B. Porter, who concludes:

> It appears to the present writer, however, that they overplay the negative evidence. On the one hand, some of the several formulae we have just been considering may some day be identified as of Spanish origin. On the other hand, none of the surviving Spanish books is intended to give a complete collection of pontifical formulae, hence its absence is not surprising.[2]

From the description in *Ant.* cited above of the placing of the chrism on the altar for the Palm Sunday mass, we may infer that the chrism was episcopally blessed at this time, although the case cannot be considered proven.[3]

The rites of Palm Sunday in Spain, as in Gaul and Milan, must have been among the most impressive of the year. The procession of palms, the presence in church of the young *competentes*, their exorcism and anointing, followed by the delivery of the creed, would have been an outstanding event in the annual cycle, particularly if it was also the occasion of the consecration of chrism. The day is called *Dies Unctionis* by *Ild.*,[4] and its gospel included the account of the anointing of Jesus at Bethany.[5]

The actual baptismal rites took place at the Easter vigil. Ildephonsus says plainly:

> That baptism be celebrated only on two days, Easter and Pentecost, at the seats (*sedes*) of legitimate bishops and in their presence, both apostolic and patristic antiquity has appointed.[6]

By the time of *L.O.* the restriction was no longer observed, and we find an *ordo* for baptism *quolibet tempore*. Like his predecessors, *Ild.* expects that the bishop will be the normal minister of baptism, and he forbids the presbyters of nearby towns to baptize, but permits it "in the

---

[1] *Ant.*, p. 249.

[2] *The Reform of Holy Baptism*, p. 331.

[3] We may compare this with the pontifical form for the solemn consecration of oil for the sick on the feast of the Holy Physicians Cosmas and Damian (*L.O.*, col. 69–71). cf. H.B. Porter, op. cit., p. 333.

[4] *Ild.*, 34.   [5] *Liber Comicus* (ed. Perez and Gonzales), Vol. I, p. 319.

[6] *Ild.*, 108 (*P.L.*, 96, 157).

churches of distant parishes". The right of administering baptism, he says, is confined to the priest, that is to the bishop and presbyter, although deacons, clerks (*clerici*), and even laymen (*fideles*) may baptize in case of necessity, "that no one may depart from this world without this life-giving (*vitale*) medicine".[1] In this Ildephonsus is faithful to the view expounded by the Spanish councils. He would, nevertheless, make no concession about the time of the rite.

> Outside these two times it is permitted to baptize at any time only on account of the necessity of death.[2]

Apparently the exception had become the rule between the seventh and eleventh centuries.

The rites of the Easter vigil began with the blessing of the paschal candle and the reading of the prophecies. After the third lesson, from Isa. 55, the bishop went to the baptistery, which had been sealed since the beginning of Lent, and reopened it with prayer. *L.O.* directs that the chrism and the Communion be placed upon the baptistery altar.[3]

The bishop then blessed the font, with the sign of the cross, exorcism, and the pouring in of oil.[4] *L.O.* does not give the prayers for the blessing at the Easter vigil, but simply states, "Baptism is then celebrated in order", and we must look for the forms in the *ordo quolibet tempore*.[5] They included the pouring of the blessed oil into the water in the form of a cross, and generally fulfil the description in *Ild.*[6]

The renunciation of the devil and baptism followed the blessing of the font. The peculiar Mozarabic features of this rite are a single immersion, and the addition of the phrase "that thou mayest have eternal life" to the baptismal formula. The single immersion was a protest against the Arians, and *Ild.* explains this as baptism into the one Godhead.[7]

The baptism was followed by the anointing with chrism. "When he is led forth from the water, while a hymn of joy at liberation is sung, he is taken to the touch of the holy chrism, that he may be anointed by

---

[1] *Ild.*, 116 (*P.L.*, 96, 159). [2] *Ild.*, 108 (*P.L.* 96, 157).

[3] *Ild.*, 107, 108; L.O., col. 217. [4] *Ild.*, 109. [5] L.O. col. 29–31.

[6] *Missale Mixtum* has a different blessing of the font, a variant of *Gal. Vet.* n. 168, which is the source of the series of short petitions in the blessing of the font in the First Prayer Book of Edward VI.

[7] *Ild.*, 110–12, 117; L.O. col. 32; cf. my "Mozarabic Baptismal Rites", in *Studia Liturgica*, Vol. 3 (1964), pp. 80ff.

the Spirit of God, and may be called Christian from the anointing and name of Christ."[1] *L.O.* directs the priest (*sacerdos*) to chrismate the neophyte, "making the sign of the cross on his forehead alone". The formula given is:

> The sign of eternal life which God the Father Almighty has given through Jesus Christ his Son to them that believe unto salvation.[2]

In the manuscripts of both *L.O.* and *Ant.* this formula is accompanied by muscial notation.

Ild. explains the meaning of the chrism at length. It is derived from the unguent compounded by Moses in Leviticus, with which the high priest and the king were anointed. But under the Christian dispensation, "not only priests and kings, but the whole Church is consecrated with the anointing of holy chrism, because it is the most holy member of the eternal King and Priest".[3] He attaches two meanings to the unction: christological and pneumatological.

From the *chrisma* we receive the name of Christian and we are united with the Χριστός as members of the royal and priestly nation whom he has called. It is also the anointing of the Holy Spirit, which bathes the inner man as the chrism anoints the exterior, and by which he comes to dwell in us to fulfil us with the fire of his love, and it is the sign with which we are sealed unto the day of redemption. Ildephonsus identifies this unction with that of 1 John 2.20–7, speaking of it as the *sacramentum* of the "invisible unction of the Holy Spirit".[4]

Having said these things about the anointing, Ildephonsus describes the laying on of hands. "After baptism the Holy Spirit is aptly given with the imposition of hands. For this the Apostle is shown to have done in the Acts of the Apostles." The example of St Paul in Acts 19.1–17 is first quoted, and then that of St Peter and St John in Acts 8.14.[5] *Ild.* also gives as a Scriptural reference for the laying on of hands the example of our Lord in Mark 10. 13, 14.[6]

Certainly there is some confusion in *Ild.* about the meaning of the laying on of hands. It seems almost as if he is giving two alternative interpretations of the rite. In the first the unction is identified with the royal and priestly calling of Christians, and the Spirit is given by the laying on of the priest's hand. The second interpretation speaks of the anointing of the Holy Spirit, and of the hand of blessing laid on the

---

[1] *Ild.*, 122.   [2] *L.O.*, col. 33.   [3] *Ild.*, 123.
[4] *Ild.*, 123–5 (*P.L.*, 96, 163).   [5] *Ild.*, 129 (*P.L.*, 96, 165).   [6] *Ild.*, 127.

faithful by the priest, following the example of Christ, who said, "Suffer the little children to come unto me."

We may, perhaps, understand the confusion if we note that Ildephonsus continues his discussion of the laying on of hands by quoting the letter of Innocent to Decentius, probably not directly, but through the *de Ecclesiasticis Officiis* of St Isidore, from which he quotes many passages.[1] Dom de Puniet has accused Ildephonsus of having "the unhappy talent of expressing the contrary of his thought",[2] and he certainly has placed passages gleaned from different sources in juxtaposition, so that he appears to ascribe identical effects to both the anointing and the laying on of hands. If we look at his summary of the rites, both in the passage quoted earlier from the *de Itinere Deserti* and in the following passages, we shall see that it is the anointing, rather than the laying on of hands, which he emphasizes:

> After the washing of the font, after the renewal of life, after the unction of the Spirit, the man is to be taught to pray with the words of truth.[3]

> After the regeneration of spiritual birth, after the grace of the heavenly unction, after the teaching of the Lord's Prayer, after the invocation of the divine Fatherhood, let him come to participate in the heavenly banquet.[4]

In *L.O.* two prayers are given for the laying on of hands. The first is for use *quolibet tempore* and the second *in Vigilia Paschae*. The first prayer speaks of the unction of chrism which God has commanded to follow the administration of baptism, concluding, "that, confirmed in the Name of the Trinity, they may be worthy through the chrism to become Christs, and through Christ to become Christians".[5] The anointing is here taken in the closest possible connection with the laying on of hands, so that Férotin can state in his notes,

> This prayer for the imposition of hands and the anointing which preceded it constitute the sacrament of confirmation.[6]

Certainly our reading of *Ild.* confirms his opinion. The second prayer expands the catalogue of the gifts of the Spirit with an *ut* clause after the mention of each gift, but it too refers to the neophytes "who have been anointed (*delibuti*) with the chrism of the divine unction'.[7]

L.O. directs that the imposition of hands be followed by the veiling

---

[1] Isidore, op. cit., 27 (*P.L.*, 83, 825–6).
[2] "Onction et Confirmation", loc. cit., p. 456.
[3] *Ild.*, 132 (*P.L.*, 96, 166A).   [4] *Ild.*, 136 (*P.L.*, 96, 186C).
[5] *L.O.*, col. 33–4.   [6] ibid., note 1.   [7] *L.O.*, col. 36–7.

of the neophytes' heads and the administration of Communion. It had ordered the chrism placed on the altar of the baptistery in the *ordo* of the Easter Vigil, and we may therefore presume that the children were communicated from the reserved Sacrament, even though the mass was to follow later in the rite. Undoubtedly in an earlier period adult catechumens would have been communicated at the Easter mass.

Ild. states that they were taught the Lord's Prayer before being communicated. The Easter *ordo* in *L.O.* continues after the baptism with the fourth lesson and the rest of the ceremonies of the vigil. Both *Ild.* and *L.O.* expect the baptismal robe to be returned on the third day after the baptism, *Ild.* providing a sermon and *L.O.* a blessing for the occasion.[1]

Our discussion of these rites would not be complete without considering the forms for the reception of those baptized in heresy. *Ild.* tells us that heretics baptized in the name of the Trinity are not to be rebaptized, "but to be cleansed by chrism alone and the laying on of a hand".[2] *L.O.* preserves three such forms: for the reconciliation of Arians, Donatists, and "him who has been baptized in heresy from the Catholic faith", together with a prayer for a converted Jew which Férotin believes to be unique in Western rites.[3] The form for the Arians was undoubtedly the most used and is the fullest. It contains a specific renunciation of the Arian christology and pneumatology, and the three credal questions. They are immediately followed by this formula:

> And I anoint thee with chrism in the name of the Father, and of the Son, and of the Holy Spirit, for the remission of all thy sins, that thou mayest have eternal life. Amen.[4]

No rubric is given, but it is clear that the priest is to anoint the person with chrism. After this he lays his hand upon him and says the *oratio confirmationis*. This is a variant of the prayer in the baptismal rite, and prays for the seven gifts of the Holy Spirit. The connection of the anointing with the laying on of hands in this order is a powerful witness to the close association in which the post-baptismal anointing and the imposition of hands were held in Spain.[5] Considering this rite in connection with that of baptism, we must agree with Dom de Puniet,

---

[1] *Ild.*, 142; *L.O.*, col. 145.   [2] *Ild.*, 121 (*P.L.*, 96, 161).   [3] *L.O.*, col. 100–7.
[4] *L.O.*, col. 102.

[5] The other two forms speak more of the reconciliation of penitent sinners than of the bestowal of any gift of the Spirit.

"For the Spaniards, to receive the anointing with chrism is to receive the Holy Spirit."[1]

The Mozarabic baptismal rites in their totality are generally similar to the Gallican rites we examined in the previous section, although they differ in particular details. They differ sharply from the Roman rite in having a single post-baptismal anointing, the signing of the forehead with the sign of the cross. Undoubtedly the Spanish presbyters, like the Sardinian presbyters of whom Gregory the Great wrote, were accustomed to perform the entire rite, including the anointing and the laying on of hands. *Ild.* and *L.O.* expect that the bishop will officiate at the solemn baptisms of Easter (and Pentecost) in his own cathedral, but in the remote parishes, and in the baptisms *quolibet tempore* when they became general, the presbyter was undoubtedly the customary officiant.

The Mozarabic writers considered the bishop to be the proper minister of baptism, but, in spite of isolated attempts to restrict the practice in accordance with Roman customs,[2] they customarily delegated presbyters to act for them, using chrism consecrated by them for the anointing, and, as long as the minister was a *sacerdos*, they considered that they were complying with ancient and apostolic custom.

Baptism in Spain was a single rite. There is no trace of a perambulation of the diocese by the bishop to administer confirmation. The decrees of the councils requiring those clinically baptized to be brought to the bishop for the *benedictio*, or laying on of hands, refer only to those baptized by deacons or laymen. The baptism, the anointing, and Communion were customarily administered together, and although those baptized under unusual circumstances might receive the anointing and the Eucharist at a later time, they were still thought of as one rite.

THE NORTH ITALIAN RITES

The principal North Italian rite is the Ambrosian liturgy of the Church of Milan, which has maintained its existence in the old archiepiscopal province of Milan to the present day. The medieval Ambrosian liturgy is preserved in the surviving Ambrosian sacramentaries, in the three volumes of Magistretti's *Monumenta Veteris Liturgiae Ambrosianae*, hereafter cited as *Pont. Amb.* and *Man. Amb.* I and II, and in *Beroldus*, hereafter cited as *Ber.*, a twelfth-century description of the ceremonial

---

[1] "Onction et Confirmation", p. 459.

[2] For example, Con. Hispanense II, Canon 7 (Mansi, X, 599).

of the cathedral church compiled by its *magister ceremoniarum* as a guide for the participants. A few fragments have also been published by Giovanni Mercati under the title *Antiche Reliquie Liturgiche Ambrosiani e Romani*, including the forms for consecrating chrism and blessing oil from the Ambrosian order for consecrating a church.

An edition of the Sacramentary of Biasca, dating from the ninth or tenth century, was projected by Dr Antonio Ceriani, prefect of the Ambrosian Library, and it exists in manuscript form in the Vatican Library and in the Capitular Library in Milan. Mohlberg plans an edition of this work in his series *Rerum Ecclesiasticarum Documenta*. The Sacramentary of Bergamo was edited by Paul Cagin in an edition published in 1900, but the volume is not readily available. A new edition by Dr Angelo Paredi, which we shall cite as *Berg.*, appeared in 1962. Dr Paredi has also published an edition of the early eleventh-century *Sacramentarium Heriberti*, but it is well hidden in a memorial volume of studies dedicated to Adriano Bernareggi, Bishop of Bergamo. Both books are in the series *Monumenta Bergomensia*. There is Ambrosian material in the *Sacramentarium Triplex*, compiled, according to Mohlberg, in 1010, but this is available only in Gerbert's *Monumenta Veteris Liturgiae Alemannicae*, issued in 1777, an edition which Bourque warns us must be used with extreme caution. An edition of this in Mohlberg's R.E.D. series is now in preparation.

In addition to the Ambrosian rites, we shall examine the North Italian rite published by Dom Lambot in the volume *North Italian Services of the Eleventh Century*, which will be cited as *North*, and that described in the three tracts on baptism ascribed to Maximus of Turin.

In an earlier section we discussed the testimony of St Ambrose, and we shall therefore pass at once to an examination of the rite as it appears in the Milanese liturgical books. In these Lent was a period of intensive preparation for Holy Baptism. The names of the *competentes* were "given" on the Sunday *de Samaritana* at the beginning of Lent.[1] Three scrutinies are assigned to the following Saturdays, called *de Abraham*, *de caeco*, and *de Lazaro*.[2] We may infer from the fact that the *traditio symboli*, placed by St Ambrose on Palm Sunday, is assigned to the fifth Saturday in *Man. Amb.* and *Berg.* that the scrutinies were originally held on the Lenten Sundays. We may also see a reflection of this in the direction in *Ber.*:

---

[1] *Man. Amb.* II, p. 135; *Ber.*, p. 82.   [2] *Man. Amb.* II, p. 169.

The same order is to be observed at each scrutiny, and [*or even*] (*et*) on Sundays, after the gospel, up to Palm Sunday.[1]

A prominent feature of the Ambrosian scrutinies was the blessing of ashes and the placing of them on a goatskin on the floor of the church.[2] St Ildephonsus of Toledo apparently knows the same custom in Spain, for he speaks of the children being led to the anointing over a carpet of goatskin.[3] *Ber.* assigns an anointing to the third scrutiny, on the *sabbatum de Lazaro*. The Roman *Canones ad Gallos* also assigned the pre-baptismal anointing to the third scrutiny.

> On the Saturday of Lazarus, all the children, male and female, are to be enrolled, and after the deacon's questioning, two presbyters vested in alb and stole stand at the doors where the catechumens are to enter, and two doorkeepers hold the sanctified oil, and anoint the children on the breast and say: *I anoint thee with the oil of salvation in Christ Jesus the Lord unto eternal life.*[4]

The same form is found in *Man. Amb.* in an order for making catechumens, apparently intended for presbyteral use outside the solemn times.[5]

The Ambrosian pre-baptismal anointing is directly connected with the exorcizing ceremonies of the scrutinies. It is clearly related to the Mozarabic pre-baptismal unction and to what we believe to have been the Gallican practice. It also has similarities to Roman usage. The *interrogatio diaconi* of *Ber.* is the renunciation of the devil, which in Ambrosian practice was repeated at each scrutiny. In Rome, as we have seen, the pre-baptismal anointing took place on Holy Saturday, following the renunciations and the *effeta*. We may, perhaps, find the connecting links between these practices in the writings of St Ambrose and John the Deacon. In *de Sacramentis* the *effeta*, the anointing with oil, and the renunciations take place in that order. In John the Deacon the *effeta*, performed with oil, and an anointing of the breast are described as "after the renunciation of the devil", but are a part of the scrutinies. In all of these descriptions the anointing is an exorcizing rite associated with the renunciation of the devil and the ending of his influence over the catechumen. It formed the climax of the preparatory rites. St

---

[1] *Ber.*, p. 83; trans. in Whitaker, p. 138.
[2] *Ber.*, p. 92; cf. my "Ambrosian Baptismal Rites", in *Studia Liturgica*, Vol. I (1962), pp. 241ff.
[3] *Ild.* 14; see above, p. 136.   [4] *Ber.*, p. 94; trans. in Whitaker, p. 140.
[5] *Man. Amb.* II, p. 467.

Ambrose does not describe any scrutinies, but he does tell of instructing his adult catechumens during Lent.[1] The rites which he describes on Holy Saturday were the completion of this preparation with the formal renunciation and anointing. John the Deacon also speaks of the *effeta* and anointing as coming at the end of the scrutinies. Canon 8 *ad Gallos* appears to refer to the custom, presumably of some Gallican bishops, of anointing on many days, and dismisses the number of anointings as of secondary importance.[2] Canon 3 of the Council of Mâcon speaks of bringing the *competentes certis diebus* for imposition of hands (i.e. exorcism) and anointing.[3] The *ordo scrutiniorum* in *North* includes an anointing at each scrutiny.[4] We may envisage the probability of several pre-baptismal anointings. The *competentes* would be anointed at each scrutiny, and at the final preparation on the morning of Holy Saturday. The point of view represented by the aforementioned canon *ad Gallos* prevailed, however, and in the rites which we have already examined all but one anointing has been dropped. Different local Churches have retained it upon different occasions, but always at the climax of their pre-baptismal ceremonies: Spain at the *traditio symboli* on Palm Sunday; Rome, originally at the corresponding ceremony of the third scrutiny, but later on Holy Saturday morning; and Milan on the *sabbatum de Lazaro*.

The Ambrosian books provide for the blessing of the baptismal oils on Maundy Thursday, for which the Milanese name is *feria quinta in authentica*. The rite is described by *Ber.* and the forms are contained in *Pont. Amb.* and *Berg.*[5] *Ber.* speaks of the blessing of the oil for the sick at this time also, but the *ordo* in *Pont. Amb.* and *Berg.* provides no form for the purpose.[6]

The blessing follows the *oratio super oblatam* of the mass. The sub-deacons go to the chapel where the oil has been prepared and bear it into the church "with great reverence". The deacon receives it and places it upon the altar. The bishop then begins the *confessio principalis chrismatis*. *Ber.* says that he begins with the exorcism, "I exorcize thee, creature of oil, through God the Father almighty." The same direction is given in the thirteenth-century manuscript called *Beroldus novus* printed by Magistretti as *II Ordo* for the blessing of the oils in *Pont.*

---

[1] *de Mysteriis*, I.I.   [2] Mansi, III, 1137.   [3] ibid., IX, 1951.
[4] *North*, p. 10.
[5] *Ber.*, pp. 102–4; *Pont. Amb.*, pp. 98ff; *Berg.* p. 155, nn. 485–7.
[6] Forms for blessing the oil of the sick are given in *Man. Amb.* I, pp. 79, 147, to be used at the visitation of the sick.

Amb.[1] This is presumably the exorcism given in *Gel.* for the exorcizing of the oil of the catechumens *ad succurendum*,[2] which is also provided for the same purpose in *Man. Amb.*[3] Two manuscripts of *Man. Amb.* direct the priest to use it to bless pre-baptismal oil in case of necessity, "if you do not have oil consecrated by the bishop". This exorcism appears to be a Roman importation into the Ambrosian rite. A Gallican-type bidding is provided in the older Ambrosian sources. This is given by Magistretti in his first *ordo*, in *Triplex*, in *Berg.*, and in Mercati's *Ordo Ambrosianus ad Consecrandam Ecclesiam*.[4] It reads:

> In unity and concord, dearest brethren, let us beseech the merciful help of God the Father almighty, that he may strengthen with heavenly benediction and the firmness of his power, this ointment, with which his people is to be clothed in regal glory, and by his shield preserve his people blessed for ever. By the mediation of our Lord Jesus Christ, who with him and the Holy Spirit liveth and reigneth throughout all ages.

We may note that the reference to being clothed in royal glory is reminiscent of the Gallican description of the chrism as a robe, and also of the anointing of kings, so prominently mentioned from the time of Hippolytus.

Our sources agree that the actual blessing of the chrism, which followed either the bidding or the exorcism, was cast in the form of a eucharistic preface of which the distinctive opening words were "dominator Domine Deus, rex unctus, auctor unguendi".[5] The preface speaks of the royal anointing of the Christian given in the name of Christ, the Anointed King, whose Name is *de chrismate*. It describes those to be anointed as "signed with this holy chrism", and the anointing itself as "the sign of the cross, the seal of the forehead (*signum frontis*), and the title of the holy warrior (*bellator*)". The chrism is primarily the means of affixing the *forma crucis* to the forehead of the Christian warrior, who is described as *signifer*. When we examine the anointing with chrism in the baptismal rite, we shall see the importance of this clear statement of the purpose of the chrism.

The consecration of the chrism is followed by the blessing of the oil of the catechumens. *Ber.* and *Beroldus novus* again direct an exorcism,

---

[1] *Ber.*, p. 103; *Pont. Amb.*, p. 106.
[2] *Gel.*, p. 97, n. 617.   [3] *Man. Amb.*, II, p. 446.
[4] *Pont. Amb.*, p. 98; Gerbert, op. cit., Vol. 1, p. 75; *Berg.*, p. 155.
[5] *Ber.*, p. 103; *Pont. Amb.*, p. 98; *Berg.*, p. 155; *Triplex*, p. 75; Mercati, op. cit., p. 21.

"I exorcize thee, creature of oil, in the name of God the Father."[1] Magistretti identifies this with the form having the same *incipit* in *Gel.*[2] The proper Ambrosian form follows. This alone is given in *Berg.* and *Codex Heriberti.*[3] The blessing itself speaks of this oil as that with which the heads and hearts of pontiffs are anointed, "whom in this creature thou hast shown the nobility of an excellent name, that through it thou mightest make them Christs". It asks for the pouring out of the Holy Spirit upon the oil:

> ... that whoever in human kind shall have been touched with it may soon pass over to a heavenly nature; nor may the ancient foe lay any claim upon him after the anointing.

Certainly the opening phrases of the prayer seem more apt for the consecration of chrism than for the oil of the catechumens. The noble name can hardly be anything other than *chrisma*. There is, of course, reason to believe that *chrisma* could bear a more general meaning than it does to-day. *Ber.*'s mention of the *principalis chrisma* lends itself readily to the idea that there were other lesser *chrismae*. The form for blessing oil of the sick in *Gel.*, which is also appointed in *Ber.*, speaks of that oil as *chrisma tuum perfectum*. Unquestionably this form raises many problems which do not admit of ready solutions. From reading the texts of the chrismal preface and the blessing of the oil, one gains the impression that the principal (or perhaps princely) chrism was an oil for signing the cross, while this lesser oil was used for anointing, whether of catechumens or bishops. Certainly the clear Roman distinction between exorcized and blessed oil is completely lacking in *Ber.*, which provides both an exorcism and a blessing for chrism, for baptismal oil, and for the oil of the sick. It is interesting that the exorcism appointed by *Ber.* for use with the chrism is provided in *Man. Amb.* for the emergency use of presbyters to exorcize oil of the catechumens. *Pont. Amb.* provides two additional blessings of oil "for catechumens or the sick", from an Ambrosian ritual of the fourteenth century.[4] The first is a general prayer for blessing oil for anointing or drinking, and the second is a form for use at the unction of the sick.

We may now turn to the actual baptismal rites of the Holy Sabbath. The renunciations, *effeta*, and anointing described by St Ambrose have disappeared. The rite begins with the *benedictio fontis*, which forms a part of the vigil ceremonies, coming after the blessing of the new fire

---

[1] *Ber.*, p. 104; *Pont. Amb.*, p. 107. [2] *Gel.*, p. 63, n. 389; see above, p. 105.
[3] *Berg.*, p. 155, n. 487; *Pont. Amb.*, p. 99. [4] *Pont. Amb.*, p. 109.

and paschal candle, and the reading of six prophecies. The blessing of
the font, which contains elements found in *Gel.*, *Gal. Vet.*, and *L.O.*,[1]
concludes with the pouring of chrism into the water. *Ber.* describes this,
in the pontifical rite, as being performed with a silver spoon (*coclear
argentum*), by means of which the archbishop pours the chrism into the
font three times in the form of a cross, saying each time:

> May this font be hallowed, sanctified, and anointed in the name of the
> Father, and of the Son, and of the Holy Ghost. Amen.[2]

In the rite described by *Ber.* only three children are baptized: three
boys to be named Peter, Paul, and John. It is the obvious intention of
the *magister ceremoniarum* to see the ancient rites of the cathedral church
performed properly, without any concession to the press of numbers.
The archbishop himself asks the three credal questions and gives orders
to a presbyter and a deacon who have entered the font, to baptize them
in the Triune Name. Three immersions are made, and the declarative
formula is used.[3]

Following the baptism a short litany is said over the neophytes,
during which the archbishop kneels.

> After the litany the archbishop chrismates the aforesaid baptized children on
> the forehead (*in frontibus*) in the form of a cross.[4]

Man. Amb. directs the presbyter to perform the anointing, "making
a cross with chrism on the child's head (*in celebro*)".[5] The prayer
assigned is the chrismal prayer which we have examined in a variety
of sources already.[6] This signing immediately after baptism is the only
unction with chrism provided in the Ambrosian books. The direction
in *Man. Amb.* that the presbyter is to anoint the *cerebrum* instead of the
frons is unquestionably a modification of the original practice in accordance with the directions of Pope Innocent I that only bishops might sign
the forehead. The wording of the prayer for consecrating the chrism
makes it clear that it is *signum frontis* which is envisaged, and the early
eleventh-century *Sacramentarium Heriberti* clearly directs the *sacerdos*
to make the chrismation *in fronte*.[7]

Distinguished Ambrosian scholars, such as Dr Marco Magistretti,
do not hesitate to call the rite described by *Ber.* confirmation, and, until

---

[1] *Man. Amb.* II, pp. 205–7; cf. also my "Ambrosian Baptismal Rites", pp. 246f.
[2] *Ber.*, pp. 111f.   [3] *Ber.*, p. 112; *Man. Amb.* II, pp. 207f.
[4] *Ber.*, p. 112 (*Beroldus novus*, *Man. Amb.* II, p. 209, n. 2, reads "in cerebro").
[5] *Man. Amb.* II, p. 209.   [6] See Diagram on p. 122 above.
[7] op. cit., ed. Paredi, p. 400.

the introduction of the Roman Pontifical in modern times, there has been no other Ambrosian rite of confirmation. The present writer fully accepts Magistretti's conclusion, and, moreover, can see no grounds for distinguishing the episcopal consignation of *Ber.* from the presbyteral signing of *Man. Amb.* If one is confirmation, the other must be accepted as confirmation as well.

When we consider Gallican, Ambrosian, and Mozarabic practice together, we see a substantial agreement. The single anointing with chrism following baptism, whether performed by bishop or presbyter, must be equated, as far as its effects are concerned, with the Roman episcopal consignation, or confirmation. The *spiritale signaculum* described by St Ambrose, like the laying on of hands known to St Hilary of Poitiers, has disappeared, and we must either assign the full effect of the initiatory rite to that rite as it stands in the Ambrosian liturgical books, or assert that a separate grace of confirmation was lost to the Churches of Milan and Gaul for a considerable period.

Actually the theological problem need not be so difficult as it is for the modern Roman Catholic theologian, who is committed to the position that there is a separate grace of confirmation for which he must find a place in any Catholic liturgy. If we believe in the essential integrity of the rite of Christian initiation, we can accept the position that certain parts of this rite, such as the laying on of hands in the East and in large parts of the West, or the anointing in the Anglican Church, can be omitted by local Churches without any loss of sacramental grace.

A further bond between the Ambrosian and Gallican rites is provided by the foot-washing, performed by the bishop after the anointing.[1] In the pontifical rite of *Ber.* the bishop leaves after the *pedelavium* to celebrate mass at the church of St Ambrose, and the presbyters return to the font to baptize and anoint the remaining children.

In addition to the solemn forms for Easter, *Man. Amb.* provides a shorter form for the baptism of the sick. The form for making a catechumen which precedes it contains the exorcism of oil previously discussed, and the form for the anointing quoted above from *Ber.* as part of the ceremonies of the Saturday of Lazarus.[2]

The baptism itself is followed by the anointing *in cerebro*, with the customary form, a single prayer and the administration of Communion by intinction.[3]

---

[1] *Ber.*, p. 112; *Man. Amb.* II, p. 209.   [2] *Man. Amb.* II, pp. 466–72.
[3] ibid. p. 473.

In addition to the Ambrosian rites of Milan, the use of North Italy is represented by a collection of ceremonies in an eleventh or twelfth-century manuscript belonging to the Ambrosian Library at Milan which has been published by the Henry Bradshaw Society under the title *North Italian Services*, which we shall abbreviate *North*. The manuscript begins with an almost illegible *ordo* of which the nature is unknown, and contains a rite for baptism *in extremis*, extensive provision for scrutinies, an order for baptism, and some other rites. Although attempts have been made to identify these forms with a particular locality,[1] their editor, Dom Lambot, assigns them simply to an unknown Italian city, perhaps as early as the eighth century.[2]

The scrutinies are highly unusual, involving at least thirteen sessions. As a prelude to the exorcisms the catechumens were anointed on the breast by a deacon (*Diaconus signet pectus cum oleo sancto*) with the formula:

I sign thee with the sign of the living God for the preservation (*ad tuitionem*) of thy life.[3]

On the Friday before Palm Sunday the *effeta* was performed.[4] The gospel was the Markan account of the healing of the deaf mute. After its reading the customary anointing of the candidates by the deacon took place, followed by consignations and exorcisms. The presbyter then touched the mouths and ears of the candidates with his own spittle, saying, "Effeta by the power of Christ our God." The anointing of the mouth rather than the nostrils, and the use of spittle appear to be deliberate imitations of the Gospel account which had been read at the service.

The repetition of the anointing before the exorcisms of each scrutiny is thoroughly consistent with our reconstruction of ancient customs. While various other Churches adopted a single anointing, the unknown city represented by *North* continued to anoint the catechumens at each pre-baptismal session.

Dom Lambot does not believe that the actual baptismal forms in *North* are as old as the *ordo scrutiniorum*, but assigns them to the class of "eighth-century Gelasian" orders.[5] The incomplete order with which the book opens is apparently a condensed order for admitting cate-

---

[1] G. Morin, "Sur la date et la provenance de l'*ordo scrutiniorum*", in *Revue Bénédictine*, Vol. 44 (1934), pp. 216–23.

[2] *North*, p. xxxiv.   [3] *North*, p. 10.   [4] *North*, pp. 15f.

[5] *North*, pp. xxxiv ff.

chumens, or for preparing them for baptism. It includes an anointing of the breast with holy oil, with the form used in the *ordo scrutiniorum*.[1] The *effeta* follows the exorcisms, and is in the Roman form. After the *effeta* are the renunciation of the devil and the anointing by the presbyter. He makes the sign of the cross on the breast and between the shoulders, saying:

> I anoint thee (*ego te unguo*) with the oil of sanctification, safe and secure unto the grace of the baptism of salvation. In the name of the Fa✠ther, and of the ✠ Son, and of the Holy✠ Ghost. Amen.[2]

These ceremonies correspond to the Roman rites for Saturday morning, and to the Ambrosian form for making a catechumen which precedes the order for private baptism in *Man. Amb.*

The actual order of baptism begins with the blessing of the font.[3] The prayers are those of *Gel.* with rubrics directing additional ceremonial. This, as we shall see, is typical of "eighth-century Gelasian" books. The chrism is poured into the font at the end of the blessing with the formula:

> In the name of the Holy Ghost the Paraclete may this font be sanctified and made fruitful, through the same Spirit who came down upon the river of Jordan.

A parallel form is found in *Ordo L*, a tenth-century Germanic composition, although without the reference to the Jordan, which, at least in the opinion of Dom Lambot, is original in the local rite of *North*.

The interrogative creed and baptism with the declarative formula follow. The presbyter is then directed to sign the neophytes, making a cross in chrism with his thumb. The chrismal prayer is given as in *Gel.*[4] The rite closes with the giving of the white garment and the Communion of the neophytes, administered in one kind.

Our remaining North Italian source is the group of three tractates on baptism traditionally ascribed to St Maximus of Turin, a fifth-century bishop.[5] Dom Bernard Capelle, in an article in *Revue Bénédictine*, has shown them to be the work of an unknown sixth-century North Italian bishop.[6]

---

[1] *North*, p. 4.   [2] *North*, p. 6.   [3] *North*, pp. 32ff.

[4] See Diagram on p. 122 above. The *incipit* is "deus pater omnipotens" and *linit* is corrected to *lineat*. Otherwise it is *Gel.*, p.74, n. 450.

[5] *P.L.*, 57, 771–8.

[6] "Les *Tractatus de Baptismo* attribués à Saint Maxime de Turin", Vol. 14 (1934), pp. 108–18.

The first tractate explains the *effeta*, the second the baptism itself, and the third the anointing with chrism. The *effeta* is performed with *oleum benedictionis*, and the ears and nostrils are anointed, to prepare us for the hearing of faith and the good odour of Christ to which we are called. The baptism itself follows the interrogative creed. In the third tractate he continues:

> When baptism is completed, we pour upon (*infundimus*) the head the chrism, that is the oil of sanctification, by which the royal and priestly dignity is shown to be conferred by the Lord upon him who has been baptized.

He continues with a catena of Biblical references, first to the Old Testament anointing of priests and kings, then to the First Epistle of St Peter, identifying the Christian believer with the *regale sacerdotium*. The final rite which he describes is the foot-washing.

Pseudo-Maximus describes no rite of laying on of hands, and only a single unction. *Infundimus* is reminiscent of the Gallican, rather than the Ambrosian method of anointing. He explains the anointing in terms which do not refer to the Holy Spirit. It is, as in Tertullian, a royal and priestly anointing. It is in the font that he sees the working of the Holy Spirit.

> The Holy Spirit indeed works in that water, that they who before baptism were charged with diverse crimes and were going to labour with the devil in the Gehenna of eternal fire, after baptism are made worthy to enter the kingdom of heaven.

The only episcopal rite which might correspond to confirmation which we have found in any of the North Italian sources is the anointing of the forehead in the solemn rites of Easter described by *Ber*.[1] It appears that in the matter of the post-baptismal anointing North Italy and Gaul represent the same tradition, that of a single chrismation. It seems clear that no additional rite was contemplated and that all of the benefits of the sacrament were conferred in a single rite, consisting of the immersion and anointing. Certainly the North Italian single anointing, like the foot-washing, is a point of contact with the rite of Gaul.

---

[1] An apparent exception is the *Liber de baptismo* of Archbishop Odilbert which includes a section *de impositione manus pontificis*. An examination of this work, however, will reveal that it is an answer to a series of questions put to various bishops by the Emperor Charlemagne on the basis of the official Roman rite, which he had introduced throughout his empire, and like the other respondents, Odilbert avoids mention of local usages and answers the questions on the basis of the Roman rite.

In North Italy, as in Spain and Gaul, baptism was a single rite, in which regeneration and the gift of the Holy Spirit were bestowed through the washing of water and the anointing with chrism. Whether the anointing was administered solemnly by the bishop or by the presbyter, it is the same anointing. There is but one blessing of the chrism, and that blessing in Milan hallowed it for the signing of the Christian warrior with the cross of his salvation, that he might bear it into the promised land.

THE GREGORIAN SACRAMENTARY

The baptismal rites of the Gregorian Sacramentary, hereafter abbreviated *Greg.*, are known to us principally through manuscripts derived from the exemplar sent by Pope Hadrian to Charlemagne, and described by him as the sacramentary of Pope Gregory.[1] The sacramentary was incomplete in many ways, lacking, for example, masses for the ordinary Sundays of the Church year, and was published with a supplement believed to be the work of Alcuin which provided additional material from Gallican or Gelasian sources. An excellent printed edition of *The Gregorian Sacramentary under Charles the Great* was edited by H. A. Wilson for the Henry Bradshaw Society from three of the most important manuscripts, Cambrai 164, Vat. Reg. 337, and Ottobonianus 313 (which includes the supplement). According to Emmanuel Bourque the *Hadrianum* represents the state of the Papal liturgy between 787 and 891.[2] We also possess a manuscript (Codex D 47 of the Capitular Library of Padua) which represents the Gregorian text as of about 683, but which, unfortunately, does not contain any of the formulas with which we are concerned. We shall therefore confine our attention to the *Hadrianum*, recognizing that it is the descendant of an earlier form of the *Gregorianum*.

Compared with the extensive initiatory material in *Gel.*, the rites of *Greg.* are simple and few. No scrutinies are provided. The blessing of oils is assigned to the single mass provided for Maundy Thursday.[3]

The blessing of the oil offered by the people takes place first, at the end of the canon before the final doxology, "per quem hec omnia domine semper bona creas . . ." The prayer is that appointed in *Gel.* for the blessing of the oil for the sick. The *benedictio chrismatis princi-*

---

[1] *P.L.*, 98, 463.
[2] *Études sur les Sacramentaires romains*, Pt. 1, p. 320.
[3] *Greg.*, pp. 48–50.

palis follows immediately in the text. There is no rubrical indication that it did not follow immediately in actual use, although both *Gel.* and the *ordines Romani* assign it a place later in the service.[1] The blessing, a *vere dignum*, is that provided in *Gel.* The *exorcismus olei* follows. The form is substantially that given in *Gel.*[2] No other special provisions are made, and the mass propers refer to the betrayal of Christ and the institution of the Eucharist. The traditional Roman order, blessing the chrism before exorcizing the oil of the catechumens, is followed, as in *Ap. Trad.* and the *ordines Romani*.

On Holy Saturday morning the *dominus papa* presides at the *redditio symboli* and delivers the final solemn exorcism. A formula for the *effeta* is not given, but the rubric directs:

> After this he touches individually the nose and ears and says to them *Effeta*. Afterward he touches the shoulders and breast with holy oil . . .[3]

The triple renunciations follow immediately, as in *Gel.* It is not clear how the *effeta* was to be performed, nor whether any formula other than the single word *effeta* was to accompany it. Presumably it would have been performed as in *Gel.*

For the vigil, only the prayers following the lessons, four in number, are given. The blessing of the font follows.[4] No form for baptism is given, but a rubric directs:

> The presbyter baptizes and anoints (*linit*) him with chrism on the head (*in cerebro*) and says.

The prayer which follows is the chrismal prayer, as in *Gel.*[5] Immediately after this prayer is the title *oratio ad infantes consignandos*, and a prayer for the sevenfold gifts of the Holy Ghost, the confirmation prayer of *Gel.*, but with the opening and closing phrases altered.[6] No rubrical indication of the ceremonial of the consignation is given, but the last line of the prayer reads:

> . . . and sign (*consigna*) them with the sign of the cross that they may have eternal life.

Fr Hanssens, who believes neither *Gel.* nor *Ap. Trad.* to be truly Roman, contends that this form is the original Roman ceremony, a

[1] *Gel.*, p. 61, n. 383; *Ordo L*, sec. 77, etc.
[2] The phrase *incrementorum et profectum spiritalium munerator* is omitted from the *Greg.* version.
[3] *Greg.*, p. 54.   [4] *Greg.*, pp. 55-8.
[5] See Diagram on p. 122 above.   [6] cf. *Gel.*, nn. 451, 615.

simple consignation, with no anointing or laying on of hands.[1] Unquestionably the signing with the cross was the important liturgical
action in the Roman rite. It was this which gave the name *consignatio*
to the ceremony. As we have seen in discussing both *Ap. Trad.* and *Gel.*,
the *manuum impositio* was probably not an actual laying on of the
bishop's hand, as it is in Anglican confirmations, but an extension of
the hands towards the candidates while the prayer was said. The
ninth or tenth-century Sacramentary of St Eloy, described by Bourque
as "mixed Gregorian"[2] contains the text of the prayers as in *Greg.*, but
its rubrics direct the *pontifex* to recite the prayer "with hand raised over
the heads of all", and after the prayer,

> When the deacon has asked the names of each, the pontiff, having dipped his
> thumb in chrism makes a cross on the forehead of each, and does the same
> individually for all.[3]

It is certainly reasonable to assume that this was, in fact, the manner in
which the form in *Greg.* was customarily used.

Greg. gives no further ceremonies for the solemn Easter baptisms,
except the propers for the mass. We may assume that the part of the
popes in the solemn rites consisted in consecrating the oils, performing
the final exorcism on Holy Saturday morning, consecrating the font,
confirming the neophytes, and celebrating the mass. It is therefore for
these ceremonies that *Greg.* provides.

No baptismal material is given for the vigil of Pentecost, but prayers
are provided *ante descensum fontis* and a mass *post ascensum fontis*.[4]
Apparently the Easter rites were intended to be used again.

The *Hadrianum* also provides, in a sort of presbyteral appendix
towards its close, a form for baptism of the sick. A short exorcism of the
water is followed by the directions:

> You baptize and anoint him with chrism on the head.[5]

The declarative baptismal formula, omitted from the solemn rite, is
then given. "Afterwards you touch him with chrism on the head (*in
capite*)." The customary chrismal prayer is again provided. The closing
rubric is, *Communicas et confirmas eum*. In *Ordo Romanus I communicas
et confirmas* means to administer the sacramental Bread and Chalice,
and if this is its meaning here, there is no reference to the consignation at

---

[1] *La Liturgie d'Hippolyte*, pp. 476–7.
[2] op. cit., Pt. 2, T. 2, p. 258.
[3] *P.L.*, 78, 90.　　　[4] *Greg.*, pp. 75–7.　　　[5] *Greg.*, p. 137.

all. If, on the other hand, *confirmas* means the episcopal consignation, then this order makes the same provisions as the corresponding section of *Gel*.[1]

It is hardly surprising that a supplement to the *Hadrianum* was needed to make it suitable for general use. Additional forms for baptism are a prominent part of Alcuin's supplement. After additional forms for the vigils of Easter and Pentecost a complete baptismal liturgy follows: making of a catechumen, giving of salt, exorcism, *effeta*, anointing, renunciation, baptism, chrismation, confirmation, and Communion.[2] The form was originally intended for use at the solemn seasons, but it apparently is intended here for use *quolibet tempore*.[3]

The *effeta* and anointing of the breast and shoulders are as in *Gel*. The priest is directed to anoint, "making a cross with his thumb and calling his name". The post-baptismal chrismation is *in vertice*, the presbyter making the sign of the cross with his thumb while he says the chrismal prayer, in the *Gel*. rather than the *Greg*. form.[4] Following the anointing the neophyte is clothed with white garments and,

> ... if the bishop is present it is fitting that he at once (*statim*) be confirmed with chrism, and afterwards communicated. And if the bishop is absent let him be communicated by the presbyter.

Confirmation is definitely an episcopal rite, and is omitted if the bishop is not present to administer it. Presumably it would be supplied on a later occasion.

These baptismal forms given in Alcuin's supplement correspond rather to the Gelasian than to the Gregorian rites, and yet they do not agree precisely with the text of *Gel*. The source from which they have been drawn is without doubt the "Eighth-Century Gelasian" sacramentaries, to which we shall now turn.

THE "EIGHTH-CENTURY GELASIAN" BAPTISMAL RITES

Edmund Bishop called the "Eighth-Century Gelasian" sacramentary (*Gel. VIII*) "The Roman Sacramentary of King Pepin",[5] and with this

---

[1] *Ordo I*, 111–16; *Gel.*, p. 96, n. 615.   [2] *Greg.* pp. 159–63.

[3] Bourque, op. cit., Pt. 2, T. 2, p. 200.

[4] The differences are significant only as a means of identifying the source of the material in the supplement. See Diagram on p. 122 above.

[5] *Liturgica Historica*, p. 152, n. 1.

designation Emmanuel Bourque concurs.[1] *Gel. VIII* was compiled in France in the period 740–50 under the auspices of King Pepin, the father of Charlemagne, in a monastery of Benedictines. The archetype of *Gel. VIII* is not known to us, and we must rely upon various copies, of which the most important is the Sacramentary of Gellone, usually dated between 770 and 795. Almost at once the new sacramentary was superseded by the *Hadrianum*, introduced by Charlemagne in 784. A second recension, nevertheless, appeared about the year 800 and received considerable usage, particularly in North Italy and in Germany. Of this recension the Sacramentary of Angoulême, and the Sacramentaries of Phillips, St Gall, Reichenau, Rheinau, Monza, and the *Gelasianum Triplex* are representative.[2]

This new sacramentary was of a syncretistic type which "enriched" the matter drawn from *Gel.* with material from *Greg.* and from Gallican sources. In spite of its brief life *Gel. VIII* is of considerable importance, for it was a principal source of the Germano–Roman Pontifical, from which the present Roman Pontifical and Ritual are derived.

No synthetic edition of *Gel. VIII* exists, although one has been promised for many years by the Henry Bradshaw Society. We shall have to make use, therefore, of the partial edition of the Sacramentary of Gellone in Martène, *de Antiquiis Ecclesiae Ritibus*,[3] the table of *initia* published by Dom de Puniet,[4] and the edition of the Sacramentary of Angoulême published by Paul Cagin in 1918.[5]

Gellone, unlike the older *Gel.*, recognizes three solemn seasons for baptism: Epiphany, Easter, and Pentecost. It provides seven scrutinies before the Easter baptism and three before both Pentecost and Epiphany.[6] The rites of the Holy Sabbath (and of the Vigil of Pentecost and Epiphany as well) take place at the sixth hour, that is in the afternoon.[7] The rubrics for the pre-baptismal anointing are fuller than in *Gel.* The priest is directed to make a cross with his thumb on the breast of the catechumen while saying, "Dost thou renounce Satan?" He makes a second cross while saying, "And all his works?" Finally, he makes a cross between the shoulders while saying, "And all his pomps?"

The rites of the vigil follow at once. At the end of the blessing of the

---

[1] Bourque, op. cit., Pt. 2, T. 2, p. 229.   [2] ibid., 3, pp. 226–35.

[3] Page references are to the Antwerp edition of 1786 (second edition).

[4] *Le Sacramentaire romain de Gellone* (*Bibliotheca Ephemerides Liturgicae*, Vol. 4).

[5] *Le Sacramentaire Gélasien d'Angoulême.*

[6] Martène, col. 98–103 (Book I, Ch. I, Art. XII, Ordo II).

[7] Martène, col. 183–6 (Book I, Ch. I, Art. XVIII, Ordo XII).

font, the priest pours chrism from a vessel into it in the form of a cross and mixes it with his hand. He then sprinkles the font and the people standing around with the blessed water. The people are also permitted to take the holy water in their own containers to use at home.

The actual baptism differs from that in *Gel.* in that the credal questions are no longer the baptismal formula. They are asked beforehand, and then the child is baptized with the declarative formula, "I baptize thee in the name of the Father, and of the Son, and of the Holy Ghost."

After baptism the presbyter anoints them, making a cross in chrism with his thumb on the top of their heads (*in vertice*), with the invocation of the Holy Trinity. The chrismal prayer from *Gel.* has the *incipit*, "Deus Pater Domini Iesu Christi . . .".

The bishop then seats himself in his chair in the church, and the children are brought to him. He gives to each a stole, a chasuble, a chrismal cloth, and ten coins. They are then arranged in a circle and he says the confirmation prayer, "over them with chrism, making a cross on their foreheads, with the invocation of the Holy Trinity, and he gives them the sevenfold grace of the Holy Spirit". The prayer and short formula for the signing are given as in *Gel.* At the end of this a rubric explains the importance of the episcopal consignation:

> Take care that this is done for all, and let them not neglect this, since then they confirm everyone who has been baptized with the name of Christianity.

There can be little doubt that the source of these additions to the baptismal rite of *Gel.* is *Ordo Romanus XI*. This *ordo* was unquestionably used with *Gel.* to produce the revision of the baptismal rite here described. The greatest change is, of course, in the actual administration of baptism. The ceremonies of the anointing, although explained in greater detail in *Gellone*, are substantially as in *Gel.*

Although the format of *Angoulême* is that of *Greg.* rather than *Gel.*, the baptismal rites of that book are almost verbatim transcripts of those in Vat. Reg. 316. *Angoulême* places all of the baptismal rites, beginning with the making of a catechumen, together, after the provisions for Good Friday.[1] The first addition to the baptismal portion of the vigil rites occurs at the end of the blessing of the font. *Angoulême* directs, "You receive chrism and pour it in the form of a cross." The text continues at once with the rubric from *Gel.*, "Then when the font is blessed, you baptize each one in order."[2] *Angoulême* agrees with *Greg.*,

---

[1] op. cit., pp. 44ff.
[2] ibid., pp. 57–8; *Gel.*, p. 74, n. 448.

however, in giving no actual description of the baptism. There is also no direction for a post-baptismal chrismation, but the rubric says, "When he shall have come up from the font, let the priest (*sacerdos*) say these words." The words are the chrismal prayer from *Gel.*, so there can be little doubt what is intended. The rubrics and prayers for the episcopal consignation follow as in *Gel.*

Like its prototype, *Angoulême* provides forms for sick baptism and various other special occasions. They are found at the end of the sacramentary, as in *Greg.*, but are themselves identical with the parallel sections in *Gel.*[1] The only difference is in the description of baptism itself, for which *Angoulême* provides a declarative formula, thereby showing itself a member of the *Gel. VIII* family.

The basic structure of the Gelasian rites remains in these eighth-century books, except for the addition of the declarative baptismal formula. The ceremonial directions become more developed, but little else is changed. *Gel. VIII* represents the Roman rite as it pushed north-ward into France and Germany. It is of importance to us chiefly because it was in this form that the rites of *Gel.* were known to the later liturgist who compiled the Germano-Roman Pontifical.

THE "ORDINES ROMANI"

In addition to the Latin sacramentaries described in the previous sections, we possess another valuable source of information about the medieval baptismal rites of the Western Church, the *ordines Romani*. Nominally Roman, these *ordines* were circulated in northern Europe to describe the ceremonies of the Roman rite for the edification and assistance of the Gallican clergy. The introduction of Roman liturgical books into Gaul necessitated the provision of directions for the clergy unfamiliar with the rites, to enable them to use the books and perform the services. It is therefore the Roman rite which the *ordines* describe, but not necessarily the Roman rite as performed at Rome, for certain adaptations were obviously necessary to accommodate the rite of the City to the needs of the Northern dioceses. To a greater or lesser extent these accommodations are reflected in the *ordines*.

The *ordines* are many in number, are represented in a variety of manuscripts, and are of varying dates and provenances. The monumental task of editing and collecting them has been accomplished in the

[1] *Angoulême*, pp. 137ff; *Gel.*, pp. 92–7, 104–7.

last thirty years by the late Michel Andrieu, Dean of the Faculty of Catholic Theology at the University of Strasbourg. His magisterial *Les Ordines Romani du Haut Moyen Âge*, in five volumes,[1] will be followed in the numbering of the *ordines*, and in citations of the text. Because of the limitations of space we shall consider only three of the most important *ordines*.

Certainly the best known of the *ordines* is *Ordo I*, the *Ordo Romanus Primus*, describing the ceremonies of papal high mass at the beginning of the eighth century. Associated with this in the oldest manuscript known to us is *Ordo XI*, describing the scrutinies and the baptismal rites. Andrieu dates this *ordo* from the seventh, or perhaps the last half of the sixth century. He assigns it to Rome, and believes that it was intended for use by the priests of the *tituli*, or parish churches of the City, in preparing young catechumens for the reception of baptism.[2] *Ordo XI* is therefore among the most ancient of the *ordines Romani* to survive to the present.

The rite of *Ordo XI* is closely related to that of *Gel.*, although it is far from clear in exactly what manner. In spite of different arrangements of the scrutinies, the two documents were used together for a considerable period. Chavasse, as we saw in our discussion of *Gel.*, considers *Ordo XI* to be dependent on *Gel.* His dating of the baptismal rites of *Gel.* assigns them to the same date and the same milieu to which Andrieu attributes *Ordo XI*.[3]

The most conspicuous difference between *Gel.* and *Ordo XI* is the arrangement of the scrutinies. *Ordo XI* provides seven scrutinies to correspond with the seven gifts of the Holy Spirit, beginning on the Wednesday in the third week in Lent, and reaching their climax in the rites of Holy Saturday morning.

The Holy Saturday rites begin at the third hour and correspond to those in *Gel.*[4] The description of the *effeta* contains the first part of the formula, "Effeta, that is be opened, for the odour of sweetness", followed by the words *et reliqua*.[5] The description of the *redditio symboli* follows at once, omitting all mention of the anointing of the breast and back and of the renunciation of the devil. Presumably the *effeta*, anointing, and renunciations were considered a single ceremony and

---

[1] This will be abbreviated And. followed by a numeral indicating the volume.
[2] And. II, pp. 409–13.
[3] Chavasse, *Le Sacramentaire Gélasien*, pp. 163–71.
[4] *Ordo XI*, 82–9 (And. II, pp. 443f); *Gel.*, pp. 67f, nn. 419–24.
[5] *Ordo XI*, 85.

were comprised in the *et reliqua*. At least, a priest attempting to use this *ordo* with *Gel.* would have so to interpret it.

Ordo XI makes it clear that the ceremonies of the vigil were to follow the dismissal of the catechumens at the end of the final scrutiny. Apparently this means that the rites *in nocte* were actually performed in the daytime of Saturday.[1]

The pouring of chrism into the font at the end of the blessing, although not provided in *Gel.*, is ordered:

> When all this is done, he pours chrism from a golden vessel over the water into the fonts in the manner of a cross. With his hand he stirs the chrism and the water, and sprinkles all the font and the people standing about.[2]

No formula is given, and the mixing was presumably done in silence. The people were then permitted to take some of the holy water for their own use.

The bishop then baptized one or two children and designated a deacon to baptize the others. The newly baptized children were handed to a presbyter who anointed them with chrism, signing the cross on their heads, and reciting the chrismal prayer.

The bishop then came up out of the font and sat in his chair in the church, where the children were brought to him. He presented each with a stole, a chasuble, a chrismal cloth, and ten coins. When they were clothed, they were arranged in a circle, and the bishop prayed over them "confirming them with the invocation of the sevenfold grace of the Holy Spirit". This *invocatio* must have been the confirmation prayer as in *Gel.* and *Greg.* It is said *super eos*, that is without necessarily any physical contact between the bishop and the children. After the prayer the bishop made the sign of the cross "with his thumb and chrism on the forehead of each". The formula here is: "In the Name of the Father and of the Son and of the Holy Ghost. Peace be with thee", rather than "The sign of Christ unto life eternal", as in *Gel.*[3]

Certainly it is the anointing which is the important liturgical act in confirmation to the compiler of *Ordo XI*, and he underscores his point by saying:

> Great care must be taken that this is not neglected, because it is at that point

---

[1] *Ordo XI*, 89.
[2] *Ordo XI*, 94 (And. II, p. 445); trans. in Whitaker, p. 193.
[3] *Ordo XI*, 94–101 (And. II, pp. 445f).

that every baptism is confirmed and justification made for the name of Christianity (*tunc omne baptismum legitimum christianitatis nomine confirmatur*).[1]

The concern of the Roman tradition with episcopal consignation is here made evident.

Ordo XI concludes its description of the rites by directing the children to go to mass and receive Communion.

Andrieu believes that this *ordo* was a source of the Sacramentary of Gellone, which he calls "a slightly amplified recension of our *Ordo XI*".[2] *Gellone*, in turn, he believes to be the source of *Ordo XV*. Certainly the sacramentaries of the *Gel. VIII* class represent attempts, as do the *ordines*, to adapt *Gel.* to the needs of the Frankish kingdom, and Andrieu's demonstration of the relationship between *Gellone* and these two *ordines* is a major step towards unravelling the confusion.

If in *Ordo XI* we breathed the air of the *tituli Romani*, when we turn to *Ordo XV* we have entered the northern lands. Andrieu dates it from the middle of the eighth century and assigns it to western Gaul.[3] It is entitled *Capitulare Ecclesiastici Ordinis*, and although it describes itself as "the manner in which it is celebrated by the Holy and Apostolic Roman Church, just as it has been handed on to us by our wise and venerable fathers", it has many marked Gallican features.[4]

The *ordo* is arranged to follow the ecclesiastical year, beginning with Advent, and describes all manner of liturgical practices. The first with which we are concerned is the *ordo* for Epiphany. The Epiphany, as we have seen in chapters III and IV, was a traditional date for solemn baptism in the East, but in the Western Church the popes had sought to restrict the solemn administration of the sacrament to Easter and Pentecost. *Ordo XV* provides for the solemn blessing of the font on Epiphany, with the administration of baptism.[5] The source upon which *Ordo XV* has drawn for its description of the rites is, as Andrieu has demonstrated, the Holy Saturday rites of the Sacramentary of Gellone.

After the blessing of the water, the presbyters and deacons went into the font and baptized the children in the Triune Name. They then handed them to the presbyter who signed them with the cross in chrism upon their heads, "with prayer and the invocation of the Holy Trinity".

The baptized children (*infantes*) are soon brought before the bishop and the sevenfold grace of the Spirit is given to them with chrism on the forehead

---

[1] *Ordo XI*, 102; trans. in Whitaker, p. 194; cf. *Gellone* on pp.158–9 above.

[2] And. III, p. 81.   [3] And. III, pp. 19–21, 92.   [4] And. III, p. 95.

[5] *Ordo XV*, 69–77 (And. III, pp. 110–12).

and the invocation of the Holy Trinity, that is the confirmation of baptism or Christianity.[1]

The phrase *cum invocatione sancte trinitatis* in both anointings is from *Gellone*.

Ordo XV describes baptism again on Holy Saturday. The opening rites are those of the final scrutiny. The exorcism is followed immediately by the anointing and renunciations:

> Then the priest touches the breasts of the children with blessed oil, making the cross twice on their breasts.[2]

These two crosses are made while the priest asks the candidate to renounce the devil and all his works. A third cross, between the shoulders, is made while the priest asks them to renounce the devil's pomp. The *effeta*, performed with saliva, follows the renunciations. In *Gellone*, to which this rite is otherwise parallel, it is in its accustomed place before the anointing.

The actual baptism is not described again, but the section concludes:

> The baptized children, if they can have the bishop present, ought to be confirmed with chrism. Which, if they are not able to obtain the bishop on the day itself, they shall do without delay, as quickly as they can obtain him.[3]

We find here again the insistence upon episcopal confirmation which we found in *Ordo XI* and in the Gelasian tradition. The close connection of the episcopal confirmation to baptism is clearly shown by the insistence that, if it is impossible for the bishop to be present at the baptism, he be obtained as quickly as possible. The continual concern of *Ordines XI* and *XV* lest the consignation be omitted is consistent with our previous findings, that confirmation was unknown except where the Roman rite was followed.

The last of the *ordines* edited by Andrieu, *Ordo L*, is of considerable importance. The text, with its introduction, comprises the entire fifth volume of his work, and was published posthumously in 1961. *Ordo L*, or *Ordo Romanus Antiquus*, is an integral part of the Germano-Roman Pontifical, of which it forms a chapter. Among its sources Andrieu counts the Leonine, Gelasian, "Eighth-Century Gelasian", and Gregor-

---

[1] *Ordo XV*, 77. This passage is missing from the principal manuscript, Sangallensis 349, but it is probably a simple oversight, as it is included in the Holy Week *ordo* of the same manuscript.

[2] *Ordo XV*, 113–14 (And. III, p. 119).

[3] *Ordo XV*, 119 (And. III, p. 120).

ian Sacramentaries, and the earlier collections of *ordines*.[1] In other words, it was compiled upon the basis of most of the Roman material we have considered thus far. *Ordo L*, unlike the earlier *ordines*, tends to give the liturgical forms in full. It is, in fact, a pontifical, providing not only guidance for the bishop in the performance of various episcopal ceremonies, but also the actual texts which he would need to perform them. Andrieu assigns the composition of *Ordo L* to the editor of the Germano-Roman Pontifical. He describes it in this way:

> About 950, a monk of St Alban, richly provided with older liturgical materials, among which we can identify most of the *ordines* of which we have knowledge, decided to gather into a single volume all the texts necessary for the performance of episcopal functions, whether they were of a fixed date or not. He realized his design, but with an exuberant *gaucherie*, weighting down his book with superfluous documents, archaic *ordines*, or didactic pieces, equally dispersed in *Ordo L* and the other parts of the Pontifical. *Ordo L* is thus but a particular chapter of the work. It was edited under the same conditions and by the same pen as its context.[2]

We may readily observe this exuberant *gaucherie* by examining the provisions of *Ordo L* for the blessing of chrism. The blessing is in chapter 25, entitled, "Concerning the Divine Office from the Supper of the Lord to the Octave of Pentecost". The blessing of the oil for the sick at the end of the canon is described first. After the Communion of the bishop, the chrism is consecrated.[3] The bishop sits in his chair while the chrism (*oleum chrismale*) is brought in. A metrical hymn, *Audi, iudex mortuorum*, is provided to be sung while the chrism is brought into the church in solemn procession. The hymn might be described as a *laus olei*. The sixth strophe is most directly relevant to the use of chrism at baptism:

> *Lota mete sacro fonte*
> *Aufugantur crimina;*
> *Uncta fronta sacrosancta*
> *Influunt carismata.*

The bishop is then directed to preach *tam ad clerum quam ad populum* concerning the making of the chrism, after which he mixes the balsam

---

[1] And. V, p. 71.   [2] And. V, pp. 78f.

[3] *Ordo L*, 25.77–92 (And. V, pp. 214–21). This is the usual Roman place for the consecration of chrism. cf. *Ordo XXIV*, 19 (And. III, p. 291); *Ordo XXVII*, 32 (And. III, p. 354); *Ordo XXVIII*, 22 (And. III, p. 396); *Ordo XXXI*, 26 (And. III, p. 495).

with the oil. Two forms are provided: a long prayer asking that the oil and balsam thus mixed may be one, and that whoever is externally anointed therewith may be internally anointed with that which will make him partaker of the heavenly kingdom; and a short formula:

> May this mixture of liquids be made for the propitiation of all who are anointed, that they may be preserved in safety for ever. Amen.

The exorcism of the chrism follows. The form is that given in *Gel.* for the exorcizing of oil *ad succurendum*.[1] This is said *lenta voce* and is followed by the *Sursum corda* and the great chrismal blessing of the Roman rite, *alta voce*.

The consecration of the chrism is followed by the exorcism of the "oil with which catechumens are to be anointed".[2] This is performed "as if reading a lesson". It consists of an exorcism followed by a blessing. The former is *Gel.*, n. 389, provided as an alternative form in *Gel.* for exorcizing oil (or perhaps chrism). The latter is the usual Roman form for exorcizing oil, as in *Gel.*[3] This order is noteworthy in that all of the material from Vat. Reg. 316 has been put to use except the two chrismal prefaces, although not in the way in which *Gel.* uses it. The order of the blessings is that of *Ap. Trad., Greg.*, and the earlier *ordines*. As in the Ambrosian *Beroldus*, both an exorcism and a blessing have been provided for each oil.

At the end of the regular provisions for Maundy Thursday, *Ordo L* gives the Ambrosian forms for blessing all three oils, and a Mozarabic form as alternatives, and two *sermones generales de confectione chrismatis*,[4] apparently for the assistance of bishops not able to preach the required sermon. Certainly these must be among the superfluous documents with which the compiler has weighted down this *ordo*.

The second sermon concludes with a description of the benefits of confirmation, which may be summed up in a single sentence:

> In baptism we are regenerated to life; after baptism we are armed and strengthened (*confirmamur*) to fight against enemies.

This is, of course, a statement of the doctrine that confirmation is an *augmentum*, an addition to the grace of baptism. It forms a part of a homily on Pentecost by the fifth-century bishop called Pseudo-Eusebius of Emesa, from which, according to Gregory Dix, it was

---

[1] *Gel.*, p. 97, n. 616.   [2] *Ordo L*, 25.92–6 (And. V, pp. 221–4).
[3] *Gel.*, p. 61, n. 384; *Greg.*, p. 50.
[4] *Ordo L*, 25.138–45 (And. V, pp. 233–44).

borrowed by the author of the Forged Decretals in the ninth century and ascribed to Pope Melchiades. In Dix's view this is the *fons et origo* of all the medieval distortions of the primitive doctrine of the bestowal of the Holy Spirit in the post-baptismal rites, against which he and Thornton and Mason took up arms. As he wryly remarks, "Confirmation addresses, like books, have their destinies."[1]

The rites of Easter Even form chapter 29. The morning rites take place after the third hour.[2] First those who are able recite the creed and the Lord's Prayer themselves. The godfathers make the *redditio* for those who cannot speak for themselves. The candidates, whom the *ordo* calls *infantes*, are then exorcized and the *effeta* performed. Each candidate is then anointed on the breast and between the shoulders with the exorcized oil. The presbyter makes the sign of the cross with his thumb and calls them by name, asking them if they renounce the devil. The three renunciations are followed by the formula:

> And I anoint (*linio*) thee with the oil of salvation in Christ Jesus our Lord, unto eternal life. Amen.

The rites of the vigil begin at the seventh hour, barely after noon. At the conclusion of the blessing of the font, the bishop pours chrism into it in the form of a cross, saying *lenta voce*:

> May this font be sanctified and made fruitful to those who are born anew in it unto eternal life.[3]

The bishop then asks the candidates to renounce the devil a final time, and asks them the credal questions. The text from this point divides into two recensions. That called A by Andrieu proceeds at once to the baptism with the declarative form, while recension B inserts a final pre-baptismal anointing, repeating the formula used at the morning rites.[4]

The post-baptismal anointing is performed by the presbyter, signing the cross *in vertice infantis* with the traditional chrismal prayer.[5] The children are then clothed and brought to the bishop, who recites the confirmation prayer in its Gregorian form "with his hand lifted up and laid upon the head of all".

When the prayer has been completed and the deacons have asked the names of each, the pontiff, having dipped his thumb in chrism, makes a cross on the

---

[1] *The Theology of Confirmation in Relation to Baptism*, p. 21.
[2] *Ordo L*, 29.2–7 (And. V, pp. 261ff).
[3] *Ordo L*, 29.52 (And. V, p. 281).   [4] ibid., 58.   [5] ibid., 64 (p. 286).

forehead of each, saying: *I confirm and sign thee* (*Confirmo et consigno te*) in the name of the Father and of the Son and of the Holy Ghost.[1]

The words *confirmo et consigno te* have been added to the Trinitarian formula of *Ordo XI*, making it parallel to the declarative *baptizo te*. A short, concise statement of what the liturgical action is intended to convey has been added to a longer prayer.

A versicle and response, a collect, and the blessing of the confirmands complete this rite of confirmation, as we must now call it. It has become a self-contained service administered after baptism, and presumably also at other times. The collect speaks of the giving of the Holy Spirit to the apostles, and through them and their successors to the faithful, and it prays that the same Spirit may come into the hearts of those whose foreheads have been signed with the cross and anointed with chrism.[2] It should be noted that in spite of the mention of the apostles, no mention is made of laying on hands after their example. It is the signing with chrism which is the external sign of the inward anointing of the Holy Ghost.

The section on confirmation closes with a repetition of the warning against omitting the rite from *Ordo XI*.[3] For Pentecost *Ordo L* directs the baptismal rites of Holy Saturday to be repeated.[4]

The baptismal rites of this *Ordo Romanus Antiquus* are not only a recapitulation and revision of those we have previously examined, they are a chapter in the Germano-Roman Pontifical, which in its turn, is the ancestor of the present Roman Rituale and Pontifical. The forms of *Ordo L* are reproduced almost without change in the twelfth-century Roman Pontifical, and are essentially those of the later editions.[5] It represents in a real sense the completion of the "shape" of the Roman baptismal rites. We may therefore conclude our study of the baptismal liturgy of the Western Church at this point, and prepare to consider our conclusions.

It is impossible to speak of a consistent testimony of the *Ordines Romani*. They speak with many voices, from many local traditions. We may, nevertheless, see in the use which they made of the material from the sacramentaries the line of development of the anointing. There is a definite tendency to provide short declarative formulas to

---

[1] *Ordo L*, 72–4 (p. 289).   [2] ibid., 29.76 (And. V, p. 291).
[3] ibid., 78.   [4] ibid., 39.15 (And. V, p. 346).
[5] cf. Andrieu, *Le Pontifical Romain du XII*e *Siècle* (Studi e Testi, Vol. 86); de Puniet, *The Roman Pontifical*, pp. 44–55; Bourque, op. cit., Pt. 2, T. 1, p. 248.

accompany liturgical action. We have seen such forms develop for the actual baptism, the pre-baptismal anointing, and the consignation. The *ordines* have made clear the importance which the Roman Church attached to confirmation, as it had begun to be called. The extended period separating baptism from confirmation familiar to modern Western Christians was not yet contemplated, but confirmation had become a separable entity.

CONCLUSION

We have now examined the baptismal anointings in the rites of the Western Church. In the case of the Roman rite, I believe that we can trace a continuous pattern of development from *Ap. Trad.* through *Gel.* to *Ordo L* and the twelfth-century Roman Pontifical.

Baptism is preceded by an anointing with exorcized oil. In *Ap. Trad.* the whole body was anointed. John the Deacon speaks of anointing the ears, the nostrils, and the breast. The Roman liturgical books know only the anointing of the breast and back. The trend, which works also in the post-baptismal anointings, is to reduce the amount of oil used. Anointings become signings with the cross, on selected, symbolic members of the body. The meaning, nevertheless, remains unchanged. It is an exorcism, guarding the body of the catechumen from the attack of the devil, so that it may become a Temple of the Holy Ghost.

The Roman rite also provides for two anointings after baptism. *Ap. Trad.* speaks of an anointing of the whole body by the presbyter, followed by an anointing of the head by the bishop, accompanied by the laying on of hands and signing of the forehead. Although our evidence of Roman practice between *Ap. Trad.* and *Gel.* is fragmentary, and we do not possess the text of any complete baptismal rite in the period, I believe that the evidence we do have is consistent with the view that the Roman Church continued the double chrismation, by presbyter and bishop. This is the rite of *Ap. Trad.* and of *Gel.* I do not believe that the evidence we have examined requires us to doubt the continuity of Roman practice.

The two anointings of the Roman rite are customarily called *unctio capitis* and *unctio frontis*. The tradition ascribed by the *Liber Pontificalis* to Pope Silvester and expounded by Pope Innocent I in his letter to Decentius directs the presbyter who baptizes *sine episcopo* to anoint the top of the head, leaving the signing of the brow to the bishop. This distinction is consistently maintained in the Roman rite.

Rome insisted that the *unctio frontis* be administered by the bishop personally. Consignation, or confirmation, came therefore to be a separable rite, administered later by the bishop. Although in the great cathedrals the bishop still presided at the solemn rites of the Easter vigil and fulfilled his liturgy in the initiation, for the vast majority of medieval Christians the *unctio capitis* administered by the parish priest was followed at once by the reception of Communion. Roman bishops were expected to make a circuit of their dioceses to administer consignation, and, at least in Italy where the dioceses were small, they were able to do so. Nevertheless, the separability of the episcopal act from the other initiatory rites led to a theological differentiation between the sacraments of baptism and confirmation. In the writings of Rabanus Maurus, a distinguished disciple of Alcuin who provided the medieval Church with a theology of confirmation, that sacrament is called a distinctive gift of the Spirit already received in the baptismal *unctio capitis*, to strengthen the Christian for the life in Christ.[1]

Outside the Roman rite the anointings followed a different pattern. The pre-baptismal anointing tended to become a blessing, rather than an exorcism. The pre-baptismal oil was considered the lesser of two holy oils and imparted a lesser blessing, and the idea of its fulfilling a different function from chrism was obscured. This is shown particularly in the Gallicanized Roman forms for blessing the holy oils. Both the chrism and the oil of the catechumens were exorcized, then blessed.

The outstanding difference between Rome and the non-Roman Western rites lies in the post-baptismal anointing. The present writer sees no evidence for more than a single anointing. In the African rites there was undoubtedly an episcopal laying on of hands after the anointing. For this we have the testimony of Tertullian, Cyprian, and Augustine. They associate the anointing with the baptism, however, not with the imposition of hands.

In the period of the extant liturgical books we find no evidence of any additional anointing or laying on of episcopal hands. In this we differ from the Roman Catholic scholars, such as Galtier, de Puniet, Coppens, and Van den Eynde, who have studied the Gallican rites. They all believe that there was a rite of episcopal confirmation in Gaul, in spite of the complete lack of evidence for its existence. They do this, in the present writer's opinion, on the *a priori* grounds that a Catholic liturgy must contain such a rite.

In Spain baptism was regularly followed by the signing of the fore-

---

[1] *De Clericorum Institutione* 1.28–30 (P.L., 107, 313–14).

head with chrism and the imposition of hands by the bishop or presbyter who performed the baptism. In Milan the single signing by presbyter or bishop after baptism is the only Ambrosian post-baptismal anointing in the ninth century. In Gaul the *infusio chrismae* followed baptism and was presumably performed by the officiating priest, whether presbyter or bishop. It is only with the introduction of the Roman rite into Gaul that we find bishops going about their dioceses to anoint those previously baptized by presbyters.

The chrism was universally consecrated by the bishop, and the Spanish theologians see in this his function in the baptismal liturgy. The bishop was the proper minister of baptism, although he might, and normally did, act through his presbyters. Thus the non-Roman Western rites, like the Eastern rites, maintained the unity of the baptismal liturgy by allowing the priest to perform the entire rite as deputy of the bishop and using episcopally consecrated chrism.

Conclusion

In the ancient world anointing with oil was the normal accompaniment of bathing. Literary evidence as ancient as Homer associates anointing with washing, while the testimony of later Roman authors proves the continuity of Greek and Roman practice. Although it would be going considerably beyond the evidence to see in this secular use of oil the origin of the Christian baptismal anointing, we must realize that to the Greek, or Roman, or Hebrew of the first and second centuries water and oil were naturally associated, and the use of oil at the sacred bath would not seem strange.

Oil was also used both by the Jews and the Romans in religious ceremonial. In Hebrew usage the priest and king were anointed with oil which conveyed the power to exercise their functions. The anointing of the priest was in the form of the Greek letter *chi*, that is, a cross.

It is in this royal anointing of Israel that we must find the ancestor of Christian baptismal anointing, or at least of the anointing with chrism. Christ was *rex unctus*, the Anointed King, and Christians are likewise anointed as members of him, and of his royal and priestly people.

We cannot, on the basis of the present evidence, state precisely at what point the anointing became a part of Christian baptism. Our *terminus ante quem* is Tertullian and Hippolytus, and we must take seriously the possibility that it was known to the author of 1 John, and to the Seer of the Apocalypse. There is no intrinsic impossibility involved in ascribing the origin of the baptismal anointing to the period of the New Testament, and the evidence for the period between the writing of 1 John and Tertullian must be considered neutral. At whatever time the actual anointing was added to the baptismal washing, it was done in the context in which the New Testament places it. As the Holy Spirit descended upon Christ at his baptism, so the Christian is anointed with the Spirit at his.

In the Syrian tradition the gift of the Holy Spirit, the *rushmâ*, is associated with the pre-baptismal anointing. There is every reason to believe that, at least in Syria, this is the original practice, and the theological interpretation of Dr T. W. Manson is a most attractive explanation of its rationale. What we may describe as the main line of Christian development, however, is that represented by *Ap. Trad.* in which the principal anointing is that which follows baptism.

There is no consistent pattern of pre-baptismal anointings among the rites of the Christian Church, and except in the case of the Syrian *rushmâ*, it is difficult to see upon what grounds its use developed. In the Roman rite its effect is negative. The oil has been exorcized, and by its application to the catechumen he is freed from possession by evil spirits and made ready for the indwelling of the Spirit of God. Neither the non-Roman Western rites nor the Eastern rites follow this usage consistently, and they often speak of this anointing as incorporating the candidate into the good olive tree, Jesus Christ, or as preparing him for combat against the devil. It is possible that there is some connection between this anointing and the pagan idea of protecting with oil those who approach the sacred mysteries.

The Roman rite, following *Ap. Trad.*, knows two post-baptismal anointings, one by the presbyter and a second by the bishop. The other rites, Eastern and Western, speak only of a single post-baptismal unction, performed by the officiating priest, whether presbyter or bishop. This single anointing with episcopally consecrated chrism is regularly described as the unction of the Holy Ghost and identified with the Messianic anointing of Christ with the Holy Spirit.

In Tertullian and Cyprian the anointing is regularly connected with the name of Christian, derived from the *chrisma*, and with the royal and priestly anointings of the Old Testament, while the giving of the Spirit is ascribed to the laying on of hands. This distinction did not survive, however, and the anointing in the West, as in the East, became identified with the gift of the Spirit. The confusion is perhaps inherent in the nature of the rite, for if Christ was anointed with the Holy Spirit at his baptism, then it becomes difficult to maintain a distinction between a christological and a pneumatological interpretation of the anointing.

The Roman tradition definitely ascribed the gift of the Spirit to the episcopal consignation with chrism, which it identified with the laying on of apostolic hands in Acts 8 and 19, but it never developed a coherent theological explanation of the two anointings until it declared that the Spirit was given in both anointings, in the first *ad habitationem Deo consecrandam*, and in the second *ad robur*.

The distinction between the two anointings in *Ap. Trad.* appears to have been functional. The presbyteral chrismation was an anointing of the whole body, performed when the neophyte emerged from the water. He was then clothed and brought into the church decently habited, where he received the anointing of his head at the hands of the bishop, who signed him on the forehead with the cross and blessed him with the imposition of his hand.

Much has been made of the famous statement of Alexander of Hales that confirmation was invented by the Church at the Council of Meaux in 845, but this examination of the baptismal anointings may enable us to see how he was led astray, even if we are unable to discover what action of this council could be so interpreted. We have found no evidence of any separate rite of episcopal confirmation, either by anointing with chrism or laying on of hands, later than the fourth or fifth century. Baptism was a single rite. It consisted of several liturgical actions, of which the most prominent were the washing, the anointing, and the laying on of hands. In most rites the laying on of hands disappeared, or was identified with the anointing. To this tendency the Coptic and Mozarabic rites are outstanding exceptions. The Roman rite stands alone, however, in providing an additional episcopal rite separate from baptism. In other rites the presbyter replaced the bishop as the usual minister of baptism, as he had earlier replaced him as the normal celebrant of the Eucharist, and performed the entire liturgy acting as deputy of the bishop and using chrism consecrated by him.

It is not our present purpose to expound the theology of confirmation in relation to baptism. This has been done many times, most notably by Mason, Dix, and Thornton on one side, and by Wirgman and Lampe on the other. It has been our intention rather to examine the liturgical evidence, allowing the rites to speak for themselves. The meanings which theologians have attached to the three sacramental actions, washing, anointing, and laying on of hands, have differed, but they have agreed that in the total rite we participate in the death and resurrection of Jesus the Christ, are freed from sin and made members of him, and receive the gift of the Holy Ghost.

Theological and pastoral considerations must share in determining the way in which a particular local Church adapts the rites of Christian initiation to its own needs, but to speak of the classic rites as comprising two sacraments, baptism and confirmation, is to introduce a distinction foreign to the rites themselves. Even when episcopal consignation became separated from baptism in practice in the Roman rite, it was still considered to be a part of the one sacramental event, to be added as quickly as possible.

Precedent for the separation of the consignation from baptism may be found in the forms for receiving heretics and for anointing those clinically baptized, and perhaps in Acts 8, but these were exceptional cases in which, for various reasons, the normal procedure could not be followed. The bishop, in these cases, confirmed what had been done by others by his approval and blessing, and supplied the omitted ceremonies.

In the pastoral adaptations of the ancient rite made in both East and West something of the primitive wholeness has been lost. Those rites which have permitted the presbyter to perform the entire baptismal liturgy have lost the immediate contact between the neophyte and the bishop, the representative of the Universal Church. Those which have separated baptism and confirmation have lost their hold upon the unity of the rite and thereby introduced manifold theological and pastoral problems.

The anointing with oil has a distinguished religious history in both Judaism and Christianity. The name of Christ means Anointed, and, as Tertullian has pointed out, we become Christs by sharing in his anointing. It is in itself an important act in Christian initiation, apart from its association with the signing of the cross and the laying on of hands. In any restoration of the rite of Christian initiation to its primitive integrity, the anointing with chrism should take its place with the washing in water, the signing with the cross, the laying on of hands, and the reception of the Eucharist as one of the rites by which we become members of the mystical Body of Christ.

APPENDIX I

Anglican Use of Baptismal Oil

Although the period of separate existence of the Anglican Communion is well outside that covered in the body of this work, it would appear to be of interest and of value to give some account of the use of baptismal oil in the Anglican Communion. Certainly many have felt that the loss of this anointing is a real impoverishment of the Prayer Book baptismal rites, and a defect which should be remedied. The antiquity of chrismation was not recognized at the time of the Reformation, and although baptism and the laying on of hands rested upon the solid rock of Scripture, the anointing was swept away as a later medieval addition.

We shall begin our survey of Anglican practice with a brief look at the rites of baptism and confirmation as they stood at the eve of the Reformation. The Sarum *Manuale* includes the baptismal rites as part of the Easter vigil, although it is clear that children were customarily baptized shortly after birth. The order for making catechumens is placed first, followed by the blessing of the font and the *ordo baptismi*.

The *effeta*, performed with spittle, is among the rites of the catechumenate,[1] but the anointing with the *oleum sanctum* stands immediately after the renunciations at the beginning of the baptismal office.[2] The priest touches the breast and back of the child, making a cross with his thumb and saying:

N. And I anoint thee with the oil of salvation in Christ Jesus our Lord that thou mayest have eternal life and live for ever and ever. Amen.

This anointing is followed at once by the interrogative creed and the baptism, performed with the threefold immersion and the traditional

[1] A. J. Collins, *Manuale ad Usum Percelebris Ecclesie Sarisburiensis* (H.B.S., Vol. 91), p. 30.
[2] ibid., p. 36.

declarative formula. The priest then anoints the neophyte with chrism, making the sign of the cross with his thumb *in vertice* and saying the traditional chrismal prayer:

> Almighty God, the Father of our Lord Jesus Christ, who has regenerated thee by water and the Holy Spirit, and who has given to thee remission of all thy sins, himself anoint thee with the chrism of salvation in the same his Son Jesus Christ our Lord unto everlasting life.[1]

After the clothing and the giving of a lighted candle is this rubric:

> If the bishop is present, he ought to be confirmed at once and afterward communicated if his age permits it.[2]

What is meant by "if his age permits" is shown by a previous rubric in English:

> God faders and godmodyrs of thys chylde whe charge you that ye charge the foder and te moder to kepe it from fyer and water and other perels to the age of vii yere, and that ye lerne or se yt be lerned the *Pater noster*, *Ave maria*, and *Credo*, after the lawe of all holy churche and in all goodly haste to be confirmed of my lorde of the dyocise or of his depute.[3]

The *confirmatio puerorum* is quite brief. The bishop recites the confirmation prayer in this form:

> Almighty everlasting God, who hast vouchsafed to regenerate these thy servants by water and the Holy Spirit: and who hast given to them remission of all their sins: send down upon them the sevenfold Holy Ghost the Paraclete from heaven. Amen. The Spirit of wisdom and understanding. Amen. The Spirit of knowledge and godliness. Amen. The Spirit of counsel and strength, ✠ Amen. And fill them with the Spirit of the fear of the Lord. ✠ Amen. And sign them with the sign of the holy cross ✠ and confirm them with the chrism of salvation unto eternal life. Amen.[4]

The bishop then "anoints his thumb with chrism" and signs their foreheads with the cross saying:

> I sign thee, N., with the sign of the cross, and I confirm thee with the chrism of salvation. In the Name of the Father ✠ and of the ✠ Son and of the Holy ✠ Ghost. Amen.

A final prayer speaks of the giving of the Spirit by the apostles and their successors. There is no mention of the laying on of hands.

---

[1] A. J. Collins, *Manuale ad Usum Percelebris Ecclesie Sarisburiensis* (H.B.S., Vol. 91), p. 37.
[2] ibid.   [3] ibid., p. 32.   [4] ibid., p. 167.

We may now consider the use made of this material by Cranmer in the First Prayer Book of Edward VI.

Publike Baptisme in the Prayer Book of 1549 combined both the order for making catechumens and the order for baptism. The blessing of the font was a separate service, to be performed monthly, when the water was changed. Of the rites of the catechumenate, a signing of the forehead and breast and a single exorcism were retained, but the *effeta* disappeared.[1] The renunciation of the devil and the interrogative creed before baptism remained, but the pre-baptismal anointing vanished.[2] After baptism the priest was directed to anoint the infant upon the head, using this form of the chrismal prayer:

> Almighty God the father of our Lorde Iesus Christ, who hathe regenerate thee by water and the holy gost, and hath geuen unto thee the remission of all thy sinnes: he vouchsaue to annoynte the with the unccyon of hys holy spirite, and bring thee to the inheritaunce of euerlasting life.[3]

Although in most respects this is an accurate translation of the Sarum prayer, Cranmer has rendered *chrismate salutis* " with the unccion of his holy spirite". This must be considered theological interpretation, rather than translation, for the only Western form which uses the phrase is the Arian Mai fragment, from which it could hardly have passed into the First Prayer Book. *Unctio spiritus sancti* is a common enough phrase among the theologians of the Middle Ages, although it was more commonly applied to the episcopal consignation.

For confirmation the First Prayer Book does not order the use of chrism. The rite begins with, "Our help is in the name of the Lord", and the confirmation prayer, as in the Sarum *Manuale*. The prayer is not in the same form as in the present Prayer Book, but is closer to its Latin model. After the opening clause it prays,

> Send downe from heauen we beseech thee (O lorde) upon them thy holy gost the coumforter, with the manifold giftes of grace.

Then, after naming the seven gifts of the Spirit, it continues:

> Signe them (o lorde) and marke them to be thine for euer, by the vertue of thy holye crosse and passion. Confirme and strengthen them with the inward unccion of thy holy gost, mercifully vnto eurelasting life. Amen.[4]

After this prayer the bishop "shal crosse them in the forehead, and laye his hande upon theyr heade saying"

---

[1] F. E. Brightman, *The English Rite*, Vol. 2, pp. 728, 730 (ed. 1915).
[2] ibid., pp. 734ff. [3] ibid. [4] ibid., p. 794.

N. I signe thee with the signe of the crosse and laye my hande upon thee. In the name of the father, and of the sonne, and of the holy gost. Amen.

The rite concludes with the *pax*, the collect based upon that in the Sarum *Manuale* which is still in the Prayer Book, and the blessing.

The rites of the First Prayer Book, although different from those of the Sarum use, have preserved the essential structure of that rite. The washing with water, the unction of the Holy Spirit, the signing with the cross, and the laying on of hands (which was not in Sarum) have all found a place. In eliminating the second anointing, that of confirmation, Cranmer had the support of the non-Roman rites of East and West. We may well note that he inserted a reference to the inward unction of the Holy Spirit into the confirmation prayer. Certainly the restoration of the laying on of hands as a distinct ceremony was a proper addition to the initiatory rites and in accordance with the Scriptural and patristic pattern.

Considered together, the initatory rites of the First Prayer Book provide the traditional sequence: washing with water, anointing with chrism, signing with the cross, and laying on of hands. If the 1549 rites of baptism and confirmation were celebrated together and followed by the Eucharist, with the reception of Communion by the neophytes, we might recognize in them the primitive pattern. Unfortunately, though inevitably, they were not used in this way.

A serious lack in the First Prayer Book was any provision for the consecration of chrism. Before this could become a problem, however, the use of oil ceased, under fire from Bucer and the reforming party.[1] In the Second Prayer Book and its successors holy oil is nowhere to be found.

The Second Prayer Book places immediately after baptism a form for signing the newly baptized child upon the forehead with the cross.[2] This has remained Anglican custom in spite of Puritan protests. The form was taken from the pre-baptismal signing in the First Prayer Book and adapted to a new use.[3] Although the anointing with chrism has been lost, at least the *signum frontis*, with which the Ambrosian Pontifical tells us the Christian warrior is armed, has been retained, and those baptized with the Anglican form receive the sacred sign on their brow. As we have seen, the signing of the forehead with the cross has

---

[1] Procter and Frere, *The Book of Common Prayer*, pp. 59, 72, 75.

[2] Brightman, op. cit., pp. 741f.

[3] ibid., p. 728.

an historic position of its own, even apart from the chrism with which it was traditionally administered to neophytes.

The anointing with chrism at baptism appears to have died officially in Anglicanism with the Prayer Book of 1552, but the anointing at confirmation has had an interesting, if intermittent, history. In 1718 that section of the Nonjurors known as the Usagers, from their desire to restore the usages of 1549, introduced a new office of confirmation.[1] It followed the order of the English Prayer Book of 1662 until it came to the confirmation prayer. This it restored to the 1549 form and then directed:

> Then all of them kneeling in order before the bishop, he shall anoint every one of them with the Chrism or Ointment, making the sign of the Cross upon their forehead.

The anointing was to be followed by the laying on of hands. The formulas provided are:

> N., I sign thee with the sign of the Cross, I anoint thee with Holy Ointment. And I lay my hand upon thee: In the Name of the Father, and of the Son, and of the Holy Ghost. Amen.

The rubrics require the bishop to keep his hand upon the person's head while he repeats also the formula from the English Prayer Book, "Defend, O Lord, this thy child...".

At the conclusion of this office is a brief form for consecrating chrism, to be used before the beginning of the confirmation office, "unless he hath some by him already consecrated". The matter of the chrism is declared to be "sweet Oil of Olives, and precious Balsam commonly called Balm of Gilead". The form of blessing asks that "all those who after Baptism shall be anointed therewith, may be cleansed and purified both in body and soul, and confirmed in godliness, and obtain the blessings of the Holy Ghost".

A copy of the English Prayer Book which had been the property of Bishop Thomas Brett is in the possession of St Mark's Library of the General Theological Seminary in New York. This book has been altered to conform to the Usages of the Nonjurors. At the end of the book this confirmation office is written in long-hand. As an examination of the manuscript copy by this writer shows that it conforms exactly to the printed text in Canon Ollard's "Confirmation in the Anglican

---

[1] Reprinted in S. L. Ollard, "Confirmation in the Anglican Communion", in *Confirmation or Laying on of Hands*, Vol. 1, pp. 231ff.

Communion", this book of Bishop Brett's does not provide us with any new material, but does confirm the actual use of this office by Nonjuring bishops.

According to Canon Ollard's learned essay, the Usages controversy involved only the new order for the Holy Eucharist, and no exception was taken to this new order for confirmation. He doubts whether it was abandoned when the new Communion Office was laid aside in 1731.[1]

A new recension of this office was issued by Bishop Thomas Deacon in his *Compleat Collection of Devotions* in 1734 and was apparently used by the section of the Nonjurors which Deacon headed until the last of their bishops died in 1805.[2]

Deacon's office differs from the earlier rite principally in the substitution of an Eastern form of anointing for that in the previous order:

> N. the servant of God is sealed with the seal of the Cross, and anointed with Holy Ointment, as an emblem of the inward unction of the Holy Spirit.

This is not the actual form of any Eastern rite, but is clearly based upon Eastern usage. The anointing was followed by the laying on of hands with the Prayer Book formula. After the confirmation a new prayer of great beauty, taken from the *Apostolic Constiuitions*, was introduced:

> O Lord God, who art unbegotten and without superior; thou Lord of all, who has made the sweet savour of the knowledge of the Gospel to go forth among all nations: Do thou now grant that this Chrism may be effectual in these baptized children that the sweet savour of thy Christ may remain firm and stable in them, and that dying with him in his death, may rise again with him in his resurrection, and live together with him; by whom and with whom, in the unity of the Holy Ghost, all honour and glory be unto thee, O Father Almighty, world without end.[3]

The form for consecrating the chrism is virtually the same as that in the earlier office, but it is to be used after the Nicene Creed at the Eucharist, rather than at the beginning of the confirmation office. The rubrics speak of the sponsors holding the children, and Ollard tells us that among this group of Nonjurors confirmation was normally administered to infants.[4] A most unusual rubric at the end of the order directs:

> Those who through necessity have received private baptism and have been

---

[1] Ollard, op. cit., p. 203.   [2] This is also printed by Ollard.
[3] cf. *Ap. Con.*, 7.44.2.   [4] Ollard, op. cit., p. 204.

anointed with the holy Chrism by a Priest, shall be confirmed by themselves;
in which case the Bishop . . . shall omit the anointing and sign of the cross,
and shall only lay his hands upon every one to be confirmed.

The rubric at "The Ministration of Private Baptism to Infants in
Houses" directs the priest after baptism to anoint the child with the
holy chrism, signing him upon the forehead and using the same form
provided for the bishop's use at confirmation.[1] The priest then com-
municates the child. No similar provision for chrismation and Communion was made in the forms for public baptism.[2] It sounds as if the
Usagers were attempting to follow the rule of the Council of Orange,
"It has been agreed that among us there shall be one chrismation".[3]
Normally this anointing would be performed by the bishop at confirmation, but in the case of clinical baptism the priest was to anoint and
communicate, and the bishop was to omit the anointing when he confirmed.

Deacon's order for public baptism, although it did not contain a
post-baptismal unction, restored the pre-baptismal anointing. It was
inserted between the questions asked of the candidate and the prayer
"O merciful God . . ." before the blessing of the font. The form was:

N., the servant of God, is anointed with holy oil, and signed with the sign of
the Cross, in token that hereafter he may not be ashamed to confess the faith
of Christ crucified . . .[4]

It continued as at the post-baptismal signing in the Prayer Book.

The oil for the pre-baptismal anointing was to be consecrated by the
bishop at the Eucharist after the Nicene Creed. It was to be "sweet Oil
of Olives". The prayer asks that the oil be consecrated in the Name of
the Lord Jesus, "that it may be subservient to the remission of sins, and
may be a strengthening preparation for Baptism".[5]

In his *Full, True and Comprehensive View of Christianity* Bishop
Deacon explained the pre-baptismal unction as "a strengthening
preparation for Baptism, when Christians are to combat in their spiritual arena", and derived it "From the ancient custom of Wrestlers
being anointed before they began to fight".[6]

In 1805 the last bishop of the Nonjuring succession died, and the

---

[1] P. Hall, *Fragmenta Liturgica*, Vol. 6, p. 197.   [2] ibid., pp. 166, 182.
[3] Canon 2 (Mansi, VI, 435).
[4] Hall, op. cit., pp. 163 (infants) and 180 (adults).   [5] ibid., p. 187.
[6] W. J. Grisbrooke, *Anglican Liturgies of the Seventeenth and Eighteenth Centuries*,
p. 121.

English Usagers, most of whom had already given up their usages and returned to the Established Church, ceased to exist. In Scotland, on the other hand, the Episcopal Church traces its ancestry through the Nonjuring bishops driven from their sees by William of Orange.

Bishop Thomas Rattray, who became Bishop of Brechin in 1723, is justly renowned as a theologian and liturgist. His *magnum opus*, *The Ancient Liturgy of the Church of Jerusalem*, exercised a profound influence upon the eucharistic faith and practice of Scottish Episcopalians. In a letter to Bishop Keith, written in 1731, Rattray acknowledges that he was himself confirmed with chrism.[1] It is possible that his was the case mentioned by Bishop Falconar in 1713 in correspondence with Bishops Gadderar and Spinckes.[2]

Bishop Falconar had been ordained presbyter in 1683 in the Church of Scotland by the Bishop of Ross, deprived in 1688, and consecrated bishop at Dundee in 1709. A form of confirmation with chrism in Falconar's own handwriting is in the Episcopal Chest at Edinburgh.[3] It is based upon the 1549 Prayer Book form and is similar to the 1718 English Nonjurors' office. It is intended for use with a single candidate and contains the confirmation prayer in the singular, with significant alterations. The petition conforms to the English Prayer Book of 1662 (and the Scottish Prayer book of 1637) in reading, "Strengthen him, O Lord . . ." instead of "Send down from heaven, O Lord, upon them . . .". Most significantly, the opening phrase has been altered to read:

> Almighty and everliving God who hath vouchsafed to sanctify this thy servant by the Laver of Baptism and hast given unto him forgiveness of all his sins . . .

This places the Scottish forms in the tradition of the Oriental versions of *Ap. Trad.* by omitting all reference to regeneration by the Holy Spirit in baptism.

The words, "Sign him and mark him . . ." as in 1549 are included, and the actual formula of administration is:

> I sign thee with this sign of ✠ the Cross, and Confirm thee with the Chrism of Salvation, and lay mine hands upon thee in the Name of the Father and of the Son and of the H. Ghost. Amen.

This is followed by the Anglican "Defend, O Lord, this thy child . . ."

---

[1] Ollard, op. cit., p. 206.   [2] ibid., p. 205 (Spinckes was an English non-Usager).
[3] Reprinted by Ollard, op. cit., pp. 235–6.

and the rite is complete. A form for consecrating the chrism is added. It consists of a single prayer, and is similar to the Byzantine prayer for consecrating chrism. It invokes the Holy Spirit upon the oil, asking:

> Make it the oil of Gladness to the sanctifying of the soul and Body, the Garment of Incorruption and a perfecting seal, Imprinting the Holy Name of thy only Begotten Son, and the Holy Spirit on this thy servant now hallowed by the water of Baptism.

Also in the Edinburgh Episcopal Chest is the order of Bishop Rattray,[1] which is identical with the order of 1718 except that the form "Defend, O Lord . . ." has been emended to read:

> Seal this thy Servant, O Lord, with the gift of thy holy Spirit, that he may continue thine forever . . .

The form for consecrating chrism has also received additions from Bishop Falconar's order, so that it combines the substance of both prayers.

At the conclusion of the order a note in a different hand indicates that in a copy of the office in Rattray's own handwriting the confirmation sentence reads:

> N. I seal thee with the Seal of the Cross ✠ I anoint thee with holy Ointment, as an Emblem of the inward Unction of the Holy Spirit. And, I lay my Hands upon thee; in the Name of the Father, and of the Son, and of the Holy Ghost.

This alteration is clearly based upon Deacon's order, although avoiding his Eastern use of the passive. The prayer translated by Deacon from *Ap. Con.*, 7 is added to complete the picture.

It was their study of the ancient liturgies which caused these bishops to revive the use of chrism. Bishop Gadderar specifically states that he has consulted the ancient liturgies "both of Greek and Latine Churches, particularly as to Chrism".[2] Canon Ollard knows of no evidence for the use of chrism in Scotland after the death of Bishop Rattray in 1743, as the revival of the penal laws following the Rebellion of '45 all but extinguished the flame of episcopacy in Scotland. It has, nevertheless, left its mark upon the Episcopal Church in Scotland. The present Scottish Prayer Book, although not providing for the use of chrism at confirmation, has returned to the forms of 1549, adding the petition "Sign them, O Lord, and mark them . . ." to the confirmation prayer

---

[1] ibid., pp. 236–40.   [2] ibid., p. 205.

of 1662, and directing the bishop to sign the forehead with the cross, using the words of 1549, followed by the form of 1662.

Other provinces of the Anglican Communion have been even more forward in restoring the use of chrism to confirmation. The South African Prayer Book permits the bishop to sign the persons being confirmed with chrism, using the form:

N., I sign thee with the sign of the Cross, and I lay my hand upon thee.

A prayer for consecrating the chrism has been authorized by the Episcopal Synod of the province since 1938. It is not in the Prayer Book, but is printed separately, as are several other offices for the use of the bishops. The prayer is an adaptation of that in the Gelasian Sacramentary, and since it is not readily available, it will be quoted in full:

It is very meet, right, and our bounden duty, that we should at all times and in all places give thanks unto thee, O Lord, Holy Father, Almighty, Everlasting God: Who among the gifts of thy loving-kindness didst in the beginning command the earth to bring forth trees bearing fruit after their kind, and didst make the olive tree to grow among the same.

For as David thy psalmist sang of the oil which thou hadst brought forth to make men a cheerful countenance, so in these latter days, when thou hast washed away our sins in the waters of Baptism, by the anointing of this oil thou makest us cheerful in spirit, and bestowest the abundance of thy peace upon us.

Wherefore, O Lord, Holy Father, Almighty, Everlasting God, we humbly beseech thee that with thy heavenly bene ✠ diction thou wouldst be pleased to hal ✠ low this oil. Sanc ✠ tify it, we beseech thee, by thy Holy Spirit through the power of thy Christ. And as thou hast anointed therewith kings and priests and prophets, so to all who are born anew of water and of the Holy Spirit, may this chrism be for anointing unto salvation; and of thy great mercy make them also to be partakers of life eternal and partners of thy glory in the world to come; through the same . . .[1]

The rubrics direct that the oil and balsam be mixed before the Eucharist and that the chrism thus compounded be placed upon a table in the sanctuary. After the consecration, or after the *Gloria in excelsis*, it is placed upon the epistle corner of the altar and there blessed.[2]

The Supplement to the Book of Common Prayer of the Church of India,

---

[1] This form is printed for the Episcopal Synod. The Lord Bishop of Natal graciously permitted me to transcribe his copy.

[2] The oil for the sick is blessed first, also with a prayer from *Gel*. The South African Church does not officially use the oil of the catechumens.

Pakistan, Burma, and Ceylon similarly provides for the use of chrism at confirmation. The forms were authorized by the Episcopal Synod in 1960. They provide for the optional use at confirmation of the form "Sign them, O Lord . . ." from 1549, and the formula from the same source, "N., I sign thee . . .". The rubric permits the bishop to make the sign of the cross "with or without the holy Chrism, at his discretion", and a further rubric provides that the chrism may be used with the form "Defend, O Lord . . .".

In the American Episcopal Church, the first of the *Prayer Book Studies* considered the revision of the initiatory rites. Although the introduction explains in full why the Liturgical Commission declined to provide for the permissive restoration of anointing to confirmation,[1] they do not appear even to have considered restoring the anointing to baptism. It would seem to this writer that the Commission is right in not wishing to restore the *permissive* use of chrism at confirmation. Certainly its addition to the initiatory rites would be far more than a mere embellishment, like the giving of the white robe or the lighted candle, which may be included or omitted *ad lib.* without theological significance. If, however, they wish to place the liturgy of the American Prayer Book on the firm ground of the historic liturgies, they would do well to consider the restoration of the anointing to baptism, where the 1549 Prayer Book placed it. Certainly, Tertullian did not consider the anointing to be an alternative to the laying on of hands, but a significant ceremony in the baptismal liturgy, making us partakers of the Christian Name and of the royal priesthood of the holy people of God. The Anglican Church would not have to give up its historic insistence upon episcopal confirmation by the laying on of hands, but it would place itself in harmony with all of the historic liturgies of the Catholic Church, Eastern and Western, if it restored the baptismal anointing to its place following the washing, perhaps, by associating it with the signing presently in that position.

This would be a departure from the present trend of other Anglican Churches to associate the anointing with the laying on of hands, but the Liturgical Commission has already rejected this course, so it should not be urged on the grounds of Anglican uniformity. If those Churches which have abandoned the laying on of hands in Christian initiation have thereby impoverished their rites, as Anglicans must almost perforce believe they have, then we too have impoverished our rite by neglecting this ancient, perhaps Scriptural anointing.

[1] *Baptism and Confirmation (Prayer Book Studies I)*, pp. 21–3.

APPENDIX II

The Seal of The Spirit

Dr Lampe's *The Seal of the Spirit* has recently been characterized by a distinguished English liturgical scholar as "the last and most skilful rearguard action on the part of the more conservative element of the Church of England who are now in retreat".[1] This is in many ways a fair estimate of the book. Lampe's main thesis is that baptism in water is the only essential and truly primitive external rite of Christian initiation, while the "seal of the Spirit" he considers to be "the inward mark or stamp of the indwelling Spirit of God which is received by the convert who is justified by faith in Christ and through Baptism is sacramentally made a partaker of him in his death and resurrection".[2] He does not regard confirmation as a part of baptism, but considers it rather to be a rite in which "the Christian who was baptized in infancy was now able to make his necessary profession of faith after due instruction, and, on so supplying the deficiency which infant baptism would otherwise suffer, to receive the blessing of the representative leader of the Christian society with prayer for his strengthening and increase in the Holy Spirit".[3] "The purpose of the Anglican service", he says, "is primarily to enable the baptized to ratify their vows."[4]

Concerning the baptismal anointing he concludes:

The Reformers were probably wise in their abandonment of the practice of chrismation. The outward sealing with the Cross, which occupied so prominent a place in the thought of the Church of the Fathers, has already taken place in Baptism, and the symbolism of the use of chrism in effecting the consignation serves only to illustrate what has also been done in Baptism—namely, that the candidate has received the priestly and kingly status which belongs to the Church as the people of the Christ. It is an edifying symbol, comparable

---

[1] C. E. Pocknee, *The Rites of Christian Initiation*, p. 15.
[2] Lampe, op. cit., p. 307. [3] ibid., p. 314. [4] ibid., p. 315.

with the ancient practice of giving milk and honey to the neophytes to illustrate their entrance into the land of promise; but it has at best no more than a relatively minor importance, and it is not appropriate to the Confirmation of those whose Baptism took place long before, since it relates to what was done then rather than to what is being performed in Confirmation.[1]

Although there is much in Lampe's work with which he must agree, the present writer finds himself in substantial disagreement with these basic conclusions. Historically, the baptismal liturgy has included the anointing with chrism at least from the second century, and possibly from the time of the writing of 1 John and the Apocalypse. As we have seen in the body of this study, it was by no means considered an unimportant rite. Although theologians disagreed about its precise meaning, it was universally considered to be an important, if not an essential, part of the rite. Lampe's contention that the laying on of hands in Acts 8 and 19 is not confirmation is disputed by many reputable scholars,[2] and is admittedly inconsistent with the use of Acts 8.14–17 at the confirmation service by the American Prayer Book and the Proposed English Book of 1928.[3]

Lampe is unquestionably right in saying, "Episcopal administration of Confirmation, or the presbyteral administration of Baptism, has serious disadvantages in the case of adult baptism",[4] but it must seem to many, including this writer, that there are similar disadvantages in the case of infant baptism. Christian initiation, whether of children or adults, is essentially one rite, and to rend it asunder, for whatever purpose, is, to say the least, fraught with serious disadvantages.

There is, nevertheless, a positive side to Lampe's work. Thornton, Dix and others, have perhaps been too ready to draw a sharp distinction between baptism in water and baptism of the Spirit and so destroy that very unity of the rite for which they are contending.[5] Water baptism is unquestionably the central act of the initiatory liturgy, but the rite included the anointing and laying on of hands as well, and it is to the rite as a whole that the effects are ascribed. To say that the prayer of consecration is the essential act of the Eucharist is not to suggest that the offertory, or the gospel, are unimportant, and most students would agree that a liturgy which lacked one or both of these was seriously deficient. If Lampe has shown that we cannot accept the view that the

---

[1] ibid., pp. 321f.
[2] ibid., pp. 66–70; cf., for example, Pocknee, op. cit., p. 16.
[3] ibid., p. 315.   [4] ibid., p. 316.   [5] ibid., pp. 206ff.

Spirit is given *de novo* in the post-baptismal rites, he has not demonstrated to this writer's satisfaction that we must consider baptism an integral whole without those rites.

Lampe is on sound liturgical and historical ground when he associates the unction with chrism with what happens at baptism, rather than at such a rite as he conceives confirmation to be. He points out quite accurately that the consignation in the Anglican rite takes place immediately after baptism, but he fails to draw what this writer considers to be the inescapable conclusion that it is therefore to baptism that the Anglican Church should restore the anointing with chrism. The reasons which he urges for the abandonment of chrismation at confirmation in no way militate against its restoration to baptism, but rather seem to recommend it.

These few paragraphs hardly constitute a refutation, or even a qualified refutation, of Lampe's position. His investigation and that which we are undertaking did not run on parallel paths. It is rather the purpose of this appendix to show the relationship of Dr Lampe's conclusions to those of this study at their point of contact, the post-baptismal anointing.

A Select Bibliography

I. Texts

A. PATRISTIC

Ambrose, *On the Sacraments and On the Mysteries*, trans. T. Thompson, London, 1950.

Apostolic Constitutions, *Didascalia et Constitutiones Apostolorum*, ed. F. X. Funk, Vol. 1–2, Paderborn, 1905–6.

Didascalia Apostolorum, ed. R. H. Connolly, Oxford, 1929.

Hippolytus, *The Apostolic Tradition of Hippolytus*, ed. B. S. Easton, Cambridge, 1934, and New Haven, 1962.

—, *The Treatise on the Apostolic Tradition of St Hippolytus, Bishop of Rome and Martyr*, ed. G. Dix, London, 1937.

—, *La Tradition Apostolique*, ed. B. Botte, Paris, 1946.

—, *La Tradition Apostolique de Saint Hippolyte*, ed. B. Botte (*Liturgiewissenschaftliche Quellen und Forschungen* 39), Münster, 1963.

Serapion, "The Sacramentary of Serapion of Thmuis", ed. F. E. Brightman, in *J.T.S.*, Vol. 1 (1899), pp. 88–113, 247–77.

—, *Bishop Sarapion's Prayer Book*, trans. J. Wordsworth, London, 1910.

B. EASTERN

Assemani, J. A., *Codex Liturgicus Ecclesiae Universae in XV Libros Distributos*, Vol. 1–3, Rome, 1749–66.

Conybeare, F. C., *Rituale Armenorum*, Oxford, 1905.

Denzinger, J., *Ritus Orientalium*, Vol. 1, Würzburg, 1863.

Goar, J., *Euchologion, sive Rituale Graecorum*, Paris, 1637.

C. WESTERN

I. ROMAN

The Gelasian Sacramentary, ed. H. A. Wilson, Oxford, 1894.

—, *Liber Sacramentorum Romanae Aeclesiae Ordinis Anni Circuli* (*Sacramentarium*

Gelasianum), ed. L. C. Mohlberg (R.E.D., Series Maior, Vol. 4), Rome, 1960.

The Gregorian Sacramentary under Charles the Great, ed. H. A. Wilson (H.B.S., Vol. 49), London, 1915.

John the Deacon, *Epistola ad Senarium*, ed. A. Wilmart, in *Analecta Reginensia* (Studi e Testi 69), Rome, 1933.

Martène, E., *De Antiquis Ecclesiae Ritibus*, Vol. 1, Antwerp, 1786.

Les Ordines Romani du Haut Moyen Âge, ed. M. Andrieu, Vol. 1–5, Louvain, 1931–61.

Le Sacramentaire Gélasien d'Angoulême, ed. P. Cagin, Angoulême, 1918.

2. GALLICAN AND CELTIC

The Bobbio Missal, ed. E. A. Lowe (H.B.S., Vol. 58), London, 1920.

(Pseudo–) Germanus, *Expositio Antiquae Liturgiae Gallicanae Germano Parisiensi Ascripta* (Opuscula et Textus 3), ed. J. Quasten, Münster, 1934.

Missale Gallicanum Vetus, ed. L. C. Mohlberg (R.E.D., Series Maior, Vol. 3), Rome, 1958.

Missale Gothicum, ed. L. C. Mohlberg (R.E.D., Series Maior, Vol. 5), Rome, 1961.

The Stowe Missal, Vol. 2, ed. G. F. Warner (H.B.S., Vol. 32), London, 1915.

3. NORTH ITALIAN

Beroldus, sive Ecclesiae Ambrosianae Mediolanensis Kalendarium et Ordines, ed. M. Magistretti, Milan, 1894.

Magistretti, *Monumenta Veteris Liturgiae Ambrosianae*: Vol. 1, *Pontificale in usum Ecclesiae Mediolanensis ex codicibus saec. IX–XV*, Milan, 1897. Vol. 2–3, *Manuale Ambrosianum ex codicibus saec. XI olim in usum Canonicae Vallis Travaliae*, Milan, 1905.

Mercati, G., *Antiche Reliquie Liturgiche Ambrosiani e Romani* (Studi e Testi 7), Rome, 1902.

North Italian Services of the Eleventh Century, ed. C. Lambot (H.B.S., Vol. 67), London, 1931.

Sacramentarium Bergomense, ed. A. Paredi (*Monumenta Bergomensia* 6), Bergamo, 1962.

Il Sacramentario di Ariberto, ed. A. Paredi, in *Miscellanea Adriano Bernereggi* (*Monumenta Bergomensia* 1), Bergamo, 1958.

4. MOZARABIC

Antifonario Visigótico Mozarabe de la Catedral de León, ed. L. Brou and J. Vives, Barcelona-Madrid, 1959.

Liber Mozarabicus Sacramentorum, ed. M. Férotin, Paris, 1912.

Le "Liber Ordinum" en usage dans l'Église Wisigothique et Mozarabe d'Espagne, ed. M. Férotin, Paris, 1904.

Orational Visigótico, ed. J. Vives, Barcelona, 1946.

II. Studies

Bourque, E., *Étude sur les Sacramentaires Romains*, Pt. I, Rome, 1948; Part II, Tome I, Quebec, 1952, Tome II, Rome, 1958.

Dix, G., "*Confirmation or the Laying on of Hands?*", London, 1936.

—, *The Theology of Confirmation in Relation to Baptism*, Westminster, 1946.

Dolger, F. J., *Sphragis*, Paderborn, 1911.

Lampe, G. W., *The Seal of the Spirit*, London, 1951.

Mason, A. J., *The Relation of Confirmation to Baptism*, New York, 1891.

Thompson, T., *The Offices of Baptism and Confirmation*, Cambridge, 1914.

Thornton, L., *Confirmation, its Place in the Baptismal Mystery*, London, 1954.

Whitaker, E. C., *Documents of the Baptismal Liturgy*, London, 1960.

Index of Subjects

Index of Proper Names

THE ALCUIN CLUB—of which Dr Walter Howard Frere was for many years the President—exists for the object of promoting liturgical studies in general, and in particular a knowledge of the history and use of the Book of Common Prayer. It encourages, by publications and other means, the practical study of the English liturgy with its ceremonial, and the arrangement of churches, their furniture, and ornaments. Since its foundation in 1897 it has published over one hundred and twenty books and pamphlets. The annual subscription is 21s. and members of the Club are entitled to the publications of the current year *gratis*. Subscriptions, applications for membership and for the list of publications, should be sent to the Assistant Secretary.

The Reverend Prebendary G. B. Timms, M.A.,
St Andrew's Vicarage, St Andrew's Street, London E.C.4.

The Reverend F. C. Walden-Aspy, M.A.,
The Rectory, Jevington, Polegate, Sussex.

The Reverend Dr G. G. Willis,
Wing Vicarage, Leighton Buzzard, Bedfordshire.

Hon. Secretary
The Reverend F. C. Walden-Aspy, M.A.

Hon. Treasurer
Prebendary G. B. Timms, M.A.

Assistant Secretary and Assistant Treasurer
Miss W. K. Medway, c/o The Dean's Office,
King's College, Strand, London W.C.2.